D0552384

The Essential Guide to London
The Best of Everything and Some of the Worst

DAVID BENEDICTUS

SPHERE BOOKS LIMITED
30–32 Gray's Inn Road, London WC1X 8JL

First published in Great Britain by
Sphere Books Ltd 1984
Copyright © 1984 by David Benedictus

TRADE
MARK

Set in Baskerville

Reproduced, printed and bound in Great Britain by
Hazell Watson & Viney Limited,
Member of the BPCC Group,
Aylesbury, Bucks

To those who love London

Acknowledgements

(Apologies to those who would have liked to be on this list and aren't; also to those who would have preferred not to be and are; also to those whose names have been misspelled.)

Olive Ainge; Lucy Antrobus; Yvonne Antrobus; Bruce Baker of Wisconsin; N. W. Bate; Jared Bernstein; Jill Brooke; Henrietta Browne-Wilkinson; Emily Carey; Danny Cohen; Lesley Cunliffe; Krsto and Celia Cviic; Tony Elliott; Jane Forman; John & Sheila Frisby; Kate Gilchrist; Anne Gobey; David Goldberg; Daniel & Benjamin Goldstein; Carol & Richard Savage; Diana Tamblyn; Nicky Henson; Jane Heslop; Bill Hootkins; Rachel Ingals; Florine Katz; Martin & Ruth Landy & friends; Roger Lloyd Pack; Sara & Charles Michell; Bru & Roger Myddleton; Mark Penfold; Paul Petzold & Jane; Clay Randall; Benedict & Sara Rich; Rosemary Anne Sisson; Hilary Smith; Sue & Nick; Nina Thomas; Angelica Toynbee-Clarke; Geoffrey Tufts; Ann Valery; Lizzie Webb; Miki van Zwanenberg; Jill Zilkha & friends.

Preface

To the immediate north of Putney Bridge you can find an ancient parish church, a palace, a sex shop, a country club and a snooker club. To the south St Mary the Virgin, raped by vandals some six years ago but currently being restored to virtue; an eccentric auctioneer's, a cinema, a curry house, and an enticing book shop. Off the bridge jumped Mary Wollstonecraft (1759-1797), authoress of *Vindication of the Rights of Women*, and under it the most famous boat race in the world is started. Within a few hundred metres may be found all that is necessary to keep a reasonable man or woman in good humour; she or he may sport or pray, lust or deal, be educated or entertained, fed or wined, or put an end to it all. Putney Bridge is London in microcosm.

The glories of Wren and Hawksmoor, Nash and Inigo Jones seem more glorious when set in opposition to the concrete coffins of the money-grubbers of the 1960s. The marvellous multiplicity of London trees is enhanced by the variety of folk who eat sandwiches under them and the variety of birds who peck up the crumbs; it is these sandwich eaters, the Londoners themselves who make the city or break it, who create what is best or worst about it, who make a book such as this a delight to research and a necessity (I hope) to buy.

The popular myth of the lovable Cockney, the friendly Bobby and the chipper Pearly King needs to be set against the psychopaths of the National Front and the crazed football fans. Graffiti in London are by no means as witty or engaging as Nigel Rees would have us believe. There are more people, it seems, prepared to sell their city for a few fast bucks than spend months carving a tree in Kensington Gardens or creating a garden from an abandoned bomb site. The street markets in which you may bargain energetically for a few pence are overlooked by the clip joints in which you may be taken for a dangerous and expensive ride. A new and revolutionary type of self-flushing lavatory is unveiled in Leicester Square with much pomp, while round the corner high pressure hoses are used to flush out the homeless from the pedestrian subways in which they contrive to sleep. The guide book which promotes the best without warning against the rest is no better than a travel agent who sells you tickets to a desert island paradise on a leaking boat, or who recommends a stretch of golden sands without mentioning the sharks who swim inshore and flash their shining teeth.

Just over a hundred years ago Charles Dickens published his

Unconventional Hand Book to London. In the preface he wrote: 'The plan of a work of this character necessarily involves the mention of names; but over statement and over recommendation made in the Dictionary is put forth either as the result of actual experience, or on perfectly trustworthy authority. No payment has been received, or ever will be received, directly or indirectly that appears in the body of this book.'

I could not have put it better myself. He also invited suggestions from his readers which might tend to the improvement of future volumes. I do the same and recommend to your attention the form at the back of this book. With the aid of your A-Z or your Nicholson London Streetfinder you may identify the best of everything in your area. *My* area is the west of London, and, if there is a westward bias in the pages which follow, as I think there may be, that, I'm afraid, is inevitable. However, I must thank all my friends who collaborated so cheerfully on the research. Those mentioned in the acknowledgements, as well as those who were too shy to bask publicly in the sunshine of my approval, deserve my gratitude. They took much trouble.

London (latest population figure: 6,696,008) is constantly changing. Nightclubbing impresarios no longer open their own premises, but hire existing ones for weekly gigs. Theatres open and (more frequently) close. At the time of writing the London theatres are just emerging from the worst slump they have ever experienced, and Covent Garden has triumphantly re-emerged. Sex shops have closed, are closing, and will continue to close. Cinemas are threatened. As for restaurants and shops, I have tried to emphasise in my recommendations those which have been in business for some time, or look as though they will be. Publishing deadlines make topicality difficult, but I've done my best and nobody, except politicians, can do more.

I trust that this volume will give service to those who buy or borrow it, and cause offence only to those who give offence.

David Benedictus, 1984

African Food

The best African food in London is at the *Calabash*, down the stairs in the Africa Centre (38 King Street, WC2; 01-836 1976). Food from many African states is deliciously prepared (expect rice, black-eyed beans, bananas, yams and fish) and cheerfully served. Since the prices as well as the food are influenced by the Third World, it is readily affordable and forms a welcome contrast to some of the rip-off joints in the adjoining Covent Garden complex. Is eating cultural? If not, cultural activities may still be found at the Africa Centre, which is heartily recommended.

Toddie's (241 Old Brompton Road, SW5; 01-373 8217) serves English food as well as African and cocktails too; after midnight on Fridays and Saturdays blues singers are featured there, but should you listen to the blues with a bulging tummy?

The very best African food is served in Paris – and Africa.

Best African food: the *Calabash*.

Alleys

The most remarkable alley in London has to be *Brydges Place*, WC2, which runs between St Martin's Lane and Bedfordbury. It measures 200 yards by (at its narrowest point) 15 inches wide. Since the buildings on either side are tall and dark and since the sun never pierces this crack in the surface of London, walking along it is not unlike falling down a well sideways.

The most beautiful alley is *Goodwin's Court*, also running between St Martin's Lane and Bedfordbury. Wrought iron gas-holders illumine a marvellous row of gently serpentine bow-front houses – shops, of course, originally. A plaque announces: 'Goodwin's Court (replacing Fishers Alley) first appeared in the Rate-Books in 1690 and it seems probable that the houses on the Court were erected in that year. LCC Survey.' Inside, however, these houses are a little disappointing.

Magnificent and unexpected is *Gentleman's Row*, Enfield. This footpath, which blossoms with bronze plaques, is flanked by enchanting houses from the 16th, 17th, 18th and 19th centuries. On the other side of the path gardens run down to the Brent with its iron footbridges and ingenuous ducks.

The gas-lit *Exchange Court*, WC2, where William Terriss, the actor-manager, was stabbed, is alarming but not so alarming as the little yards and alleys around *Aldgate*, where the ghosts of Jack the Ripper's victims cry out for retribution.

Post Office Alley, Strand-on-the-Green, W4, is too cute for its own good; like something on a film set. *Crown Passage*, St James's, SW1, has elements of cuteness, but Chubby's Sandwich Bar and Supersam Snacks present a healthily vulgar front to passers-by.

Also recommended are *Crown Passage* and *Harrow Passage* in Kingston; *Church Path*, Mortlake, from which you can listen to one of the oldest peals of eight bells in the country; *Holland Path*, W8, where you get a good class of voyeur watching the schoolgirls; *Cox's Walk*, Dulwich and the fast disappearing *Clink Street*, SE1.

Best alley: *Goodwin's Court*, WC2.
Worst alley: *Cons Street*, Waterloo.

All-Night Eating

(a) Grand
The *Carlton Tower* and the *Kensington Hilton*, catering as they do for jet-lagged foreigners who find Greenwich Mean Time as confusing as pounds, shillings and pence used to be, will provide food at all hours – even, if nagged, to non-residents. The *Strand Palace Hotel* serves snacks as a matter of course, but beware of the spaghetti.

(b) Not so grand
Wurst Max (75 Westbourne Grove, W2; 01-229 3771) is lively. Open till 4 a.m. You can eat hot sausages and sauerkraut – in the garden if it's a balmy summer's night. Also take away.

Calamitees (104 Heath Street, NW3; 01-435 2145) serves hamburgers to hungry Hampstead intellectuals till 3 a.m., while *Up All Night* (325 Fulham Road, SW10; 01-352 1998) does the same until 6 a.m. for famished Fulham fops. Chinese somnabulists walk to the *Diamond* (23 Lisle Street, WC2; 01-437 2517) – Cantonese food till 4 a.m.

(c) Basic
Mick's Cafe in Fleet Street might look squalid to most of us, but journalists seldom notice their surroundings unless paid to. *The Pie Stand* at Chelsea Bridge is popular with taxi drivers and famous for its brown sauce. *The kiosk* at Caxton Hall and the *Beigel*

Shop in Brick Lane attract a better class of insomniac than the *Wimpy* opposite King's Cross Station, which is depressing. Many of the *Kentucky Fried Chicken* branches open 24 hours a day for their battery customers, who throw the chicken bones on the ground for my dogs to crunch up. But their corn on the cob is an analgesic to a tormented soul.

Best all-night eating: the *Beigel Shop*.

All-Night Petrol

On your behalf I asked the AA for an up-to-date list of all night garages in the centre of London, but, as you might expect from a motoring organisation, they don't have one. However . . .

The nearer you are to Piccadilly Circus the more expensive is the petrol. So, should you be desperate, the *Fountain Garage* (83 Park Lane, W1; 01-629 4151) will sell you petrol, but don't fill the tank. That you can do at any of the 24-hour garages listed below (a geographically diverse selection):

City Petroleum, 276 Upper Street, N1.
Esso, Camden Road, NW1.
Esso, 617 Finchley Road, NW3.
Heron Garage, 430 Old Kent Road, SE1.
Chelsea Cloisters, Chiswick Flyover, W4.
Mount Pleasant Filling Station, 39 King's Cross Road, WC1.
National Garage, Sloane Avenue, SW3.

It's always worth considering converting to diesel fuel. Diesel engines are fifty per cent more efficient than petrol, and can run on a variety of fuels (after shave might be worth a try in extremis), all of which are lead-free. But then you have to ask a cabbie for a 24-hour diesel garage – there's one at Shepherd's Bush.

Arcades

The Burlington Arcade off Piccadilly contains thirty-eight Regency shops built between 1815 and 1819 by Lord George Cavendish and his architect, Samuel Ware, author of an essay on vaulting – architectural not gymnastic. The stated purpose of the arcade was, 'for the gratification of the publick and to give employment to industrious females'. The idea of the arcade was that gallery lighting would flatter both shops and shoppers equally, but sadly Ware's designs were tampered with by the late Professor Beresford Pite, who replaced the original façade with what Sir John Summerson calls 'cynically outrageous baroque'. The back entrance in Burlington Gardens is better. Nor is it only the architecture which is baroque, for the arcade is policed by three liveried beadles, who ensure that there shall be no undue whistling, humming, hurrying or unfurling of umbrellas throughout the precinct. However, despite the beadles the arcade is fly-posted with warnings about unattended parcels. The shops are expensive and some of them are classy, notably the two tobacconists at No 34 and No 60, the Irish linen at No 35, the women's shirts at No 3 and the Chester Barrie tweed jackets at No 50, if you want to look like an American film star trying to look like an English gentleman.

On the south side of Piccadilly is the *Piccadilly Arcade*, recently refurbished. The marble floor, the narrow bow-fronts of the shops and the tiny upstairs rooms put one in mind of an elaborate Regency toy, but there are interesting purchases to be made. Ignore the rather dull modern pottery and porcelain and go instead for the sponges, the medals and the beautiful antiquarian books. *Prince's Arcade* to the south of Jermyn Street and the *Royal Arcade*, where you can buy Charbonnel & Walker's Boîtes Blanches of chocolates, are both elite, but even more exclusive is the *Halkin Arcade* off Knightsbridge. Every establishment in this exuberant art deco court shimmers with chic, none more so than No 3, the Chiu Gallery, which is like the Bauhaus redesigned by the Marquis de Sade.

The *Opera Arcade*, off the Haymarket, a vaulted passage with shops along one side (compare the Rue de Rivoli) is a fortunate survival of what had once been a magnificent design by Nash and Repton. Though in a less fashionable area than the other arcades it oozes elegance.

Best arcade: *Halkin Arcade.*
Worst arcade: *Oxford Walk.*

Arches

Marble Arch, designed by John Nash after the Arch of Constantine in Rome, was intended to stand as the entrance to Buckingham

Palace, but it was too narrow to permit the state coach to pass through, so was moved to its present ominous position, at the top of Park Lane, where Tyburn gallows once stood. And there it sits, a massive traffic island, quite at a loss, like an elephant on a croquet lawn.

Constitution Arch, otherwise called *Wellington Arch*, because the Duke of Wellington once rode his horse on the top of it, where Boadicea now drives her chariot, is also a traffic island, but a more impressive one, and Boadicea casts a giant shadow across Green Park. Within this arch is a police station. At the far end of the Mall between Trafalgar Square and St James's Park stands *The Admiralty Arch*, designed by Sir Aston Webb and intended as part of the national memorial to Queen Victoria. Although hideous it does give a certain dignified formality to a drive up the Mall.

These three grandiose lumps of masonry are all very well, but none of them can stand comparison with the *Doric Arch* at Euston, swept away by bureaucratic vandals in 1962. Gone but not forgiven.

St John's Gate, Clerkenwell, once the entry to the Priory of the Knights Hospitallers, has survived since it was rebuilt in 1504. It is almost all that does remain of the Priory, and above it is the Council Chamber, where once Edward Cave, founder of the *Gentleman's Magazine*, sucked the end of his gentlemanly quill. It is now available for banquets – the Chamber, that is, not the quill.

The arches of the old London-Greenwich railway line form a viaduct which is the most interesting architectural feature of south east London – some would say the *only* IAF of SEL. Many of the arches have been filled in to form alarmingly dark recesses in which men called Alf and Dave regrind crankshafts and sell one another greyhounds brought over from Ireland. Others shelter bats and meths drinkers.

What remains of the original Tudor brick archway leading into the yard of the old Bishop's Palace in Richmond (or Sheen as it used to be called, hence East Sheen) built by Henry VII upon the ashes of an earlier palace, is impressive and romantic; but even finer is the Norman archway which once formed part of the ancient monastery of *Merton Priory*. In 1977 the Philistines put up a garage only a few yards away from this unique survival – and that's the way we do things here.

Best arch: *Merton Priory.*
Worst arch: *Knightsbridge Barracks* (see next entry).

Architecture

London architecture is both instantly recognisable and entirely unpredictable. It is the brick of the early Victorian terraced houses in Islington, Bloomsbury and Southwark, it is the villas in Parson's Green and the suburbs, it is the gloomy philanthropy of the Peabody Estates. It is the stucco of the Nash Terraces, the wit of the Palladian Lodges, the fantasy of the Victorian Gothic. It is the domestic friendliness of iron balconies and fanlights, and the public arrogance of railway stations. It is statues everywhere.

There were the periods of great speculative building which produced the handsome London squares, and the periods of disastrous speculative vandalism which pulled them down again – whatever happened to *Portman Square*? The Great Fire of 1666 destroyed four-fifths of the City, the great fires of the Blitz destroyed rather less. The first fire made way for Wren and Gibbs and Dance, Vanbrugh and Hawksmoor, men of vision and taste, the later fires made way for towers of concrete and glass which could not be lived in, but could be borrowed against.

Had it not been for *St Paul's* surviving triumphantly in the midst of chaos and proving beyond argument that when men aspire to God they become as gods, architects might have forgotten what they were there for; fortunately a few – very few – remembered. But it is salutary to compare the *Chelsea Hospital*, built by Wren and Hawksmoor for the pensioners, with the *Knightsbridge Barracks*, built by Sir Basil Spence some 250 years later for serving men; salutary and dispiriting. And so often the best of London architecture is molested by the worst. The charmingly eccentric churches along the *Marylebone Road* are crushed by flyovers and skyscrapers. The pretty façade of the *Victoria Palace Theatre* is insulted by *Portland House* behind, and what madness possessed the BBC when they erected their yellow brick offices behind *All Souls'*, Langham Place, I cannot imagine. Much of what isn't molested or raped is destroyed – sometimes by bulldozers under cover of darkness. In this way went the lively Firestone art deco building in west London, and even something as charming and unpretentious as the *Kew Gardens Station Precinct* is currently under threat from anonymous developers and no one seems to care.

Later in this book you may find architecture dealt with in greater detail under such headings as Crescents, Big and Small Houses, Palaces, Squares, Underground Lines and Stations, Streets, Modern and Commercial Buildings etc, but for the moment let me nominate:

Best architecture: the *Wren Churches.*

Worst architecture: *59/67 Portland Place,* where one fifth of an Adam Terrace has been sliced off through pediment, pilaster and all, to squeeze in a 1930s building of total mediocrity.

I can recommend the excellent book *A Guide to the Architecture of London* by Edward Jones and Christopher Woodward (Weidenfeld & Nicolson £12.95 & £8.50) and the classic *Georgian London* by John Summerson (3rd Edition Barnie & Jenkins 1978).

Art Galleries

If it's pictures you're after, it has to be the *National Gallery.* Titian, Leonardo, Turner, Reynolds, Fra Angelico, Tintoretto, Rubens, Rembrandt, Vermeer, El Greco, and a superb selection from the French School, these are just some of the artists who make this collection a celebration of the optimism of the human race. But the quality and the scope of the pictures on display does not ensure that a visit to the *National Gallery* is necessarily a success. It's not unlike being tied down with silken ropes and having vintage champagne dripped onto your head while Mozart plays incessantly in the background and a pedigree Pomeranian licks your toes. If sensibly you decide to 'do' one room per visit, you still have to walk blindfolded through the others or risk premature artistic ejaculation. The Velasquez room is too cool; the impressionist room next door too hot and the pictures are unimaginatively hung.

When the *Tate* stirs itself it can mount an exhibition of international repute, but it has been going through tough times since it destroyed its splendid extension and forfeited much of the goodwill that went with it. Let us hope that the soon to be opened Turner rooms compensate. There is much that is impressive. Hogarth and Blake and the civilised English painters of the 19th century, who painted as they lived, with style and decorum; Matisse and Picasso ('that brute Picasso' – Evelyn Waugh); and the best of the modern Brits – Bacon and Hockney, Peter Blake and Freud. But many of the post-war acquisitions now look jaded, and Warhol and Pollack and Liechstenstein do not deserve their wall space. Nor is Rex Whistler's *Pursuit of Rare Meats* in the restaurant any real compensation for weak coffee at more than five bob a gulp.

Compare the *Dulwich Picture Gallery* (College Road, SE21; 01-693 5254 – closed daily for lunch, so be warned), London's oldest public art gallery and designed by Sir John Soane. This is what J. C. Smetham wrote in 1891:

'How kind! How civil! How silent! You write your name in the visitors' book, and see that yesterday John Ruskin was here . . . All is sober and uncrowded, and well-lighted and profoundly still . . . The keeper of the Gallery comes and peers at you over his spectacles. He is not quite sure in his little room which are the pictures and which are the visitors, and he's come to see.'

The design, which incorporates a mausoleum containing the bodies of the principal benefactor of the gallery and his friends, is superb. What if the pictures are not so fine? There is always a Rembrandt, a Gainsborough, a Claude Lorraine and a Guido Reni which redeem the rest. The Reni, in which John the Baptist is depicted as young and handsome, is as fresh and unexpected as the day it was painted.

To qualify for inclusion in the *National Portrait Gallery* (round the corner from the *National Gallery*) you have to be famous or royal and ten years dead. It has been computed that since several of the works on display are crowd scenes there are some 45,000 faces on view at this gallery, and what a fascinating place it is! The photographs – Beardsley with his bony nose and spatulate fingers, Thomas Hardy so grey and undistinguished – are often even more illuminating than the portraits, but the whole exhibition is an essential reminder that these people, Henry Moore and Henry VII, Sir Thomas More and Sir Thomas Beecham, John Donne and T. S. Eliot, *lived*. History being about chaps, this is the best place to go and study history.

The *Hayward* is confusing. It's a building of notorious hideousness, concealed within the serpentine coils of the South Bank complex, and is expensive, but it does feature Arts Council Loan Exhibitions of considerable significance. The *Whitechapel Art Gallery* (adjoining Aldgate East tube station) is a splendid example of art nouveau architecture, light and airy and imaginatively run. The *Courtauld Institute Galleries* (not at the Courtauld Institute but in Woburn Square), the *Photographers' Gallery* (5 Great Newport Street, WC2), *Illustrator's Art* (16a D'Arblay Street, W1) and the *Workshop* (81 Lamb's Conduit Street, WC1) for book illustrations and cartoons respectively, are all recommended. *Thomas Agnew* (43 Old Bond Street, W1) is the place if you wish to buy an old master. *Nigel Greenwood's* (41 Sloane Gardens, SW1), the *Mayor Gallery* (22a Cork Street, W1; 01-734 3558), Anthony d'Offay (9 Dering Street, W1; 01-629 1578) and the *Lisson Gallery* (56 Whitfield Street, W1; 01-631

0942) are the best of the avant garde specialists, particularly the last named. The *Juda Annely* (11 Tottenham Mews, W1; 01-637 5517) is noted for modern exhibitions of high seriousness.

The *Royal Academy* summer show is erratic. An amusing cartoon at the *National Portrait Gallery* poking gentle fun at the selection process might explain this. The pictures on display along Piccadilly and the Bayswater Road of a Sunday are usually of great hideosity. Many of those selling the pictures are not, as you might suppose, the artists, but merely salesmen for the mass producers. Be warned! The *Serpentine Gallery* mounts two summer shows of the works of young and little known artists. Last year more than 6000 slides were submitted for consideration. The *Marianne North Gallery* in Kew Gardens is a beautiful dream (see under Florists).

Best gallery for old pictures: *The National Gallery.*
Best gallery for modern pictures: *The Lisson Gallery.*
Best gallery qua gallery: *Dulwich Picture Gallery.*
Most interesting gallery: *National Portrait Gallery.*
Worst gallery (for pictures): *Royal Academy Summer Exhibition.*
Worst gallery (for atmosphere): *Hayward.*

If you've only time or the inclination for one picture, try:

National Gallery: 'Young Woman Standing at the Virginals' (Vermeer). (Room XI)
National Portrait Gallery: 'The Brontë Sisters' (Branwell Brontë). (Room XXI)
Tate Gallery: 'Swan Upping' (Stanley Spencer).
Dulwich Picture Gallery: 'John the Baptist' (Guido Reni).
Wallace Collection, Hertford House: 'The Swing' (Fragonard). (Room XVIII)
Sir John Soane's Museum: 'The Rake's Progress' (Hogarth). (The Picture Room)

Arts and Crafts

Liberty's in Regent Street ('Tudor revival at its most exuberant') is the Mecca of arts and crafts. Founded in 1875, it still retains something of its original quaint earnestness, and bearded artisans in open-toed sandals may still be seen flashing Barclaycards amongst the Paisley shawls and leather rhinosceri. At the *Portmeirion Shop* (5 Pont Street, SW1; 01-235 7601) look out for old patchwork quilts and brass bedsteads.

Specifically British crafts may be viewed at the *British Crafts Centre* (43 Earlham Street, WC2; 01-836 6993 – Tuesday, Friday and Saturday) and at *Naturally British* (13 New Row, WC2; 01-240 0551); exhibits are for sale, as they are at the *Design Centre* in the Haymarket. Here the emphasis tends towards what Betjeman calls 'ghastly good taste'. For healthy vulgarity try Petticoat Lane.

For arty crafty materials *Cass* (once Craftsmith, a branch of W. H. Smith, but no longer) carry an extensive stock. Their writing paper and envelopes in mind-blowing colours can be bought by the weight, like barley-sugar at Wimbledon. The *Arts and Crafts Shop* in Abbey Road, NW8 (junction of Belsize Road) will attempt to mend, alter or repair anything with good grace. Also recommended: *Yarncraft* (112a Westbourne Grove, W2; 01-229 1432) for the homeyweavey set and *Hobbyhorse* (15 Langton Street, SW10; 01-351 1913).

Best arts and crafts: *Cass* (various branches).
Worst arts and crafts: those pottery ewers you see in florists' shops.

Arts Centres

Arts should not properly be in centres. Administrators like to put them there so that they can keep an eye on them, and performers rather like them so that they can be fed and wined without having to emerge into the rain. But once you have a centre with an ocean of wall space the problems begin. What to hang on them? What to put on in your two or three theatres/cinemas/concert halls? What if – as is invariably the case – there just isn't enough worthwhile 'art' to go round? Inevitably what there is is diluted, and standards begin to fall. More seriously, audiences come to believe that because the building (rightly in the case of the *Barbican* called a 'complex') is so splendid, all that goes on in it must be artistically splendid too. Peter Brook, a bright lad, has realised this and takes his plays to drill halls and African villages and traffic islands and wherever.

The best arts centre in London is probably the *Riverside* in Hammersmith. It is friendly and tatty and seems to get some of the best – if not the most reputable – of the visiting companies. As a result it lives on a financial tight-rope and suffers from stringencies which its posh cousin, the *Lyric* up the road, is (comparatively) free from.

The *ICA* in the Mall is full of loonies. On my last visit there I was subjected to an improvised concert of great banality followed by a horror film in three dimensions. The radical book store was not much of a comfort. The Concert Hall is either suffocating (with the windows shut) or noisy (with them open). But the snacks are excellent.

The *Barbican* is a monster. Apart from Trevor Nunn and his immediate entourage, the entire staff work underground, like creatures in a novel of the future. That would matter less if the air conditioning worked better. The *Barbican* boasts the best safety curtain and arguably the worst food in London.

The *National*, like the *Royal Shakespeare Company*, is very hot on production values. Their shows are impeccably mounted and competently acted. But they have quite failed to find worthwhile new plays or playwrights and have revived some very second-rate old plays as a result.

While sight lines are excellent at both these new centres, and the audiences never feel remote from the action as they do at, say, Drury Lane, acoustics remain untrustworthy. Theatre and concert-hall architects have much to learn about sound waves.

Best arts centre: *Riverside Studios.*
Worst arts centre: *Barbican.*

Auctions

An auctioneer: 'One who admires *all* works of art' – Oscar Wilde.

For somebody like myself who is hooked on auctions, London is the place. Currently, prices at London salerooms are running at about 10-20% lower than prices at the major provincial salerooms. Indeed it is now commonplace for a dealer to send a prime piece of furniture to Bath or Birmingham or Sevenoaks, where he may confidently expect it to fetch a higher price than in boring old London. An important consideration however must be the infamous buyer's premium by which 10% is added on to the hammer price. *Christie's* have reduced their premium to 8% (no premium at their South Kensington branch); there is VAT at 15% of the premium to be added additionally to the premium.

As a vendor you should certainly use the major London houses (*Sotheby's, Christie's*, and, to a lesser extent, *Phillips* and *Bonhams*) if you have a masterpiece which requires international exposure; also if you have items of a specialist nature, such as art nouveau and art deco, model soldiers, antiquities, post cards, textiles, cameras, gramophones and records and so on. The best place to sell general goods is *Bonsor Pennington's* of Eden Street, Kingston (01-546 0022). For some reason goods sold in their spacious salerooms (too hot in summer and too cold in winter) seem to raise some 15% more than anywhere else. Although they do not exact a premium their commission rate (17½%) is hefty.

My favourite hunting grounds for bargains have been *Dowell Lloyds* by Putney Bridge, *Phillips* in Marylebone (Hayes Place next to Lisson Grove), and *Harvey's* in Neal Street, Covent Garden. *Dowell Lloyds* is mouldering and cobwebby but fun. *Phillips* is junky with vast job lots of glassware, toys, books and so on; you need to be sharp and quick, for the auctioneer rattles through the lots at 140-150 per hour. At *Harvey's* the 'antiques' and furniture come first, but the bankrupt stock 'by order of the sheriff' is where the real bargains are to be had. You want fifty gross of leather uppers? *Harvey's* is the place to get them, though parking is a serious problem. The auctioneer at *Harvey's* used to regale you with selections from Broadway musicals, but has become a bit solemn since they moved to their smart new premises. Extremely cheerful is the *Lots Road Galleries* (71 Lots Road, SW10; 01-352 2349). If you bring goods in on Wednesday they will sell them the following Monday, and pay ten days later. The goods may be modest but the auctions are fun. However they have imposed a minimum commission of £5 per lot, so that when I sold 24 lots recently for £474, with two 'bought in', I received less than £300 after deductions. Be warned!

There are numerous other sales in London; the *Daily Telegraph* on Mondays, *The Times* on Tuesdays, and the various antique magazines give details.

Best auction for buying: *Christie's* (South Kensington) – no premium.
Best auction for selling: *Bonsor Pennington's* of Kingston.

Ballet

London ballet is not enjoying a golden age. At the *Royal Ballet* it is alarming to note that the average age of the principal dancers has now passed forty. A few younger dancers, such as Patrick Armand, Ashley Page, Ravenna Tucker, Alessandra Ferri, Bryony Brind, and Fiona Chadwick, grab eagerly at such chances as present themselves, but there are few enough of these. Those who work outside the main companies (Laurie Booth, Janet Smith, whose work is gentle, and the magnificent black pair, Stewart Arnold and Paul Henry, whose work is anything but) risk more and achieve more, while Wayne Sleep, through such shows as *Dash* and *Song and Dance*, has almost single-handedly shown that dance can be popular, exuberant and fun. The tours abroad by such companies as the *Ballet Rambert* (Lucy Burge is superb) and the *London Contemporary Dance Theatre* have enhanced the reputation of British dancers (Charlotte Kirkpatrick is rather special at the *LCDT*, which will find it difficult to replace Robert Cohan). Richard Alston, Siobhan Davies and Ian Spinks work at their *Second Stride Company* and some of the energetic and theatrical ballets at *Extemporary Dance* offer hope for the future (under the directorship of Emilyn Claid). And a new contemporary group, *Dance Alliance*, led by Mary Fulkerson, head of dance at Dartington College, has made an excellent start. Between the tried and tested and the mad and modern there is a great gulf fixed. The *London Festival Ballet* and the *Sadler's Wells Royal Ballet* are doing little to help and the inadequate playing of many of the ballet orchestras is a serious impediment.

The old established *Freed* (94 St Martin's Lane, WC2; 01-240 0432) and its off-shoot *Turning Points* (46 Monmouth Street, WC2; 01-936 9919) are best for individually fitted ballet-shoes. For books on ballet try *Dance Books* or *French's* (see under Bookshops).

Best ballet company: *Royal Ballet* (but with so many decrepit dancers and such a paucity of new work it must be in danger of losing its Michelin star).

Best modern company: *LCDT* (energetic and tough).

Best experimental company: *Second Stride*.

Best male dancer: *Ashley Page*.

Best female dancer: *Elaine McDonald* OBE (when she comes to London).

Best choreographer: up for grabs.

Banks

After Edward I was unwise enough to expel the Jews, control of the money supply passed to *Lombards*; hence Lombard Street, the centre of banking today. And what a business to be in during the seventies and early eighties! As interest rates rose, so did profits; the inheritance is a mass of shining edifices (the NatWest Building supreme) which o'ertop the city's churches, and even St Paul's, proving that religion is all very well so far as it goes, but it doesn't get half as near to God as money does.

Indeed there are few good banks in London. In almost all of them the cashiers sneer openly when you ask them for money, they close when you need them to be open (a few *Barclays* branches now open on Saturday mornings), and their much advertised cash points are not to be trusted. The *TSB* remains open to 4 p.m. on weekdays, the *Giro Bank* keeps normal post office hours, and *Co-op* customers can cash cheques at some *Co-op* branches, but if you are desperate for cash at an unsociable hour, try Heathrow.

Now for the exceptions. *Hoares*, with only two branches, is a venerable family bank offering the sort of services the big five used to offer. Its head office, at the sign of the Golden Bottle in Fleet Street, is a dignified architectural delight. *Lloyds Bank* in St James's Street is well-proportioned in the manner of one of the adjacent London clubs. *Barclays*, just off Park Lane, is a remarkable example of Lysergic gothic, while the *NatWest* in Victoria Street, SW1 displays, above a model house, two stone squirrels hoarding nuts. *Drummond's Royal Bank of Scotland* in Spring Gardens, Trafalgar Square, is the only drive-in bank. *Coutts* seem to care.

I had one pleasant bank manager, who sang tenor in *Belshazzar's Feast* at the Albert Hall, and another, Mr Bate, who was sympathetically inclined, but nothing can erase the dreadful memory of Mr L. who, holding up a huge pair of scissors, brought to him specially by his secretary, announced: 'I want you to watch this,' as he sliced my Barclaycard in half. I crawled from *Barclays* a broken man, my voice an octave higher than when I went in. Mrs Barley has done what she can to restore my masculine pride.

Best bank: *Hoares*.

Benches

The very essence of a bench is that it should not draw attention to itself. But it is hard not to take pleasure from the benches along the *Victoria Embankment*. At their ends are iron camels rampant, which match, I'm sure, the camel in the *Embankment Gardens* (see under Statues). As consoling is the circular bench around the tree in Oriel Place, NW3. Very fine – except that you are not allowed to sit on them – are the striped benches along the walls of the striped dining room in the Adam-designed Apsley House, the home of the great Duke of Wellington and choc-a-block with his loot including a vast (11 feet high) naked (all but a fig-leaf) statue of Napoleon in white marble by Canova.

The traditional benches in the *Great Chamber* in the Inner Court of the Law Courts are good solid oak with good solid carved feet. Sitting on them does *not* make you a bencher; you need to be a senior member of one of the four Inns of Court to merit that honour. Sitting on a bench in a *McDonalds* hamburger restaurant is anything but an honour. Like as not it will throw you off again. This discourages customers from lingering too long over their grub. When the new *Euston Station* was built there was a public outcry because no benches had been provided. Commented a spokesman: 'They would make the place look untidy.' There are a few there now, but quite inadequate.

Best benches: *Victoria Embankment.*

Betting Shops

The mid-sixties were not just great for photographers and property developers. Punters had the time of their lives as well. It was possible in *Olympia* – which is where I then lived – to find a betting shop which would happily offer one third the odds for a place in a race even if the favourite was odds on. These were the years in which the big money men like Mr Bird and Mr Bull made their fortunes; with no tax to be paid there was really no excuse for losing.

Things are now sadly changed. There is little point in shopping around, for most betting shops offer the same odds. Only at the race tracks does the punter have any advantage, for there the tax is a mere 4% instead of 10%.

Currently the distressing odds on offer for place betting are as follows:

6 or 7 horses: ¼ the odds
8 or more horses, non handicap, favourite odds on: 1/6th the odds
8 or more horses, non handicap, favourite odds against: 1/5th the odds
8-11 horses, handicaps: 1/5 the odds

12-15 horses, handicaps: ¼ the odds
16-21 horses, handicaps: 1/5 the odds, 4 places
22 and more horses, handicaps: ¼ the odds, 4 places

If you can find a betting shop offering better odds than these, go there. It will not, however, be one of the big conglomerates.

Amongst the major bookmakers off the racecourse the only shopping around to be done is in the ante-post market. Here *Heathorn's* offer a big concession. Their advertised prices on the morning of a big race are guaranteed until midday.

At the racetrack (q.v.), it can be profitable and fun to shop around, but few of the bookmakers in the ring are prepared to take each way bets, although account customers can always bet each way.

The only way you can hope to win without psychic powers is to bet once in your lifetime, hugely, to win, tax paid, on a horse that is well fancied. There is the story of a very rich man at Monte Carlo, who asked the management if they would remove the limits for him to bet that evening. The casino manager asked, was he standing at the tables or sitting? Sitting, said the croupier. In that case, said the manager let him bet as heavily as he wishes. Evelyn Waugh, in whose collected letters this anecdote may be found, commented correctly that all the casino feared was one massive bet on an even chance. The moral is clear.

My favourite betting shops are those in which I have won. These include *Barnett Racing* in Richmond Road, Twickenham, where the counter clerk has an endearing dog, *William Hill* in Shepherd Market, W1 and *Mecca* in South Molton Lane. Mecca branches now take cheques with credit cards. A disastrous innovation! Recommended too are *Ladbroke* in Leadenhall Street and *William Hill* in Swallow Street, W1. Amazingly in Acton there is a betting shop called *James Joyce*.

Bicycles

On a bicycle you can pedal 1,600 miles before you have used the energy equivalent to one gallon of petrol, but it can be dangerous. The best protection is to wear a fluorescent belt, or at least clothes which are visible on the darkest of days, and a helmet. The 'Bell' helmet (available from *Beta Bikes*, 275 West End Lane, NW6; 01-794 4133 or *F. W. Evans*, 77 The Cut, SE1; 01-928 4785) is best. You can transport your bicycle free on British Rail and on the Circle, Metropolitan and District lines of the Underground system (though not during the rush hour). To buy a new bike I can recommend *Alan's Cycles* (79 Wandsworth Road, SW8; 01-622 9077) and *E. J. Barnes* (285 Westbourne Grove, W11; 01-727 5147), both of whom will part exchange. The *Paolo Garbini Cycle Centre Ltd* (36 Great Pulteney Street, W1; 01-734 9912) imports the famous Alan frame from Italy and has a wide stock of racing cycles. Paolo used to race. His daughter sells cyclists' macs, and other sports equipment. *Covent Garden Cycles* (41 Shorts Gardens, WC2; 01-836 1752) and the *Victoria Cycle Company* (53-55 Pimlico Road, SW1; 01-730 6898) are also reliable. Second-hand bikes are best bought either through the small ads of your local paper or the advertisement boards outside your local newsagent or by auction from *General Auctions*, 53 Garratt Lane, SW18; 01-870 3909 (Mondays at 10 a.m.). These auctioned machines have been stolen and unclaimed. Hire a bicycle through the Yellow Pages or from the *London Bicycle Company* (41 Floral Street, WC2; 01-836 2969) which runs the largest bicycle hire operation in London and has painted all its hire bikes yellow. A ten pound deposit with evidence of identity is necessary; the charge is two pounds a day or ten pounds a week.

Best for repairs is *The Bicycle Workshop*, 42 Lancaster Road, W11 (open afternoons) and *Bell Street Bikes* (73 Bell Street, NW1; 01-724 0456). For tandems try the *Tandem Centre*, (281 Old Kent Road, SE1; 01-231 1641). The bicycle stall in Leather Lane (see under *Street Markets*) is run by helpful, sensible people.

A useful handbook, *The Cycling Guide to London* is available at seventy-five pence from PDC (01-837 1460) and in most cycle shops. Even better is *On Your Bike* (85p from shops or £1 inc p&p from the London Cycling Campaign, Colombo Street, SE1 8DP), which includes 16 pages of maps to help you avoid London's traffic. From the same publishers at 55p (inc p&p) is the *South London Route Guide*.

Birds

There are extraordinary birds to be observed even in London. A greenish warbler was confirmed in Dollis Hill, and a cormorant was reported floating on the Thames by an apparently sober onlooker, while in our forty-feet urban garden my wife has identified goldcrests, siskins, and a flock of long-tailed tits. Any of the London reservoirs are worth watching, and south London is especially honoured by magpies, jays and crows. In *Tower Hamlets Cemetery*, Southern Grove, E3, over one hundred species of birds have been recorded. *The London Natural History Society* at the *Natural History Museum* (01-589 6323) has a strong ornithological section, and organises field meetings and weekend trips. The *London Wildlife Trust* (2 Selous Street, NW1; 01-403 2078) co-ordinates conservation within the City.

Adjacent to London are *Broxbourne Woods*, Herts (nightingales and nightjars), *Epping Forest* (redstarts and tree pipits), the *Hilfield Park Reservoir*, Herts (a multitude of ducks and gulls), the *Perry Oaks Sewage Farm* (west of Heathrow – waders and plovers), the *Queen Mary Reservoir*, Ashford, Middlesex (gulls, grebes, terns), *Rainham Marshes*, Essex (waders), the *Rye Meads Sewage Works*, Herts (ducks and warblers), the *Staines Reservoir* (waders, terns, and a flock of black-necked grebe), and *Walton Heath*, Surrey (warblers and great grey shrike).

Within the London A-Z area the following sites are particularly rewarding:

Barn Elms Reservoir (access only by permit from the Metropolitan Water Board, New River Head, Rosebery Avenue, EC1); turn east along Merthyr Terrace SW13 – the tenth best ornithological site for wildfowl in Britain.
(a) Winter: duck including smew.
(b) Spring and autumn: waders and terns.

Beddington Sewage Farm (access only by permit from Beddington Sewage Treatment Works, Beddington Lane, Croydon, Surrey); near Hackbridge Station.
(a) Summer: yellow wagtail, snipe, redshank.
(b) Other seasons: waders, snipe, short-eared owls, green sandpipers.

Regents Park (Baker Street Underground).
(a) Spring: willow warbler, chiffchaff, whitethroat, lesser whitethroat, spotted flycatcher.
(b) Autumn: pied flycatcher, redstart, wheatear, warblers, finches, thrushes, pipits, redpoll, tree sparrows, brambling.

Stoke Newington Reservoirs (no access but easily visible from aqueduct bridge); Lordship Road, near Manor House Station.
Winter: tufted duck, pochard, great crested grebe. (These waters stay ice-free longer than others in the London area, so that in hard weather a congregation of birds gather here.)

Walthamstow Reservoirs (access only by permit from the Metropolitan Water Board; see under Barn Elms); the twelve reservoirs are best approached from Ferry Lane (Tottenham Hale Station). The heronry may be seen from Coppermill Lane (Walthamstow Station).
(a) Winter: tufted duck, smew, great crested grebe.
(b) Summer: heron, great crested grebe.

Wimbledon Common/Putney Heath (free access). Various heath and woodland birds, especially rich in the summer months.

Best London bird-watching: *Barn Elms Reservoir.*
Worst London bird-watching: *Any underground carpark.*
Best London birds: *Green finches.*
Worst London birds: *The highly volatile ravens at the Tower.*

PS Exquisite miniature birds made by the jeweller, Alexander Fried, may be spotted and purchased at *Sarah Jones, 14 Basinghall Street, EC2, or at Stall 16 Covent Garden Market on Tuesdays.*

Blue Plaques

William Ewart MP, founder of the free public library, had the idea in 1863. A year later, after the scheme had been predictably rejected by the government, it found favour with the Royal Society of Arts, who commented that memorials to persons 'eminent in the arts, manufactures and commerce' might give pleasure to 'travellers up and down in omnibuses etc.' who would thus beguile 'a not very rapid progress through the streets.' How little London has changed! A hundred years after Ewart had his brainwave, he too was commemorated by a plaque at 16 Eaton Place, SW1.

By 1981, 438 official plaques had been erected in London besides those rogue plaques put up by individuals and societies. Over one hundred blue plaques are to be found in Westminster, while, at the time of writing, Barking, Enfield, Havering, Hillingdon, Kingston and Waltham Forest cannot muster one plaque between them.

The memorial to *Arthur Lucan* ('Old Mother Riley') at 11 Forty Lane, Wembley was opposed in 1978 by the Conservative GLC member for Brent North who claimed that the Labour controlled Council wanted the plaque 'as a misguided effort to curry popular favour'. But music hall entertainers have fared well as have insignificant British artists. *Karl Marx's* plaque has been smashed on two occasions and he now has one high up on the wall at Leoni's Quo Vadis Restaurant in Dean Street, Soho. *Lenin* received one when 16 Percy Street, W1 where he stayed in 1905, became the Royal Scot Hotel in 1972. The previous building on the site had been a vicarage!

The 'best' can only be a matter of taste. How gratifying that *Annie Besant*, organiser of the Match Girls, is remembered at 39 Colby Road, SE19. Similarly commemorated are *Mark Gertler* (32 Elder Street, E1), a brilliant but tormented artist, *Harry Relph*, alias Little Tich (93 Shirehall Park, NW4), who had an extra finger on each hand and still made folk bellow with laughter, *Violette Szabo* GC (18 Burnley Road, SW9), who gave her life for the French Resistance and *Chaim Weizmann* (67 Addison Road, W14), who helped to win the Great War and found the state of Israel.

The blue plaque on Chatham House, St James's Square, SW1, commemorates *three* Prime Ministers. The worst plaques must be those naming *John Dryden* (Gerrard Street, W1), *Joshua Reynolds* (Great Newport Street, WC2), and *Lady Di* and *Topham Beauclerk* at Great Russell Street, WC2. All are attached to the wrong houses. But perhaps the most ill-advised plaque, in the light of later events, is that to *Charles de Gaulle* (14 Carlton Gardens, SW1). In the words of Winston Churchill: 'He had to be rude to the British to prove to French eyes that he was not a British puppet. He certainly carried out this policy with perseverance.' For further details see Caroline Dakers's excellent *The Blue Plaque Guide to London* (Macmillan).

Bollards

Most Georgian bollards were made from disused cannon, their mouths blocked for ever with cannon balls. This, a 19th-century version of swords into ploughshares, accounts for the traditional shape, which may be seen in excellent repair in *India Street*, EC3, at the North end of Old Barge House Alley, Blackfriars, and elsewhere throughout London. Two fine old bollards marked 'SOMMERS TOWN 1817' may be spied in Pancras Road, and four bollards, survivors of the old clink and dated 1812 and 1826 are in Great Suffolk Street. A magnificent row of seven old bollards stands guard over Puma Court, beloved of Dickens, and just off Commercial St, E1.

There are bollards shaped like antique rockets in the *Strand*, and bollards made from shells outside the *Imperial War Museum*. In *Gracechurch Street*, EC3, the bollards are inset with coats of arms, and in *Cavendish Court*, W1, they are extremely suggestive. *Gough Square*, EC4, where Dr Johnson's House stands amidst the alien concrete, is generously sprinkled with attractive examples, but amongst the worst bollards, those in *Leicester Square* (a square which defies anything anyone seems able to do to improve it) are reminiscent of amputated limbs.

I am indebted to a Barclay's bank manager for directing my attention to some of the above. A bank manager who is tired of bollards is tired of life.

Best bollards: *India Street.*
Worst bollards: *Leicester Square* and *Browning Road*, E11.

Bookshops

There have never been so many beautiful bookshops in London, and it is a pleasure to write about them.

Take, for example, *Richard Worth* (9 Richmond Road, SW15; 01-788 9006). He adores books, has a comprehensive stock, but will get his customers anything not on his shelves. Or what about *Hatchards*? (187 Piccadilly, W1; 01-439 9921). This is the oldest bookshop in London, architecturally delightful and awash with enthusiasm and new fiction; it is not easy to leave such a bookshop empty-handed.

At the *Kensington Bookshop* (140 Kensington Church Street, W8; 01-727 0544) where they have one of the best children's departments, the staff are deeply committed – ask for Fred. *The Kilburn Bookshop* (8 Kilburn High Road, NW6; 01-388 7071) will also 'get anything', and at the celebrated *Heywood Hill Bookshop* (10 Curzon Street, W1; 01-629 0647) they not only know their books but have also read them. Those who report that 'it is not what it was' may be referring to the days when Nancy Mitford served there.

Maggs in Berkeley Square (No 50; 01-499 2501), which is very grand and has a good line in private press books and autographed letters, is a family concern par excellence. Their shop is haunted but the ghosts seem to be a little soporific these days (see under Ghosts). *Maggs* and *Bertram Rota* (4 Savile Row, W1; 01-734 3860 – strong in first and limited editions) have been staunch in their continuing campaign against the Ring, more active in the world of book auctions than elsewhere. The most remarkable examples of antique manuscripts and texts can be found at *Quaritch* (3 Lower John Street, W1; 01-734 2983).

Dillons (1 Malet Street, WC1; 01-636 1577), the academic specialist, has possibly the most knowledgeable staff of all and a carefully selected and arranged stock, but they have started charging their customers when ordering books for them. *Grant and Cutler* (11 Buckingham Street, WC2; 01-839 3136) is excellent for foreign language books. *Mandarin Books* (22 Notting Hill Gate, W11; 01-229 0327) is chaotic, but you will find books there that you will find nowhere else. Thus too *Compendium* (234 Camden High Street, NW1; 01-485 8944/267 1525). At *Compendium* you can buy American literature and choose from a wide selection of books which will help you to save the world. If you wish to save the world cheaply I suggest a visit to *Collets* (129 Charing Cross Road, W1; 01-734 0782).

The miniature bookshop which specialises in miniature books is *Bondy* (16 Little Russell Street, W1; 01-405 2737) and *Zwemmer* (76-80 Charing Cross Road, W1; 01-836 4710) is unparalleled for books on art and architecture. *Cecil Court*, between St Martin's Lane and the Charing Cross Road, is worth half an hour of anybody's time. Amongst intriguing shops there is *Dance Books* (9 Cecil Court, WC2; 01-836 2314). This of course is conveniently near to Floral Street, WC2; where everybody dances and the Coliseum, where ballerinas do. Actors go to the *Samuel French Theatre Bookshop* (52 Fitzroy Street, W1; 01-387 9373) which contains a vast selection of playscripts as well as sound effects, records, and books on the theatre. Horsey people clip clop to *J. A. Allen* (1 Lower Grosvenor Place, Buckingham Palace Road, SW1; 01-834 5606), a charmingly decorative little place. The best shop for 20th-century first editions is *Bell, Book & Radmall Ltd* (80 Long Acre, WC2; 01-240 2161). For Penguins, Pelicans and Puffins try the two *Penguin Bookshops* (10 The Market, WC2; 01-379 7650 and 10 King Street, Richmond, Surrey; 01-940 0483).

High Hill Bookshop (6 Hampstead High Street; 01-435 2218) combines great professionalism with vast enthusiasm. Local authors will be particularly well-treated there while *The Owl Bookshop* in Kentish Town, the *Gallery Bookshop* in Dulwich Village and *Hooks for Books* in Bromley South Precinct, all have passionate adherents.

Living in Twickenham, I have ten excellent bookshops within easy walking distance of my front door. Perhaps most whimsical is *Baldur Books* (44 Hill Rise, Richmond; 01-940 1214) where Eric, who presides over the place like Buddha and knows everything that is worth knowing about cricket, is a bookseller of substance. Two excellent children's bookshops in the area are *Langton's* (Church Street, Twickenham; 01-892 3800 – adult books too), and the *Lion and Unicorn* (19 King Street, Richmond; 01-940 0483), where there is a mat for children to sit on and a wide range of picture books.

The shop it is most difficult to walk out of must be *Bernard Stone's Turret Bookshop* (43 Floral Street, WC2; 01-836 7557), whose eccentric stock seems to suggest that life is actually less important than books – which it may very well be – and that, just as nature isn't artistic unless and until you put a frame around it, so life is nothing until it is bound and catalogued. Stone's greatest strength lies in his new and second-hand volumes of poetry.

For legal, naval and military subjects try *Francis Edwards* (83 Marylebone High Street, W1; 01-935 9221) in splendid new purpose-built premises. *The Costume Bookshop* (Queen's Elm Parade, Fulham Rd., Old Church St, SW3 is best for Costume and *The Travel Bookshop* (13 Blenheim Crescent, W11) is best for – wait for it! – travel.

Sadly there are also shops in London where books remain principally merchandise. *Words and Music* and *Susan Reynolds* (various branches) specialise in buying quantities of books which have outlived their usefulness and selling them at cut prices in end of lease premises; and while *W. H. Smith* probably sell more books than all other British bookshops put together, even in the larger branches the staff seem to know little and care less about books and authors.

And what about *Foyles?* Christina's policy towards her staff and the antiquated system, which makes it almost impossible to buy and pay for books without giving up your entire holidays so to do, make a trip to *Foyles* an experience many would not like to repeat. A friend requesting information at the enquiry desk about a particular book, was asked by the assistant: 'Book? Vot ees book?' However it is only fair to add that *Foyles'* stock is one of the wonders of the world, and that, where any normal bookshop would have two or three copies of books about Ruskin or Czechoslovakian wildlife, *Foyles* will have thirty-seven. Life without *Foyles* would be blander and duller and less frustrating.

Best bookshop: *Turret Bookshop*, 43 Floral Street, WC2.

PS An invaluable adjunct to any bibliophile is *Bookshops of Inner London* by Diana Stephenson (Roger Lascelles). Alternatively *The Bookshops of London* by Martha Redding Pease (Junction Books).

Bottlenecks and How to Avoid Them

The worst bottlenecks in London are:

(a) Westway/Marylebone Road/Euston Road

What makes this bottleneck particularly depressing is the continuing views of planners' blight as you sit sniffing the carbon monoxide. The underpass proved a waste of time and money. How to avoid it?

(Going east) up Cosway Street, right into Shroton Street, left up Lisson Grove, right into St John's Wood Road, right into Park Road, into Regent's Park at Hanover Gate, left around the Outer Circle, out of the park at Gloucester Gate, left along Parkway, right along Camden High Street, left along Crowndale Road into Pancras Road, and through to King's Cross.

(Going west) into Regent's Park at Park Crescent, left along Outer Circle, out of the Park at Hanover Gate, right along Park Street, left along Lodge Road, left along Lisson Grove, right along Church Street, straight over Edgware Road (by the cinema), left around Paddington Green, right into the Harrow Road and follow the signs for the A40(M).

(b) Knightsbridge

Should be avoided whenever possible, either by use of South Carriage in Hyde Park (enter either at Exhibition Road or Park Close) or via Beauchamp Place/Pont Street/Chesham Place/Chapel Street into Grosvenor Place.

(c) Hammersmith Flyover and the Great West Road

Can best be avoided by using (going west) Hammersmith Bridge, turning right along Lonsdale Road/The Terrace/Mortlake High Street and the Lower Richmond Road, recrossing the river (if you wish to) at Twickenham Bridge and so to the M4 or – better since it's usually clear – the M3 and the M25. The same system works just as well going east.

(d) Hampstead's Heath Street and Fitzjohn's Avenue

Can be desperate. Frognal Lane, Frognal and Lower Terrace may be your salvation (a pretty route anyway). Use West End Lane rather than Finchley Road to get to Frognal Lane, but don't try it on Friday evenings at all.

(e) Staples Corner, where the Edgware Road crosses the North Circular

There is a way of avoiding this mess, but, alas, I'm sworn to secrecy. The North Circular is, with the Western Avenue at

Perivale, quite the worst London road for traffic (worse even than the South Circular), but for journeys which skirt North London there seems no sensible alternative. Get a decent stereo set in your car and let Mozart's flute concertos ease away your cares.

(f) Archway Road, N6
Bad going north *and* south. Use Highgate Hill/Highgate High Street/North Road and North Hill.

(g) Southampton Row
This may be avoided by the cunning use of Bloomsbury Square, Bedford Place or Montague Street, and Russell Square.

(h) Old Kent Road and New Cross
Use Rotherhithe New Road/Evelyn Street and Creek Road to Greenwich (or the same in reverse). This is usually a worthwhile diversion, especially during the rush hours.

(i) Streatham High Street
Travelling north between midday and 3 p.m. Don't.

As a general rule it saves petrol (and pollution) to switch off your engine if you're likely to remain static for more than thirty seconds. Hyde Park Corner has the highest accident rate; hence the despised traffic lights. Safe journey.

Bowls

Once you have your set of woods – they have glamorous names such as Tyrolites, Lignoids, Jackfinders and Henselites – which should last your lifetime, bowls is one of the cheaper sports. It is ideal, of course, for those who no longer care to leap around. The most select club is the *Royal Household Club*, whose members are the royal staff at Windsor Castle and Buckingham Palace and who bowl at Home Park, Windsor. One of their regular fixtures is with another exclusive club, the one at Wormwood Scrubs Prison.

The City Institutions play at *Finsbury Circus Gardens*, but the most famous London club is *Paddington*, a green glade amidst the concrete jungle. For full details the English Bowling Association (2A Iddesleigh Road, Bournemouth. Tel 22233) should be contacted. It is remarkable that in Britain more people play bowls than any other sport.

Best bowling: *Paddington*.

Bread

If you think a baguette is where you put the baby to sleep, this entry is not for you.

Harrods can offer the customer 130 kinds of loaf, though none of them is baked on the premises, but since you normally eat only one at a time, I recommend either *Dugdale and Adams* (3 Gerrard Street, W1; 01-437 3864) for their French loaves, *Bonne Bouche* (22 Bute Street, SW7; 01-584 9839) for their black bread, *Justin de Blank's Hygienic Bakery* (46 Walton Street, SW3; 01-589 4734) for its entire range, or the *Bamboo Grove Wholefoods* (100 Park Avenue, NW10; 01-965 8549) for its granaries. *Goswell Bakeries Ltd* (Caxton Street North, E16; 01-474 6141), which also specialises in 'natural' breads, will deliver. *W. H. Summers* (323 Fulham Road, SW10; 01-352 8286) bakes bread throughout the day. The best Jewish bread for Friday nights (if you can't bake it yourself) comes from *Grodzinski* (13 Brewer Street, W1; 01-437 6007 and other branches).

If I had to choose one from all these I would go for *Dugdale and Adams*, which has a fan club of passionate officeworkers, whose lunch-time would be drab indeed without their daily fix. The bread is cooked in 100-year-old Vienna ovens with low ceilings and steam injection. They supply Buckingham Palace and many Soho restaurants.

Best baker: *Dugdale and Adams.*

PS Mother's Pride thick white sliced makes quite the best fried bread.

Breakfasts/Brunches

For a grand occasion try the *Connaught Hotel* (Carlos Place, W1; 01-499 7070) where a typical menu reads as follows:
Fresh orange juice
Papayas in syrup
Grapenuts and cream with bananas
Pheasant kedgeree
Mixed grill
Coffee
and toast, marmalade etc.

But friendlier is the *Cosmo* (5 Northways Parade, NW3; 01-722

2627), where you may eat excellent croissants (q.v.) or massive fry-ups and sit as long as you wish over them. Chefs on their mornings off eat breakfast at the *Regent Palace Hotel* (12 Sherwood St, W1; 01-734 7000) and chefs ought to know.

Also powerfully recommended are the breakfasts at *Bacon and Eggs* (South Molton Street, W1); *La Capannina* (5 Vigo Street, W1; 01-734 8353); *The Cherry Top* (Paddington Street, W1); *Chubbies* (22-23 Liverpool Street, EC2; 01-283 3504); *Diana's Diner* (30 Endell Street, WC2; 01-240 0272), where porridge is served; *Old Burlington* (140 Old Burlington Street, W1; 01-734 6177) and the *Quality Chop House* (94 Farringdon Street, EC1 – porridge *and* kippers); also the *Betjeman Room* in the *Charing Cross Hotel* adjoining the station, where British Rail maintains the tradition of Cooper's Marmalade. Coffee too is usually first rate in British Rail hotels. Rough and ready is *Arthur's Restaurant* in Smithfield (60 Long Lane, EC1; 01-600 8243); specialities are black pudding and fried bread. Also in Smithfield try the 'Full House' (£2.95), a massive fry-up at the *Fox and Anchor* (115 Charterhouse Street, EC1; 01-253 4838).

At the *Albert Pub* (Victoria Street, SW1), which has installed a division bell for MPs, kippers, kidneys, kedgeree and bacon and eggs are served, and not just to sitting members.

Best breakfast: *Cosmo.*

Breweries

No doubt about the best brewery in London. The accolade goes to *Young's Ram Brewery* in Wandsworth High Street. Not only is there a beautiful brewer's house attached to the brewery and a friendly tap with real ale, but in the back yard you may meet several geese beak to beak, as well as Gertie the goat and, naturally enough, a ram. There is also a golden one on the weather-cock. From this brewery there is a horse-drawn delivery (by dray horses) to establishments within three miles.

Whitbread's Brewery in Chiswell Street, EC1, incorporates a courtyard enclosed by well-restored 18th-century buildings. But the most intriguing feature of the Brewery may be found in the *Porter Tun Room*, an impressive place in which to give a banquet, for it boasts a king-post roof, sixty feet high. On the wall is displayed the Overlord Embroidery, which was sewn by twenty embroiderers at the Royal School of Needlework. It is 272 feet long and depicts the story of the Normandy landings (Operation Overlord). Also at *Whitbread's* is the Speaker's Coach, built in 1698, and portraits of the first three Samuel Whitbreads painted by Reynolds, Gainsborough and George Richmond.

Another fine old brewery is *Truman's* in Brick Lane, E1, against whose wall grows a fine fig tree. Both the building – residential as well as commerical – and, I suspect, the tree is late Regency.

Best brewery: *Young's Ram Brewery.*

Bridges

There are twenty-seven bridges between Teddington and the Tower. For several centuries there was only one permanent structure, that being *London Bridge* (c 1200 AD) which was replaced in 1832 with a granite bridge, designed by the Rennie family. This replacement was itself sold in 1968 to a consortium of Arizonan businessmen who believed, according to some rumours, that what they were paying for was *Tower Bridge*. So now we have a third and regrettable *London Bridge*. *Tower Bridge*, the most distinctive by far of London's bridges, would have been worth buying. It may not be beautiful ('steel skeletons clothed with stone,' was the architect's description), but it has raised and lowered its twin bascules, each weighing 1,000 tons, some half million times since the bridge was built almost a hundred years ago. The pedestrian way was such an attraction to suicides that it had to be closed but recently it has been redeveloped as a tourist attraction.

Waterloo Bridge, a clean and graceful design by Gilbert Scott, completed in 1939, is renowned more for the view *from* than the view *of* it ('earth hath not anything to show more fair . . .'). *Albert Bridge*, a cantilever and suspension affair (R. W. Ordish, 1873) looks especially glamorous at night and has more distinction than most of the Thames bridges. Myself, I have a silly fondness for *Hammersmith Bridge*, a suspension bridge designed by Bazalgette (1887). It is painted an improbable colour and is improbably furnished with statues underneath where there shouldn't be statues – there was money left over from the subscriptions – and over-elaborate lights on top; but it works.

Richmond Bridge is a fine old bridge, 250 years old, beautifully proportioned and perfectly placed where the river curves. It looks best from the water however, or from a couple of hundred yards up the Surrey bank.

Despite the claims of *Tower, Waterloo, Albert, Hammersmith* and *Richmond bridges*, and with a happy sigh for Telford's retractable iron bridge at St Katharine's Docks, I think the prize belongs to *Rennie's* five-arched stone bridge over the Serpentine. Everybody loves it and the views from it, and rightly so, but driving over it you scarcely notice it. Since we've lost two of *Rennie's* bridges, we should treasure this one.

There are numerous bad bridges. *Vauxhall and Hungerford railway bridge, Battersea* (Bazalgette again) and *Cannon Street* are without much distinction. Many dislike the railway bridge between Strand-on-the-Green and Kew; I like it for its iron soul. Another fine iron bridge crosses the Regent's Canal at *Camden Lock*; this too makes few claims to beauty and so achieves it.

Best bridge: *The Rennie Serpentine Bridge.*
Worst bridge: *Cannon Street Railway Bridge.*

Brothels

The trouble with brothels is that one only gets to hear of them after they have closed down. 'Ah yes,' someone is bound to say, 'there *used* to be a brothel in *Clarges Street*, but I don't think it's there now.' Currently London has no brothel worthy of the name and only three madames, the best and most expensive being called Brigitte. The delightful Cynthia Payne had her establishment in *Ambleside Avenue*, Streatham, but the police moved in after the politicians and the bishops and Madame Sin moved out. Latterly she returned with an authorised biography and literary critics, chat-show hosts and media persons in hot pursuit. Similarly with the *Spartacus Club* in Barnes, a haven for cherry-pickers until the sharpies arrived.

I thought I knew of one brothel which has been and still is open for business as usual, although I never fancied it would be one of your fin-de-siècle, chandelier and whalebone type of places, as featured in popular culture. This one in Mayfair has a red neon sign advertising private French lessons. Your intrepid guide rang the bell and, having been studied through the spyhole, was greeted by a French lady of uncertain years. I told her my tale; this book I was writing and so on . . . She pursed her lips: 'In zees,' she said, 'I am not interesting,' and shut the door in my face. It seems I must have been mistaken. There *is* a brothel somewhere behind Bonham's salerooms; I'm not quite sure where.

A correspondent writes to me from the New King's Road: 'Brothels? There was one next door, but we found it noisy and got rid of it. Really, David!' Of course there are brothels of a kind in London, and they are to be found in *Stamford Hill, Finsbury Park, Bedford Hill, Balham, Amhurst Park*, N16 and the *Argyle Square* area of *King's Cross*, especially the Hillview Estate. They are squalid, dangerous, and ideal only for those who like their sex furtive and hasty.

Incidentally there is still a pub – the *Silver Cross*, 33 Whitehall, SW1 – whose licence to run a brothel, issued by Charles I, has never been revoked. But it is not exploited either.

Worst brothel: *University College car park.*
See also under Sex.

Budget Restaurants

'Bad food is never cheap.'

It's no use living in the past. It's not helpful to remember that when I was at Oxford I used to lunch at *George's* in the market where for two shillings (10p) you could get steak and three vegetables with apple crumble for a further ten-pence (4p) and custard free. Now your only chance of eating substantially for under a pound is to opt for fish and chips (q.v.) or an unfashionable pub.

The best quality food at really modest prices is to be found at those theatres, art galleries and cinemas that take the trouble to cater. I can confidently recommend the *Lyric* Hammersmith, the *National Film Theatre* and the *National Gallery* cafeterias. On my latest visit to the *Barbican* the snacks were chaotically organised and not really worth the hassle. The *Churchill Theatre* (Bromley), the *Oval House* (Kennington), and the *Royal Festival Hall* are a good deal better than the *Natural History Museum*, *Madame Tussauds*, or the *Albery Theatre*. The *National Theatre* has several eating places, but the chocolate cake at any of them sits on your stomach like four hours of Peer Gynt, and the coffee is as weak as at the *Tate* – which is saying something.

The two *Cooke's* eel and pie houses, one at 41 Kingsland Road, E8 (01-254 2878), the other at the Cut, SE1 (01-928 5931), are crowded, unlicensed, and excellent value at no more than £3.50 a head. At the first you sit at marble tables and the cabaret consists of live eels in a tank; at the second it's wooden benches and formica surfaces. If the idea of eel pie and mash revolts you, *Le Steak Nicole*, 72-73 Wilton Road, SW1 (01-834 7301) is an effective antidote. Downstairs you can pay £5.50 inclusive and get a delicious steak with chips, salad, and all the accessories, served in the French manner. The *Cafe Jardin* does a steak in a herb sauce with all the pommes frites you can tuck away and a salad for £6.95. The elegant *Au Jardin des Gourmets* (5 Greek Street, W1; 01-437 1816) serves an excellent *prix fixe* menu at £9.50 inclusive, and the *Gavroche* (!) does a fixed price lunch for £16.50, which I suppose must by their standards rank as a budget meal. But back to basics.

The Quality Chop House (94 Farringdon Road, EC1; 01-837 5093) is unlicensed and closes at tea-time. But its very glamorous wooden interior, its excellent English food, and nourishing breakfasts make it a 'working class caterers' of the highest quality.

Nontas (16 Camden High Street, NW1; 01-387 4579) is bustling and friendly and serves home-made sausage and meat loaf, toasted cheese and jugged hare, all at genial prices. *Luba's Bistro* (6 Yeoman's Row, SW3; 01-589 2950) is wonderfully left bank and unchanged from the fifties. It would be no surprise to find Juliette Greco being nihilistic here. The food is . . . robust, and the stuffed mushrooms are especially good. It's noisy, unlicensed (but no corkage if you bring your own), the kitchen is entertainingly visible, and the lavatories don't always flush – but then you can't have everything!

The best pancake house (it's smart to call them crêperies) is *My Old Dutch* (132 High Holborn, WC2; 01-404 5008) with a choice of some 200 fillings. I had been advised to try the *galettes* (buckwheat pancakes) at *Obelix* (294 Westbourne Grove, W11; 01-229 1877), but found them not unlike shoe-leather for texture and shredded wheat for flavour. As for the *Crêperie* (56a South Molton Street, W1; 01-629 4794) I can only report that the pancake I had was neither tasty nor cheap, and that the pepper poured out of the pepper-pot like soft sand in a cliff fall.

There is a *Spud-u-Like* (who thought up *that* name?) in Shepherd's Bush (north side of the green) and this chain is likely to do as well down south as it has in the northern outback. Potatoes are baked with a variety of fillings and you can take them away; come to think of it, these too are substantial and less than a pound a spud.

Luigi and Paolo have two snack bars, one in Blenheim Street, adjacent to Phillips Auctions, one at 21 Woodstock Road, W1 (01-629 5039). Both are excellent, and notable for good humour and custard tarts.

Vegetable samosas at *The Jerusalem Restaurant* (150 Shaftesbury Avenue, WC2; 01-836 7145) are a sensational thirty-pence worth.

Finally a sad story. *Mrs Beeton's Restaurant* (58 Hill Rise, Richmond; 01-948 2787) provides bored housewives with the opportunity to become professional restaurateurs. They operate a rota, and you can sometimes be lucky and eat well and cheaply. But on my last visit everything was off. It was 1.15 p.m. *Everything*. Miserably the waitress admitted that there was no food left, but no one had got round to putting 'closed' on the door.

Best budget restaurant: *Lyric Theatre*, Hammersmith.

For detailed information see *The Good Caff Guide* by M. Fletcher (Wildwood).

Just a Bite, Egon Ronay's Lucas Guide 1983, is useful, but my views seldom coincide with those of the Ronay inspectors. However Egon himself has done much to improve standards at Motorway Caffs, a task which would have exercised Hercules to the ultimate.

Buskers

If Ken Livingstone is remembered for nothing else he will be remembered with gratitude by London commuters for his efforts to legalise the life-enhancing activities of the London buskers.

I do not know what happened to the charming fellows in fezzes and aprons who used to do silly dances in Leicester Square, nor to the celebrated escapologist who performed there to cinema queues. Maybe he tried to escape once too often. However a sighting of an escapologist in *Portobello Road* has recently been reported and he may indeed be – let us hope he is – the same one. But in *Green Park, Tottenham Court Road* and *Charing Cross* tube stations, in the *King's Road* next to Safeways, and above all in *Covent Garden*, buskers have never been so numerous, so talented, and, I hope, so profitable.

To busk in Covent Garden (the Piazza outside the Actor's Church is the prime location, but you can also be busked these days in King Street and James Street) you need a performer's licence (details from the Covent Garden Community Association,

45 Short's Gardens, WC2; 01-836 5555). They may audition you – more likely not.

The best London busker is the one who plays Bach Violin Partitas in undergrounds and subways, where the acoustics are most favourable; a stylish flautist – not note-perfect, but near enough – enlivens *Brewer Street* and *Old Compton Street*, Soho, but it is years since I saw or heard a one-man band. The worst buskers are the ones who play 'Stairway to Paradise' in the Leicester Square tube so out of tune that even my niece can tell they are out of tune.

Bus Routes

Let us take the good ones first. The *7* meanders through the back streets of Ladbroke Grove in the general direction of Oxford Circus with a cheerful disregard for schedules. The *11* strikes out boldly from Chelsea to the City and has even made it on occasions. (London bus drivers are a determined race; if their route required them to terminate at the source of the Nile they would certainly get there in due course and probably in convoy.) The *53* is a common occurrence but always comes when you are awaiting something else; the *221* is much admired by connoisseurs. As for the *185*, it is admirably regular and frequent, but, frustratingly, does not go anywhere much. The following may be recommended: *7, 11, 15* (very scenic), *16, 24, 53, 74, 88, 134, 159, 185, 221* and *227*. Also all Bayswater Road buses.

Now for the bad news. The *2* and *2B* are disasters. The *9* seldom comes, which is a shame, because it is such a useful route and takes in the best bits of Kensington. By the time the *22* arrives one is so relieved (a sixty minute wait is not unusual) that one smiles all the way from Putney to Liverpool Street. I have waited an hour and a half for a *176* (it was raining) and the notorious *54* seldom if ever completes its journey. The *53* (Camden Town to Plumstead) has to cope with the interminable Elephant and Castle–Old Kent Road stretch and often can't. The *104* and *187* hibernate for ten months of the year, and the *68* is virtually extinct despite a World Wildlife Fund Appeal. The *'Bloody 33'* is only described so rudely because it always comes when one wants a *90B*.

Best bus route: *15* east to west, north of the river, including the City and Limehouse.

Worst bus routes: *37* east to west, south of the river and *137* north to south, through the West End (RIP).

PS Carl Davis's *Variations on a Bus Route* selected the 31 for special attention. Does he know something we don't know?
PPS The GLC Central Zone Travelcard which enables you to mix tube and bus travel on a single ticket is a welcome innovation.

Butchers

The qualities I look for in a butchers: blue and white tiles, men in striped aprons with no fingers missing, a cashier partitioned well away from the meat, a willingness to prepare a crown, or obtain mutton, or sell boiling fowl or capons, or find good solid marrow bones for dogs. Surprisingly there are a great many such butchers in London.

But recently a new kind of butcher has emerged, a specialist who supplies restaurants and private clients with meat prepared for cordon bleu standard cooking. *Marc Beaujeu* will roll pork with prunes, alternate layers of veal and shallot or pistachio stuffing, create sophisticated hamburgers for expatriate Democrat Professors on sabbatical from Stanford. At *Boucherie Lamartine* (22 Ebury Street, SW1; 01-730 4175) he does all this and, even more importantly, ensures that the quality of meat he serves is the best available. His beef is Aberdeen Angus, his lamb comes from the west country, his rabbits from his own garden in Sussex, his game from Newbury, his chickens from Bresse.

By common consent the best of the old-fashioned butchers is *C. Lidgate* (10 Holland Park Avenue, W11; 01-727 8243) who passes all these tests with ease but who also sells fresh poultry and game, and sensational sausages and pies. *Bailey's and Allen's* in Mount Street, W1 run them close. *J. Bailey* (116 Mount St, W1; 01-499 1833) is a glazed symphony to dead birds and beasts but, since they also serve free range poultry and eggs, one cannot regard them as callous. They claim to be the oldest poulterers in the country and have Royal warrants dating back 150 years. *Slater & Cooke, Bisney & Jones* (67 Brewer St, W1; 01-437 2026) are unusual in that they provide special counters for separate meats. It's a splendidly clean, air-conditioned place where a request for haggis will not faze them. Haggis and baby goat have been spotted also at *John Lane* (6 Walkers Court, W1; 01-437 8903). Good kosher butchers include *M. Taylor* (31 D'Arblay Street, W1;

01-437 4119) and *I. Zell* (14 Newburgh St, W1; 01-437 2176). *Robert Portwine* (24 Earlham Street, WC2; 01-836 2353) is for connoisseurs, while *Harrods* (for variety), *Leadenhall Market* (for value and freshness), *Bifulco* (St John's Wood and Frith Street, for Italian cuts), *Randall & Aubin* (16 Brewer St, W1; 01-437 3507, for calves' tongues and feet, brains and tripe), *Bartholdi* (4 Charlotte Street, W1; 01-636 3762, for smoked meats), *J. and J. Dalli* (78 Brewer St, W1; 01-437 8870, for Toulouse and Marquez sausages), and *Fenn's* (Unit 6 Covent Garden, WC2; 01-379 6427, for game and venison) may safely be recommended. London's first organic butcher is called just that (*Organic Butcher*, 217 Holloway Road, N7; 01-609 7016). All David Mullen's meat is free range and guaranteed free of chemical additives.

The Bromley branch of *Manson's* is recommended, but not other branches, and it's worth considering that on Saturday afternoons from about four o'clock onwards *Murrays* (9 Church St, NW8; 01-723 6245) sell off assorted cuts at plebeian prices. *Sainsbury's* branches are dependable. *Dewhurst's* put too much colouring and such into their mince.

Best butcher: *Boucherie Lamartine.*
Best traditional butcher: *C. Lidgate.*

Butterflies

The most beautiful place in London, quite without exception, is the Butterfly House at *Syon Park*, Brentford (01-560 0881). You walk into what appears to be a large tropical conservatory and all around your head flutter these fragile brightly coloured bits of nonsense. They fly in pairs but appear to have no knowledge that there is such a thing as evil in the world. Any insects that might mean them harm are kept down through the cooperation of baby quail, and the whole environment has the surreal atmosphere of a dream. Children love it. There is also a modest display of stick insects, locusts and so forth, the prize exhibit being a red-legged tarantula which just sits there looking glum. The souvenir shop sells quality goods, and you can buy pupae of tortoiseshell butterflies which you take home to increase the population spread of these enchanting creatures. You can study the extraordinary complexity of lepidoptera in the display cases, but dead butterflies are no substitute for live ones.

Dead ones may also be viewed on the walls of *G. Dionysus*, the

Greek restaurant in Heath Street, Hampstead, and can be bought in the shop next to Sainsbury's in Streatham. A variety of live butterflies may be seen in London cemeteries, including the following species: Common Blue, Large Skipper, Peacock, Orange Tip, Tortoiseshell and Wall.

On the first night of Peter Brook's production 'U.S.' for the RSC at the Aldwych a butterfly was removed from a matchbox and a match applied to its wings. The RSPCA threatened to take Mr Brook to court. He explained to them that the butterfly only *appeared* to be burned, but that, if anyone was told, a butterfly would in fact be burned the following night.

Best butterflies: *Syon Park*, Brentford.

Buttons

There are two wonderful button retailers in London: *The Button Queen* and the *Button Box*. The former (19 Marylebone Lane, W1; 01-935 1505) specialises in rare and antique buttons, while the greatest strength of the latter (44 Bedford Street, WC2; 01-240 2716) is in supplying buttons in modern materials, many of which are weird and wonderful. It is no big thing to remove your dreary high street store buttons from your off-the-peg purchase and replace them with something astonishing from the *Button Box*, which also operates in Covent Garden Market on Tuesday and Wednesday and on Saturday in Camden Lock.

Cabarets

A healthy new trend towards iconoclastic cabaret has been observed by town-watchers. At the old *Comedy Store* in Meard Street the great Alexei Sayle had his baptism and any who wished to chance their arm at stand-up comedy were encouraged to do so, and then given the bird by a sharp and sadistic late-night audience. *The Comedy Store* has not only survived but has moved to new premises at 28 Leicester Square, WC2; (01-437-6455) where at midnight every Saturday the young comedians risk everything and the old hands gong them off the stage. Those who survive are tough and funny and politically sophisticated. Whatever you do don't miss the Oblivion Boys, should they come your way; the Joeys are also riding high.

Regular venues include *The Cornet* (Lavender Gardens, SW11, every Friday); for others see the events magazines.

Best Cabaret: *The Comedy Store.*

Canals

The best – and one of the very few – London canals is the *Regent's Canal*, built in 1820 to link the Grand Union with the Thames at Limehouse. It can be fished in and walked along from Bethnal Green to Uxbridge if you are energetic; one can live on it in one of the houseboats moored in Little Venice, eat on it in a not particularly good floating restaurant, or travel on it via Jason's Barge. A recently opened tow-path at Noel Road, Islington, makes a pleasant stroll, but don't stroll too far because it goes underground for more than half a mile. The most picturesque stretch is at the back of St Pancras, the most interesting between the M4 Motorway and Southall, for within a mile or so you find sewage works, gas works, burial grounds, and a series of locks. Further west at Harlesden amongst the cemeteries, car-breaking plants, freight-line depots and railway hostels, picturesqueness runs riot and the charms of the canal become esoteric. An excellent companion is *London's Canal Walks* by Marie Rodda (published by the London Tourist Board, the GLC, the British Waterways Board and Capital Radio – free from LTB offices).

Canteens

The willingness with which experienced Londoners pay large sums of money for moderate lunches amazes me, when an excellent alternative is available. I mean of course canteens.

It is all a matter of confidence. If you look as though you work for the establishment whose lunch you intend to sample you are unlikely to be asked for your credentials. Only at broadcasting establishments and television companies have things been tightened up somewhat and then, if you can get an appointment with somebody working in the building, you have no further problems about your subsidised lunch. Now it goes without saying that I am not *suggesting* that you should do any such thing as take possession of a pork pie under false pretences – that would be most improper – but it is possible . . .

The best canteen food I have recently enjoyed was at *Goldsmiths' College* in New Cross where Parson's Hat, the chef's special, turned out to be a sensationally good haddock and pastry dish. At the *National Film Theatre* canteen, which is first-rate value, the public wander in and out, and nobody checks membership cards.

Other recommended cantéens: the *Royal College of Art*, the *Barbican Staff Canteen* (the staff eat better than the public and why not?), the *Crown Court* behind Harrods, the *National Theatre* (excellent value and coffee at 10p), the *Civic Centre*, Bromley and the *Liverpool Victoria Friendly Society* building in Southampton Row. The *London School of Economics* canteen is variable. If you are smartly dressed and look like a budding executive there is no reason why you should not survive on the free food available at conferences. The *UK Press Gazette* gives a list of forthcoming press conferences so that, if you have sufficient chutzpah or a press card, you need not starve.

Best canteen: *Goldsmiths' College*.

Car Parks

(See also under Parking Meters)

Heal's in Tottenham Court Road is well run and usefully located for Soho; avoid it at Christmas time however. *Harrods* car park just off the Brompton Road is hopeless during the sales, but useful at other seasons. The *National Theatre Car Park* is highly recommended and adds significantly to the pleasure of a visit to that theatre; but remember where you left the car! It is charitable to assume that the *Barbican* car park is still getting itself together; at the time of writing it is chaotic. The *Charing Cross Garage* under the arches is cheap enough at £1 for 24 hours. At weekends it gets taken up by stall-holders from Collector's Corner. Useful though.

The best of the public car parks are at *Bedfordbury*, WC2, *Spring Gardens*, SW1, and *Brewer Street*, Soho, where the staff are friendly and great spielers. *Space House*, Kingsway, WC2 is attended for 24 hours, and costs less (£1) after 5 p.m.

Disastrous experiences have been reported at the car park in *St Martin's Lane*, at the multi-storey car park in *Whitcomb Street*, WC2, at *Tesco's* in Ballards Lane, Finchley, where you can get neither in nor out, at the *Swiss Centre* in Coventry Street with a s-l-o-w hydraulic lift, and at *Marble Arch*, which is so huge that you can walk about a mile before discovering that you (and your car) are lost. Strong men weep in that underground limbo, which is also a pound for the clamped and the crazed but it is not the worst . . .

Best car park: *Heal's.*
Worst car park: *Terminal 2, Heathrow.*

Car Washes

The best car washes in London are those where the work is done by hand. There is such a one in Wood Lane opposite White City and another next to the Victoria Coach Station, which is very posh but expensive. In Lowndes Square a car wash by hand is priced at £3, even if you have a Rolls. Another hand car wash may be found in Russell Road, W8, at the back of the Motorail Terminal. There is also a car wash in North End, NW3 which my research suggests is the only one with special wheel brushes. Also recommended: NCP, Brewer Street, and the Wellington Garage, NW8. At 69p (currently) Persepolis in the Chertsey Road, Chiswick is quick and good value. It appears that cars are cleaner north of the river.

Once upon a time little boys used to wash your cars for you while you watched a play at the Theatre Royal, Stratford East. Big boys sometimes offer the same service in Soho Square, and can get nasty if you say no. There were two little boys who used to operate a similar service on the corner of Avonmore Road, W8. One would say: 'Give me sixpence and my friend here won't throw a stone at you.'

Best Car Wash: *Lowndes Square.*

Cathedrals

St Paul's (see Architecture) is a miracle of course. *Southwark Cathedral* is a delightful amalgam of early 13th century Gothic (the fine Tower and the massive Choir) and late Victorian Gothic (the Nave by Sir Arthur Blomfield). There are memorials to John Fletcher and Philip Massinger, the playwrights, and to Shakespeare's baby brother, Edmund, the actor. The Harvard Chapel, commemorating the founder of the University and the charming Lady Chapel (restored) are both significant. Southwark has one window of Elizabethan glass, and several fine modern examples of stained glass.

Westminster Cathedral was inspired – if that is the word – by St

Mark's, Venice. It can seat a congregation of 2,000 and is the principal Roman Catholic Church in England. Hesketh Pearson found the right phrase when he described its style as 'later marzipan period'; Hugh Kingsmill thought it an 'incipient Turkish bath'.

Amidst all this grandeur, spare a thought for the *Ukrainian Catholic Cathedral of the Holy Family in Exile*, Duke Street, W1.

Best Cathedral: *St Paul's.*

Cats

> For he keeps the Lord's watch in the night against the adversary.
> For he counteracts the power of darkness by his electrical skin and glaring eyes.
> For he counteracts the Devil, who is death, by brisking about the life.
> For in his morning orisons he loves the Sun and the Sun loves him.
> For he is of the tribe of Tiger.
> From *Jubilate Agno* by Christopher Smart (1722-1771)

The most remarkable cat in London is *Binks*, a huge tabby. Binks (1921-1926) resided at Bates, the hatters, of 21a Jermyn Street, W1, where he would sit in the window in a top hat with a simulated cigarette between his rakish lips. He still does, although now he observes the passing scene from a glass case and through glass eyes. The *fattest* (live) cat in London presides regally over the ladies' lavatory at Paddington Station. The *largest* cat in London, and probably the world, may be seen poised over the Catford Shopping Precinct, back arched as though mousing or sniffing the dogs at the dog track down the road.

Dick Whittington's cat is made of stone and was added to the statue of Dick Whittington on Highgate Hill in 1964. It has its head turned as though listening to the bells from Bow, which supposedly strengthened Dick's resolve to turn back and become a hero in fish-net tights. Whittington was a mercer, wool exporter, royal banker, and four times Lord Mayor. His cat is probably legendary.

The *worst* cats in London are to be found in Dirty Dick's pub (202 Bishopsgate, EC2; 01-283 5888); they are mummified and mouldering.

For buyers and sellers of cats (though not real ones) I can recommend Erika Bruce who has a stall in Grays-in-the-Mews Antique Market (1 Davies Mews, W1), and is a confirmed felinophile. Cherry Saltzer's shop, Catz (25 Bedfordbury, WC2; 01-836 6513), is another purr-lined paradise.

Best cat: *Binks.*
Worst cats: *Dirty Dick's.*

Cemeteries

Hugh Meller's *Illustrated Guide and Gazetteer to London Cemeteries* (invaluable) lists exactly 100 cemeteries within the London A-Z map area. They range from half an acre (the *Jewish Cemetery* in Kingsbury Road, N1) to 182 acres (*St Pancras and Islington Cemetery*, High Road, East Finchley, N12). The finest are *Highgate, Brompton, Kensal Green* and *Norwood*, and the oldest *Bunhill* (corrupted from Bonehill) *Fields*.

(a) Brompton
The catacombs have been full for over half a century and their gloomy gates – snakes twining around inverted torches symbolising eternity triumphing over life extinguished – would deter any but the most intrepid. The cemetery is also closed for burials. The finest monuments are both to pre-Raphaelites, Frederick Leyland's tomb, ornately extravagant in the arts and crafts style, and the Gothic sarcophagus in Sienese marble memorialising Valentine Prinsep. Other notable residents include: Emmeline Pankhurst, Lionel Monckton, Gentleman John Jackson, Sir Squire Bancroft, George Henty, Richard Tauber and Brandon Thomas. One can imagine that crowd enjoying quite a lively party in the hereafter.

(b) Highgate
Wild and overgrown and full of interest. Professor Girouard: 'There is a vast army of Victorian merchants, officers, widows and judges gently crumbling into anonymity beneath ivy and saplings and lushly sinister mares' tails.' The Egyptian catacombs, Julius Beer's mausoleum, based on the original at Halicarnassus, and Karl and Eleanor Marx's memorial (by Lawrence Bradshaw 1956 in the new part of the cemetery), are not to be missed, but there are also: a lion (commemorating a lion-tamer), a horse (commemorating a horse-slaughterer), and a dog which led the

mourning procession at his prize-fighter master's funeral. Lying there also: Jacob Bronowski, John Brinsmead, Charles Cruft, George Eliot, William Foyle, Quaritch and Colnaghi, the book dealers, Galsworthy, Radclyffe Hall buried with her first lover, Charles Green, the balloonist, Philip Harben, the chef, Rowland Hill, 'Hutch', Frederick Lillywhite, who introduced round-arm bowling to cricket, Carl Rosa, Mrs Henry Wood, Herbert Spencer, the Rossetti Family, and Patrick Wymark, much missed.

(c) Kensal Green

An historic cemetery with the widest range of mausolea, temples, obelisks, caryatids and follies in the country. Lying there: Bartolozzi the engraver, Blondin, who kept on crossing Niagara Falls on a tight-rope and once on stilts as well, Marc Brunel who built tunnels and his son, Isambard, who built bridges, Decimus Burton, Cassell and Murray, the publishers, Cruikshank and Leech, the caricaturists, Hood and Leigh Hunt, the poets, Thackeray, Wilkie Collins and Trollope, the novelists, Sydney Smith, and William Whiteley and James Pope-Hennessey, both murdered under similarly tragic circumstances.

(d) Norwood (the South Metropolitan Cemetery)

Battered by time and vandals, both official and unofficial, Norwood has a splendid array of crumbling monuments, including a Doric Temple (for the Ralli family), a fine sarcophagus (for Alexander Berens, linen-draper), and a magnificent monolith (for the antiquary John Britton).

A variegated group of residents include: Isabella Beeton and Mr B., the publisher, Charles Bravo, Sir Henry Doulton, David Cox the younger and Samuel Prout, artists, Sir Henry Tate, and James Epps, the man whose splendid contribution to our well-being was to introduce cocoa to Britain.

(e) Bunhill Fields

Specifically for dissenters, Bunhill is remarkable for the quality of the men and women who lie there. These include: Bunyan, Blake, Defoe, Quare – the clockmaker, Watts – the hymnwriter, Buxton – the philanthropist, Robert Tilling – the murderer, fourteen assorted Cromwells, and Hugh Pugh, the Welsh Harpist.

The *Royal Hospital Burial Ground* is notable, as you might expect, for the longevity of its inhabitants with two old soldiers who lived to be 112, and William Hiseland (1620-1732) who served eighty years in the army, and married when a centenarian. Also two women who joined the army in masquerade to search for their soldier husbands. One, Hannah Snell, served in the navy too, was once punished with 500 lashes, published her memoirs in 1750, went on the stage, and died insane.

Don't miss: the waterfall at *Crystal Palace*; the crocuses at *Golders Green*; the rhubarb at *Mortlake* R.C. Cemetery, and the Muslims with their flowers and joss-sticks at Tottenham Park. The five Iranian terrorists who died in the Embassy Siege lie in an unmarked grave at the neglected *Woodgrange Park. Brockley* Cemetery is renowned for the names of those who lie there. Here are a few: Alberta Codbolt, Absalom Dandridge, Amelia Gossage, Horace Lermit, Alice Pyefinch, Philadelphia Sampson and Benjamin Sloss.

What happened, I wonder, to all the Pyefinches and Slosses? There are only two of each in the current London Telephone Directory.

Best cemetery: *Kensal Green.*
Worst cemetery: *Lee Cemetery* (the new section), Verdant Lane, SE6.

Chapels

The *Chapel of the Savoy* squats beside the huge hotel like a small tug half-hidden behind the luxury liner it has been towing into port. It is the official chapel of the Queen – the royal pews to the west end of the Chapel are slightly raised so as to be a few feet nearer to God – and the Royal Victorian Order, and is itself Victorian, having been rebuilt from a late Perpendicular original after a fire in 1864. It is notable for a stained glass window to D'Oyly Carte, an old wooden roof, and a plaque commemorating a Mr Gosling who died in 1586:

'So well inclined to poor and rich
God send more Goslings to be sich.'

According to *Brideshead Revisited* it is a poky little place in which divorced people got married, as Julia tragically does.

The *Chapel-of-Ease* in South Audley Street, built of brick and stone c 1750 is full of charm. Designed by a carpenter (Benjamin Timbrell), it has just the qualities you might expect; artisan and delightful.

Within the *Holy Sepulchre Church*, Newgate, whose graveyard was once particularly popular with bodysnatchers, is a Musicians' Chapel, which has windows celebrating Sir Henry Wood, one-time deputy organist there, John Ireland, Dame Nellie Melba and many other musicians. Characteristically Sir Malcolm Sargent has his own niche in the sanctuary. The Church has a Cecilian Festival every November.

St Paul's contains several chapels; the *Jesus Chapel* to the east of the High Altar, has a memorial to 28,000 Americans who died fighting in the last war. This affects me more than *All Souls' Chapel* which is chock-full of marble and dedicated to Kitchener.

The Chapel Royal in St James's Palace has been much renovated since it was supposedly built to a Holbein design, but its ceiling still bears a monogram H and A for Henry VIII and Anne of Cleves.

Finally do not miss the *Chapel* at Greenwich Hospital (adjoining the amazing Painted Hall). Rebuilt by James 'Athenian' Stuart with statues and an altar-piece by Benjamin West, it is quite something. Stuart was first a painter of fans, but a visit to Greece changed all that. The Adam brothers owe him a fortune.

Best chapel: *Chapel-of-Ease*, South Audley Street.

Characters

London's most distinguished characters have come from modest homes. *Chaucer* was born in the Vintry, *Sir Thomas More* in Milk Street, *John Donne* and *John Milton* in Bread Street. *Defoe* was a butcher's boy, *Pope* came from a linen-draper's shop, and *Browning* was born in Camberwell. I'm not sure about Falstaff, Sweeney Todd or Pickwick!

The most public 'characters' in London may be found on Sundays at Speaker's Corner, both speechifying and heckling. (The right of free speech does *not* incidentally apply there, Irish demagogues having been arrested quite recently for arguing that British troops should get out of Northern Ireland.) These orators are somewhat stagey and have been characterised on the stage by *Heathcote Williams*, himself a very weird character. More endearing is the elderly lady in white shorts who used to arrive at the British Museum every morning on a racing cycle to spend the day in the Reading Room (see V. S. Pritchett). Then there's *Lord Glancarty*, who is convinced (and why not?) that the North Pole has a hole in it through which flying saucers are ejected a bit like clay pigeons. But the House of Lords is stacked high with eccentrics. *Dave Little*, well-known south of the river, is larger than life. Once a schoolmaster his classes were more than the system could stand, and he became a grave-digger, building up his graves into miniature gardens. Last heard of he was running antique fairs, where most of the interesting characters congregate. One is *Rita*, a well-built lady who sells bits and bobs at the Streatham Fair on Thursday mornings (next to the ice rink). She buys her stock at jumble sales, wheels it to the market on a shopping trolley, and gives much of it away to children. My postman is a delight. 'Nothing but brown envelopes,' I complained. 'Why don't you bring me something from Hollywood, California?' The next morning all my letters (including the bank statement) had been inscribed 'Hollywood, California' at the top.

Despite the claims of 'Red', the Irish late night snack-seller in Soho, and most metropolitan judges and magistrates (the Master of the Rolls sucks blackcurrant sweets on the bench) the most loved character is the *Queen Mother*, who on the Royal Yacht apparently telephoned to some of the staff: 'I don't know what you old queens are doing, but this old queen could do with a whisky . . .'

Best character: *The Queen Mother.*

Cheese

Paxton and Whitfield of 93 Jermyn Street, SW1 (01-930 0259) run a cheese club. You pay £9 a month and receive five different cheeses, of which one at least will be British. *P & W*, who also deal deliciously in hams, have realised that in London appreciation of cheese has lagged a long way behind appreciation of beer, with which it is partnered so amiably. Their Stilton is the best in the world and their manager, Mr MacEwen, is one of only four cheese Chevaliers in the country. An even broader selection of the sixty plus known British cheeses may be found at *Mainly English* (14 Buckingham Palace Road, SW1; 01-828 3967); amongst the most delicious are Swaledale, Luscombe Blue and Cotherstone. Lymeswold is *not* amongst the most delicious. Typically *Harrods Food Hall* offers no fewer than 450 cheeses, even if it does take so long to get served that you can watch a Brie ripen as you wait. Try Dolcelatte (Italian) or Chaume or Caprice de Dieu (French). Mr Bowen, the buyer, is also a Chevalier of cheese.

Also recommended: *Mace & Potts* at the corner of the Strand and Essex Street, *Fratelli Camisa* (1a Berwick Street, W1; 01-437 7120), *G. Parmigiani Figlio* (43 Frith Street, W1; 01-437 4728) for Italian cheeses and *Neal's Yard Dairy* where they make it *and* sell it. It's worth a trip to the *Prince Regent* pub in Marylebone High Street to see their imposing collection of cheese dishes, and it's worth reading *The Great British Cheese Book* by Patrick Rance (*Macmillan*) or *Guide du Fromage* (revised English edition published by Aidan Ellis) on your way.

Best cheeses: *Paxton and Whitfield.*

Worst cheeses: *Anything* bought in a supermarket of a squidgy consistency wrapped in a triangle of tin foil with a picture of a laughing peasant on it.

Chess

The sad news is that *Prompt Corner* in Parliament Hill Fields, a chess café where you could suck spaghetti all day while considering the modern Benoni, has closed. I would have been a regular there, had my dog not vomited on the feet of a most serious group of players, who scarcely blinked, even when I mopped round their odorous feet with a sopping rag. In its place is the *Chequers* (18 Chalk Farm Road, NW1). There is chess every night of the week there and at the *King's Head* pub in Moscow Road, W2, where lightning tournaments are run most amicably, on Mondays. You can also play at the *Hole-in-the-Wall* (12 Sutton Lane, Chiswick, W4; 01-994 4107) which has an intriguing inn sign and the *Black Lion* (2 South Black Lion Lane, W6). The best clubs are *Streatham, Morley College, the Athenaeum*, and *Richmond and Twickenham*.

The venue for matches in the London League is the top room at the *St Bride's Institute*, where, behind glass doors, there is a fascinating library of antique books on chess puzzles and problems. *St Bride's* is ideal for chess, being gloomy, airless and intense. The worst chess experience is attending the over-crowded annual *Phillips and Drew* tournament and paying £3 for the privilege. Open-air chess is played on *Clapham Common*, and the best chess set is a fine old Staunton downstairs at *Simpsons-in-the-Strand*, for long associated with chess players.

Game Advice, the north London chess centre (1 Holmes Road, London, NW5; 01-485 4226, closed 2 p.m.-3 p.m.), has a huge selection of books, sets, boards and clocks; the specialists for chess computers are *Competence* (263A Eversholt Street, NW1; 01-380 0666), and for antiquarian chess books *Caissa Books* at Strand A 18/19 (01-629 3644) in the basement of *Gray's Antique Market* (1-7 Davies Mews, W1) are recommended.

The best opening for White is the Giuoco Piano, and for Black the French Defence.

Children's London

(See also such entries as Bookshops, Butterflies, Farms, Hamburgers, Kites, Mexican Food, Model Boats, Museums, Swimming, Theatres, Toys etc.)

A few suggestions for twitchy parents of bored children:

Phone *Kidsline* (01-222 8070) between 9 a.m. and 4 p.m. weekdays, or send for a booklet of ideas and events to Kidsline, 44 Earlham Street, WC2. Or try *Children's London* (01-246 8007) for Ed 'Stewpot' Stewart's topical hints. *What's On for Youngsters* (SAE to Information Office, Dept for Recreation and the Arts, County Hall, SE1) gives a complete list of activities in GLC Parks and Open Spaces. There should be a copy in your local library. The *One o'clock Clubs* for under-5s can be life-savers. The Children's pages of *City Limits* and *Time Out* are also useful, particularly if you like organic picnics and Third World puppet shows.

To hire cassettes or to send them as presents I recommend *Tapeworm*, 36 Boileau Road, W5 (01-997 8291). For long car journeys pre-recorded stories on tape are indispensable.

Morley College (61 Westminster Bridge Road, SE1; 01-928 8501) run monthly family concerts with participation. The *Purcell Room* (South Bank, SE1; 01-928 3002) holds mini-concerts for five-year-olds and over once or twice a month on Sunday afternoons.

The Factory (Chippenham Mews, Marylands Road, W9; 01-286 1656) runs Saturday morning (11-12.30) theatre workshops for under-12s. The *Cockpit Theatre* (Gateforth Street, NW8; 01-262 6935) has one of the liveliest TIE schemes in London. The *Polka Theatre* (240 The Broadway, SW19; 01-542 4888) is the best children's theatre. The *Screen-on-the-Hill* (see Cinemas) runs a Saturday morning Kids' Cinema Club, at which adults are admitted only as guests of young members.

I took my children to *Staveley's* fish and chip restaurant (642 King's Road, SW6; 01-731 4248), because it advertises a children's disco at lunchtime Saturdays and Sundays, but although we were assured several times that it would begin 'any moment now', it never did. *Bentley's* at the Ace of Spades, Kingston-by-Pass, Surbiton (01-397 8752) runs a Sunday Funday with dancing and games and a children's menu. Other restaurants which cater particularly for children (and which I haven't mentioned elsewhere) include the *Pizza Huts* (they provide high chairs, crayons and paper) and the Soda Fountain in the *Tree House* toy shop (237 Kensington High Street, W8; 01-937 7497). Talking of tree houses most children will enjoy being taken to *The Gardens* (99 Kensington High Street, W8; 01-937 7994), the old roof gardens of Derry and Toms. Exotic birds stroll through the shrubberies in the rarefied air above Kensington. Sunday lunch is best.

Or try the excellent Sunday carvery at the *Holiday Inn* (17 Sloane Street, W1; 01-235 4377). While you linger over your coffee, you can watch the children frolic in the handsome pool.

Chimney Sweeps

From William Hone's *Table Book* (1826):

On Monday, the first of May, 1826, the first anniversary dinner of the 'United Society of Master Chimney Sweepers' took place at the Eyre Tavern, St John's Wood, Marylebone:

About eleven o'clock, two hundred of their apprentices proceeded in great regularity through the principal streets and squares at the west end of the town, accompanied by an excellent band of music. The clean and wholesome appearance of the lads, certainly, reflected much credit on their masters . . . the boys were regaled with a substantial repast of roast beef and plum pudding; after which the masters themselves sat down to a very excellent dinner provided for the occasion . . .

Mr Bennett, of Welbeck Street, addressed the company on the subject of cleansing chimnies with the machine, the introduction of which he was confident would never answer the intended purposes. He urged the absolute necessity of climbing boys in their trade; and instanced several cases in which the machines were rendered perfectly useless: most of the chimnies in the great houses at the west end of the town were constructed in such a manner that it was utterly impossible to clear them of soot, unless a human being was sent up for that purpose . . .

The best chimney sweep in London is *Mr A. L. Ashby* (143 Harvist Road, NW6; 01-969 1633) who still uses the old-fashioned brush method and charges a gentlemanly £3.50 a go. But he doesn't send boys up the chimney.

Best sweep: *Mr Ashby.*

Chinese Restaurants

For many years after the first Chinese restaurants opened in Brighton, the British public believed that Chinese food consisted of wun ton soup, sweet and sour pork in greasy batter, chow mein and bean shoots, with ice cream or lychees as afters. This, of course, was a libel on an ancient civilisation for whom eating was a philosophy. The best Chinese food in the world may now be had in Hong Kong, but London is not far behind.

The cluster of restaurants around Gerrard Street, London's Chinatown, the *Rendezvous* restaurants and the *Red Lion* in Richmond, the Cantonese pioneers who opened the *Good Friends* and the *New Friends* in Dockland, and the trendy West End establishments of *Mr Chow* have brought a welcome variety and sophistication to those who enjoy oriental food. Diners can choose between Cantonese, Pekinese, and Szechuan food, but the best Chinese restaurant currently in London claims to be the first to specialise in food from Hunan province.

At the *Hunan* (51 Pimlico Road, SW1; 01-730 5712) you will be brought julienned cucumber with hoysin sauce while you study the menu. If this seems rather like taking a Masters degree in oriental studies, you may request Hunan's special Leave-It-To-Us Feast. Particularly delicious is the shredded chicken in sesame dressing, the roast Hunan duck basted in honey and soya, the stuffed phoenix chicken and the black beans, typically spicy with a flavour of smoke. I haven't and won't try the sliced jelly fish – I'm funny that way – but I can strongly recommend the Dynasty Wine from China and the marvellous Mei Kwei Lu, a golden liqueur flavoured with wild roses.

Almost as good is the *I Ching* (40 Earls Court Road, W8; 01-937 4707) notable for its Chinese mussels and its chicken fillet sautéed in oyster sauce and served in Yam Birds Nest. *Memories of China* (67 Ebury Street, SW1; 01-730 7734) is a clear third best, but also strongly recommended are: *The Kew Rendezvous* (110 Kew Road, Richmond; 01-940 1334) which is the best designed modern restaurant in Greater London, the *New Friends* (53 West India Dock Road, E14; 01-987 1139), *Poon's* (4 Leicester Street, WC2;

01-437 1528) economical and to be preferred to their Covent Garden branch, *Raffles* (319 Kilburn High Road, NW6; 01-328 9070), *Golden Duck* (6 Hollywood Road, SW10; 01-352 4498) and *Paper Tiger* (10 Exhibition Road, SW7; 01-584 3737).

And the uniquely chaotic *Cheun Chang Ku* (7 Wardour Street, W1; 01-734 3509) has the best fried rice in London and dim sun to dream about.

With so many excellent Chinese restaurants to choose from, it would be pointless to mention the worst. The obsessed should join the *Chinese Gourmet Club* (249 Sandycombe Road, Kew, Surrey; 01-940 5714).

Best Chinese restaurant: *Hunan.*

Chocolates

There have been only two significant moments in my development as a human being. The first took place in Elgin Avenue in the early sixties and I prefer not to speak of it (does anyone still wear roll-ons?). The second was the day I discovered *Bendick's bittermints*. The bittermint is a plain dark chocolate filled with mint and surrounded by foil. A single mouthful and you are participating in the decline and fall of the Roman Empire. It is obtainable from its HQ (Bendicks, 195 Sloane Street, SW1; 01-235 4749) and other Bendick's branches in Royal Exchange, New Bond St, Throgmorton Street, and Wigmore Street, W1, as well as most serious-minded delicatessens, but, besides Bendicks, London is choc-a-bloc with chocs.

Ackerman's Chocolates (9 Goldhurst Terrace, NW6; 01-924 2742) not only do a mischievous line in champagne truffles and noisettes, but they can also supply a chocolate zoo and delectables for diabetics, who deserve a bit of luxury. At *Quirk's* (76 St John's Wood High Street, NW8; 01-586 9525), where you must expect to pay £4 a pound, they enjoy pouring melted chocolate on fresh strawberries. At *Charbonnel et Walker* (1 Royal Arcade, 28 Old Bond Street, W1; 01-629 4396) you can buy a boîte blanche with a greeting spelt out in gold-wrapped chocolates or chocolates for children with animals on top. *Thornton's* (2 The Market, WC2; 01-836 2173) sells handmade chocolates but specialise in toffee, while *Lessiter's Chocolatiers* (167a Finchley Road, NW3; 01-624 5925) have attracted adherents who will be stretched on the rack before they will part with a rum truffle.

On the subject of truffles the best in London, at 25p a truf, come from *Prestat* (40 South Molton St, W1; 01-629 4838). Actually that is not so expensive. At *Teuscher* near the Rockefeller Center, New York, truffles are 92 cents each. (At least the one I ate was.) A one pound carton of Napoleon truffles costs a mere £7.70, but will never be forgotten (incidentally truffles will keep for over six months in a deep freeze). Furthermore Prestat, founded in 1908, has exclusive rights to chocolate moulded Paddington Bears. A little bear is £2.50, a giant one £9.50 milk or plain. (Personal shoppers only.) Belgian hand-made chocolates are obtainable from the Regent Emporium (8/12 Quadrant Arcade and 80/82 Regent St, W1; 01-437 4513).

Best chocolates: *Bendick's.*

Worst chocolates: The confectionery machine, westward District Line, South Kensington, fails to deliver any. *Which* magazine reports that one out of four attempts to get chocolate out of such machines ends in failure, and one out of eight in the loss of the money!

Churches

How is it possible to choose between Wren and Hawksmoor, Vanbrugh, Butterfield and Gibbs? Between *St Bartholomew-the-Great*, the oldest parish church in London, and Norman architecture at its noblest with a brick tower and a wooden turret housing a complete ring of bells, though these are never rung lest the patients in Bart's Hospital are disturbed, and the Gibbs baroque of *St Mary-le-Strand*, the finest traffic island in the world? Between the prettiness of *St John's, Downshire Hill, Hinde Street Methodist Church*, the Victorian Gothic of *St Augustine*, Kilburn and the high splendours of *St Mary the Virgin*, Bourne Street, SW1 with its small but excellent professional choir? It isn't possible.

St Dunstan's in Stepney Green within its seven-acre country churchyard is miraculous. It escaped the Blitz, which was half a miracle, and it boasts a majestic east window by Hugh Easton, representing the risen Christ above the rubble of the East End. And is it fair to compare *St Magnus-the-Martyr*, whose interior T. S. Eliot described as 'inexplicable splendour of Ionian white and gold', *St Bride's*, the Cathedral of Fleet Street, whose 226-feet Wren spire inspired a local baker to invent the wedding cake (within the Cathedral's bowels were discovered seven earlier churches and 5,000 skeletons), *St Mary Woolnoth*, and *Christ Church*, Spitalfields, two of Hawksmoor's masterpieces, and *St Andrew Undershaft*? To choose between them is like choosing between spring and autumn or Donne and Herbert.

So the choice must be instantaneous: *St Ethelburga-the-Virgin-Within-Bishopsgate*. The virgin saint behaved so impeccably during a 7th-century plague that Bede remarked: 'No person who knew her ought to question but that the heavenly kingdom was opened to her, when she departed this world.' Her brother, St Erconwald, was also a saint – that couldn't have been easy – and her father possibly the King of East Anglia. Anyway her church is tiny, merely 56½ feet long and 30 feet high, and dates back to the early 15th century, though the doorway could be even earlier. The west front of common ragstone with a silly little bell-turret on top reminds me of a small bull terrier standing staunchly against the encroaching bulls of Bishopsgate. It survived both Great Wars and the Great Fire but has been much renovated. The organ, described by those who know about such things, as having a mellow tone with an admirable violin diapason and great flute stops, fills much of the interior, and three attractive windows tell the story of the voyages of Henry Hudson, he of the Hudson River, and his gallant crew. Having vicariously shared their adventures you may, by permission of the verger, pass into the tiny garden at the rear of the church. Here pigeons drink from the terracotta bowl of the fountain, this and the octagonal pool around it being the gift of the Billiter Literary Society in June 1923. Even in rough weather the garden may be enjoyed for there's a covered loggia.

Overlooked as it is by skyscrapers and office buildings this must be the most peaceful place in the City of London. On the way out you step over a motto taken from the ancient temple of Aesculapius: *Bonus Intra, Melior Exi* – 'Come in Good, Go out Better'. *St Ethelburga's Church* is an architectural muddle, unassuming, little written about by the posh church-fanciers, but all the same *one does*.

Best church: *St Ethelburga-the-Virgin-Within-Bishopsgate*, SW1.

PS There are many books on London churches. *The Good Church Guide* (Ed. Anthony Kilmister – Blond & Briggs/Penguin) is a splendid read, with an excellent section on London.

Cinemas

The home video boom in Britain, where video has proved more popular than anywhere in the world, is making it even tougher for London cinemas to survive. Yet most of the 'good' ones flourish. By 'good' I mean those which offer interesting films in comfortable surroundings and project these films expertly at affordable prices to interested audiences. I shall be specific. The following are good: The *National Film Theatre*, the *Screen-on-the-Green*, the *Screen-on-the-Hill*, the *Gate* chain, the *Camden Plaza*, the *Curzon*, the *Academy*, the *Minema*, the *Everyman*, the *Electric*, the *Ritzy*, Brixton Road, the *Roxie*, Wardour Street, the *Rio*, Dalston, and the *Sherlock Holmes Centre*, Baker Street. The *Barbican* runs a repertory cinema with an interesting repertory policy, and the newish *Lumière* in St Martin's Lane promises well.

Bad cinemas are those which offer bad films badly projected in minimal comfort to boorish audiences. In such circumstances the price is immaterial; one would be better off at home. Bad, in one way or another, are these: The *Eros*, the *ABC*, *Coronet*, Holloway Road, the *Ritz*, Leicester Square, the *Odeons* at Lewisham and Swiss Cottage, the *Cinecenta* cinemas, and the *Kilburn Classic*.

Good features of the good ones: The *Curzon*, which is not cheap, and *Gate 2* are luxuriously comfortable. So are the *Camden Plaza* and the *Lumière*. The *Minema* is delightfully intimate. The *Academy* shows worthwhile shorts and will run a film that is losing money if it believes that it deserves to succeed. The late *Paris Pullman* used to show excellent late-night films every night of the week; now only the *Classic*, Leicester Square has programmes every night, and they are not always worth staying awake for. The *Sherlock Holmes Centre* has well-balanced double-features. The *Electric* is eclectic and committed. It has a season ticket scheme; £17.50 for a book of ten tickets to be used at your pleasure, but its closure is imminent. The *Ritzy* is fun, but has financial problems too. The *Rio* and the *Roxie* are brave. The *Everyman* is hooked on the classics.

The *Screens* on Green and Hill, which like the *NFT*, the *Gates*, the *Electric*, the *Ritzy* and the *Roxie*, are clubs with reciprocal membership arrangements and instant membership, are remarkably in touch with current trends and respect their audiences, not starting their main feature until all the paying public are in their seats. (At a recent visit to the *Screen-on-the-Hill* the film had been running a half hour when the box office manager rushed into the auditorium and shouted: 'Jesus Christ!

We've been robbed!' But what could *I* do?) The *NFT* offers remarkable value, interesting lectures, informative literature and excellent cheap food, though its booking services could be improved. The *Scala Cinema Club* (275/277 Pentonville Road, N1; 01-278 8052), once a porn place, is now showing interesting films, including, occasionally all-night 'trash' programmes.

Bad features of the bad ones: The Swiss Cottage *Odeon* has 'scarily situated lavatories'. The *Ritz*, Leicester Square, built by Jack Buchanan, is draughty, over-priced with bad projection and promotion. It has also removed its lovely art deco ladies from its walls. The *Cinecentas*, while sensibly staggering the times of their programmes, have tiny screens which are hard to see and poor sound which is hard to hear. The *Eros* shows terrible films. The Thorn-EMI circuit duopoly is a continuing scandal and discourages a new generation of concerned cinema-goers.

Best cinemas: The *NFT* and the *Curzon*.

Clairvoyants

Whether it is auragraph readings, psychic development, electro-crystal therapy, self-hypnosis, or merely old-fashioned clair-voyance you're after, 33 Belgrave Square, SW1 should be your first port of call, for this is the centre of the *Spiritualist Association of Great Britain*. In the Conan Doyle Room, decorated with an imposing chandelier and plastic flowers, I attended a public demonstration by *Janet Smithers*, the cheeriest of mediums. She encouraged me to believe that the book you are now reading would be a success, and passed on a message for me from 'Cyril'. *Cyril?* There are meetings at the centre (01-235 3351) every afternoon (3.30 p.m.) and evening (7.15 p.m.) and the charges are modest. *Paul McElhoney* specialises in apport seances and the production of ectoplasm, but the clairvoyant currently held in the highest regard is *Mr Benjamin*.

My appointment to see a Romany clairvoyant at *Mysteries* (Monmouth Street, WC2; 01-240 3688) got off to a shaky start when they wrote down the date and the time of the appointment incorrectly. When finally I got to see the Romany who had been most strongly recommended (at £12 a throw I needed a strong recommendation) she got my age wrong by eleven years, and just about everything else wrong as well. But a variety of fortune-tellers, using palmistry, psychometry and crystal balls, are available at *Mysteries*, and I may have been unfortunate.

A recent squabble between Zak Martin who runs the *London Psychic Centre* (weekends at the Sherlock Holmes Hotel, Baker St, 01-486 6161)) and the mystical stall-holders at the *Camden New Age Psychic Centre*, Camden High Street, is currently unresolved.

A word of warning. Don't expect to receive alarming messages from the beyond. British clairvoyants seem extremely anxious to tell you what you wish to hear. Their messages tend too towards vagueness and admit of many interpretations; they *never* give you the winner of tomorrow's three thirty.

Best Clairvoyants: the *Spiritualist Association of GB*.*

Clocks

Should you find yourself in Fleet Street on the stroke of noon, hurry to *St-Dunstan-in-the-West* (an interesting church anyway, for John Donne was once its vicar and Izaac Walton its vestryman). In a niche stands the only known contemporary statue of Elizabeth I. But the church's chief claim to renown is its clock, removed when the old church was pulled down – Charles Lamb wept to see it go – and returned from sanctuary in St Dunstan's Lodge, Regent's Park, in 1936. The clock (Thomas Harris, 1671) projects over the pavement, and behind the dials stand the two giants variously referred to as 'savages', 'wooden horologists', 'bell-thumpers' and 'Gog and Magog'. The mechanism is basic and the giants strike the bell 'so indolently', writes an anonymous author, although in fact they only *appear* to strike it, 'that spectators often complained that they were not well up to their work'. Despite this, and despite their being 'nude almost to impropriety' they were universally admired and 'Punch was hardly so popular'.

Other interesting clocks include the one at the *Horniman Museum*, which has a whole tower to itself, like a pip-squeak *Big Ben* (even pipper and squeaker is the pathetic little thing outside *Victoria Station*); the *Fortnum and Mason's* clock, which chimes the quarters and on the hour the founders trot out to make sure that everything in Piccadilly is as it should be – incidentally William Fortnum was a footman to Queen Anne; the much loved *Selfridge's* clock, and of course *Big Ben* himself. The name properly applies not to the clock but to the 13½ ton bell, struck at

---

* They will also supply you with a list of Spiritualist churches in your neighbourhood.

the Whitechapel Bell Foundry, which happily still survives. A huge fob watch complete with winder overhangs *Arthur Saunders*, watchmaker, of Southampton Row. But the best clock in and around London has to be the astronomical clock (Nicholas Oursian, 1540) over the Anne Boleyn Gateway at *Hampton Court Palace*. Still working, cunning and beautiful, it is quite a clock.

Don't omit – if you love clocks – to visit the fine collection in the *Guildhall Library*, where a marvellous reference section on London history is housed. And if you wish to buy a fine antique clock, try *Strike One* (51 Camden Passage, N1; 01-226 9709) with a selection of long cases.

Best clock: *Astronomical Clock*, Hampton Court.
Worst clock: At *World's End*, Chelsea, a fashion boutique, is displayed above the entrance a clock with 13 hours on its dial. The hands spin extremely fast backwards night and day. That way madness lies.

Cocktails

Cocktails and laughter
But what comes after
Nobody knows . . . Noël Coward

The American Bar at the *Savoy* is for well-heeled old-timers; Harry's Bar at the *Park Lane* is for Hemingway types, although Harry has been replaced by David. At the Nichols Bar of the *Cafe Royal* the ghost of Oscar Wilde sips at a weak hock and seltzer and Augustus Johns line the walls, while, if you wish to fantasise that you're meeting Faye Dunaway for a natter about old times, the Palm Court at the *Ritz* with its gold-leaved fountain is the place to be. If you care to get your nose hopelessly entangled in lotus blossoms and water-lilies Trader Vic's at the *Park Lane Hilton* is for you, but waiters with too many teeth in Hawaiian shirts (the waiters not the teeth in the shirts) are not my scene. I prefer the contemporary style of cocktail bar, as *The Palm* (539 Battersea Park Road, SW11), *Fridays* (24/26 Great Russell Street, WC1), the *Zanzibar* (30 Great Queen Street, WC2) or *Rumours* (33 Wellington St, WC2 and 41 Mackennal St, NW8). *Rumours* has the proper cocktail air of frivolity with most cocktails priced at £2 between 11 a.m. and 3 p.m. and 5.30 p.m. and 7.30 p.m. Here you may drink a Killer Zombie or a Suffering Bastard, a Dr Funk ('says more about you than American Express') or an Impatient

Virgin ('an adventure into the unknown'). Fun.

Cyril Ray, who knows about such things, adjudges that the best cocktail is the Sidecar, so-called from the officers of Pershing's Army in Paris, who travelled to Harry's Bar in sidecars. In those days it was equal parts of lemon juice, cointreau and cognac, but they make them stronger than that these days. Set 'em up, Joe.

Best cocktail bar: (traditional) Palm Court at the *Ritz*;
(trendy) *Rumours*.

Coffee

Let's not beat about the bush. *H. R. Higgins* (coffee-man) *Ltd* is my man. His aromatic emporium (42 South Molton Street, W1; 01-629 3913) glows with shafts of golden light reflecting off antique copper containers and his display of old wooden grinders is a delight to the eye. His original coffees include Tanzanian Chagga farmed by the Wa-Chagga tribe who live on the slopes of Mount Kilimanjaro, his Colombian Libano Supreme, exceptionally full-flavoured, and his Nicaraguan Dark Roasted, mild without acidity. Higgins's blended coffees are cheaper than his originals, but the very dark roasted coffees (Santiago, Creole, Sultan and Continental Blends) are to ordinary blends as curry is to mince. Once you have been initiated there is no turning back. Mr Tony Higgins and Miss Audrey Higgins are prepared to lecture on coffee on request.

Marcus Coffee (13 Connaught Street, SW2; 01-723 4020) can offer thirty-two varieties of bean, while at the *Algerian Coffee Stores* (52 Old Compton Street, W1; 01-437 2480) you can buy coffee sacks and coffee machines as well as burgundies, ports, teas . . . and coffee. Their most popular lines are their Esotico ('rich and nutty') and their Velluto Nero ('subtle and silky'). *The Drury Tea and Coffee Company* (1-3 Mepham Street, SW1; 01-928 2551 – also in New Row, WC1) is old fashioned in the best sense, while at the *Monmouth Coffee House* (27 Monmouth Street, WC2; 01-836 2572) you can try a cup of coffee on the premises before committing yourself to buying. Although they do not stock a great variety, their coffee is amongst the cheapest in London. *A. Angelucci* (23b Frith Street, W1; 01-437 5889) has been established fifty years and knows his beans, and at *Coffee Campaign* (52 Acre Lane, SW2; 01-737 4144) you can be certain that the coffee you buy will not be abetting wicked bosses with rhino whips to exploit starving peasants. Apparently Tanzanian coffee is the most acceptable to grass roots socialists, but that brings us back to the Chagga tribe and Mr Higgins. Also recommended with confidence is *L. Fern & Co.* (27 Rathbone Place, W1; 01-636 2237 and two branches). They've been roasting and blending for ninety years.

It is too depressing to list the abominations served in most cafés and canteens; they sully the good name of coffee. Indian restaurants are notorious. The best coffee from a machine comes from *Channel 4* in Charlotte Street, which could be why the programmes are so laid back.

Best coffee: *H. R. Higgins.*
Worst coffee: in the buffets of British Rail trains.

Concert Halls

It all depends on what you want. *Fairfield Halls* in Croydon is a deeply depressing pile of a place, in deeply depressing Croydon, but the acoustics are superb, the best in London. The *Wigmore Hall* is ideal for recitals and is charmingly staffed, but the dire murals are discouraging. For Mahler and Bruckner and the Last Night of the Proms, the *Albert Hall* is irreplaceable, but 'pack 'em in and hang the sound' seems often to be the attitude. It's like listening to music from within the belly of an elephant. On the South Bank the choice is between the *Royal Festival Hall* (capacity 3,000 with room for 250 musicians on the platform), the *Queen Elizabeth Hall* (seats 1,100), where the cheap seats are every bit as good as the expensive ones, and the delightful *Purcell Room* (seats 372), where, while enjoying excellent chamber music at half the price of an LP, you may have to suffer from the vagaries of eccentric page-turners.

At the *Barbican Hall*, London's newest concert hall, singers are able to exploit the gentlest of pianissimi, and the audience are close enough to the musicians to feel deeply involved in a Brahms love song or a Chopin nocturne. But the whole *Barbican* complex has serious sound-proofing and air-conditioning problems, and the acoustics for a full orchestra are deadening. The worst acoustics in London are at the *Logan Hall*, University of London. Its atmosphere is unhelpful too.

A fine summer evening at *Kneller Hall*, Whitton, Middx, the home of the Royal Military School of Music, where concerts are given under the stars is unforgettable, but *Kenwood* can be even more seductive. The ornamental lakes, alive with nightingales and kingfishers and owls, form a magical setting for open air music on warm June evenings.

St John's, Smith Square, rebuilt after the Blitz is now used for concerts and lectures. It also has a wine bar. Consulted on the design, Queen Anne kicked her footstool over and snapped: 'Oh why not build it like that?', which the architect did. Nonetheless this Footstool Church has a certain baroque charm and pleasant acoustics.

Best concert hall: *Purcell Room.*
Worst concert hall: *Logan Hall.*

Cosmetics and Body Care

> '*Le nez de Cleopatre, s'il eût été plus court, toute la face de la terre aurait changé.*' Blaise Pascal (1623-1662)

The Body Shops (six branches since its inception five years ago) sell only natural lotions, creams, oils, shampoos etc in refillable containers. They have been recommended to me by a walking advertisement for their properties. *Joan Price's Face Places* (33 Cadogan Street, SW3; 01-589 9062 and 31 Connaught Street, W2; 01-723 6671) allow you to try out their beauty products before parting with good (is there any other sort?) money. They are stockists for most of the leading brands, which means that you can compare lipsticks *at one counter* – a service not readily available elsewhere.

Elizabeth Arden (20 New Bond Street, W1; 01-629 1200) is to beauty salons as a Daimler is to other cars. I doubt whether they would agree to insert a safety pin through your cheek, but in other particulars provide a complete body service top to toe, and their standards are universally reliable. *Estée Lauder* Cosmetics (71 Grosvenor Street, W1; 01-493 9271) are extremely pricey. To pay such sums to be made more beautiful hints at desperation.

Animal Aid (111 High Street, Tonbridge, Kent; Tonbridge 364546) will let you know which cosmetic firms refuse to abuse animals in their research. Any products marked 'Beauty without Cruelty' are safe, as are *Boots* own brand cosmetics, *Yardleys* and *Innoxa*.

The parade of the demi-mondaine in the cosmetic department at Harrods is like something out of De Maupassant.

Best cosmetics: *The Face Place.*

PS Are people really deceived by packing such tiny bottles of scent in such large boxes?

Cottages

In Victorian London there was a craze for building miniature houses, often Gothic and usually topped with a tea-cosy of thatch. The most famous of these *fermes ornées* were *Ivy Cottage* at Parson's Green, *Queen's Cottage* in Kew Gardens and *Craven Cottage* at Fulham. One of the few survivors besides *Queen's Cottage* is *Hunter's Grove* in Belsize Lane, NW3, very charming and rather silly as the fashion required. An earlier example is *The Hermitage*, 8 Church Road, Hanwell; with its whitewashed walls and ogival doorway it is reminiscent of a Beatrix Potter illustration.

Less fey are the 18th-century cottages at *1-6 Pond Square*, Highgate. But the essence of an ideal cottage is that it should be delightful, lived in and unexpected, and I must therefore refer you to *Lisson Grove Cottages* – follow the alley beside the quaint Lisson Grove post office – described by Geoffrey Fletcher as 'industrial revolution combined with Peabody'. Dated 1855 these cottages are certainly an unlikely survival. So too are *Chester Cottages* and *Sparke's Cottages*, both so improbably sited behind the Royal Court Theatre as not even to figure in the A-Z. Rose-bedecked and winsome, they are nevertheless real working cottages. The terrace of cottages (c 1810) in *Old Palace Lane*, Richmond, next to the White Swan, are best in the bleak midwinter when the crowds of pubby tourists stay at home. The lock-keeper's cottage at *St Pancras Lock* on the Regent's Canal amidst its chrysanthemums appears as isolated as if it were in the depths of the country.

Best cottages: *Chester Cottages*, SW1.

PS 'Cottaging' is not hunting for cottages by the way. If you want to know what it is, read *Prick Up Your Ears*, the biography of Joe Orton, or ask anyone in the Joe Orton Bar at the King Edward VI pub, 25 Bromfield Street, N1. They'll tell you. They may even show you.

Crescents

For several years I lived in the handsomest crescent in London. This was, and remains, *The Paragon*, Blackheath, and consists of a cluster of mansions linked by colonnades, designed by Michael Searles circa 1790, bombed and extensively rebuilt as flats. With fine landscaped gardens at the rear, and spell-binding trees and daffodils in the front, *The Paragon* is all very grand, but living there had its drawbacks. We were not permitted to feed the birds, my dog chased the air-vice-marshal's cat, and children were never conceived nor born on the premises. Adjacent to *The Paragon* and almost as impressive is *Morden College*, brick almshouses almost certainly designed by Wren.

Very satisfactory is *Pelham Crescent*, which, like much of Belgravia, was built by George Basevi, Sir John Soane's pupil. The houses here and in Pelham Place (1820-1830) are exactly as town houses should be with iron railings and balconies, elegant cornices, good, solid front doors, and high moulded ceilings. Gainsboroughs should hang on the walls. Even more to my taste is *Wilton Crescent*, built a few years later. How handsome are the house numbers here and in Kinnerton Street, which cuddles *Wilton Crescent*, and is itself a half-crescent. As Gascoigne, one of London's worst poets, wrote:

> I sing Belgravia! that fair spot of ground
> Where all that worldlings covet most is found!
> Of this stupendous town, this mighty heart!
> Of England's frame, the Fashionable part!

The Crescent (1827) in Crescent Grove, Clapham, is quite beautiful. Julius Caesar Czarnikow, the merchant, was once a resident. *Annett's Crescent* at 246-290 Essex Road, NI, is another late Georgian gem, and I have always enjoyed driving round the *Aldwych* which reminds me of a vast plunger for unblocking the drains which embouch into the Thames – Kingsway, of course, being the handle.

But the most spectacular crescent in London is Nash's *Park Crescent*. The rebuilt façades have copied the destroyed ones in every particular, and what finer gateway to a park could there be? But it's a shame that one has to stare at it so balefully from traffic jams, and that so much of it is lit internally with neon. This crescent of 1812 was the first major construction in Parkes' Roman Cement, thus inaugurating the age of stucco.

Best crescent: *Wilton Crescent* (Belgravia is more lived in than Regent's Park).
Worst crescent: *Albacore Crescent*, Catford.

Cricket

> Patient, dramatic, serious, genial
> From over to over the game goes on,
> Weaving a pattern of hardy perennial
> Civilisations under the sun.

Gerald Bullet

Well, it has to be *Lord's*, despite everything. But what would the doctor, who played for England for some forty years and is commemorated in the Grace Memorial Gates, have said about the screaming advertisements around the boundary? What would he have said about Lillee wagering £10 at 500 to 1 that his own side, the Australians, would lose the Test – though on that occasion the bet was struck at Trent Bridge? And what – I dare not imagine – would he have had to say about some of the Packer-inspired innovations? He might not have minded paying £9 for admission to the ground on Benson & Hedges Cup Final day, but I did. Despite everything it has to be *Lord's*, preferably during a three-day County game, early in June, when there's nobody much about, and you can take a P. G. Wodehouse and some corned beef and tomato sandwiches with you. Midweek of course. Should the rain come down there's always the Cricket Museum and the Royal Tennis Courts. I don't much enjoy cricket at the *Oval* (the House of Commons to the House of Lords); one is too far from the wicket, and it's too far to walk around the boundary, and the gasometers are all very well but don't enhance the scene. Is that snobbery?

There is still plenty of village cricket in and around London; *Kew Green, Roehampton, Richmond Green* or *South Park*, Fulham are the pleasantest places to watch or play. Mike Brearley is, or was, the best London cricketer, or at least the wiliest captain. He confessed to me once that he hums to himself the first four bars of the Razumovsky Quartet while waiting for a fast bowler to deliver the ball; he also adores curry; quite a guy.

Best cricket ground: *Kew Green.*

Croissants

A strong black cup of unblended coffee, a hot crisp croissant with black cherry jam like they used to serve – and maybe still do – at the buffet in *Basle Railway Station*, why there's a breakfast fit for heroes! Unchronicled and unsung (well it doesn't rhyme with anything much) the croissant is enjoying something of a revival, with the opening of, for instance, the *Croissant Show* at the Trafalgar Square end of the Strand, *Croissant Variées* in Fleet Street, and a croissant stall at *Liverpool Street Station* and at *Waterloo Station*.

There are five places in London where superb croissants may be found.

(a) *Maison Sagne*, 105 Marylebone High Street, W1.

(b) *Maison Bouquillon*, 4 Moscow Road, W2 with a second branch around the corner at 28 Westbourne Grove.

(c) *Cafe Matthiae*, Kew Road, Richmond.

(d) *The Original Maids of Honour*, further up the same road towards Kew Bridge.

(e) *Paris Croissants*, next to the giant HMV emporium in Oxford Street.

A word of warning, however. Those who are not content to leave well alone have been developing the croissant in disastrous ways. While the Croques Dorés may be all very fine, the Pains du Chocolat are an unfortunate hybrid.

Best croissant: *Maison Sagne*.

Croquet

Although croquet may be played seriously at the *Wimbledon All-England Lawn Tennis Club* and at the *Lansdowne Club* in Berkeley Square and at the *Roehampton Club* and in the Dulwich garden of my brother-in-law the QC, the best place for croquet in London, in Britain, and, so far as I know, in the world is the *Hurlingham Club*, Fulham, SW6 (01-736 8411), which is the national headquarters for the game. Here, while bishops' daughters sip china tea under blue and white striped awnings, the clink of a Jacques mallet upon a Jacques ball as a young blade from the Baltic Exchange executes a mischievous roquet upon an Anglo-Indian administrator, indicates that all is well with the Empire. Says the club secretary, Mr D. F. A. Trewby: 'You could scarcely have anything else on these lawns. Two people moving about is all right; bowls would be a crowd!'

Best croquet: the *Hurlingham Club*.

Darts

The *Sussex Pub* is the place. At 21 London Street, W2 (01-402 9602) it runs nine teams and counts four internationals amongst its regular players. Other good pubs for darts players include *The Skiddaw* (46 Chippenham Road, W9), the *World's End* (459 Kings Road, SW10) with matches on Thursdays, and, for the less competitive, the *Angel* (11 Roehampton High Street, SW15), which has a charming pub sign and clusters of roses. The *Cambridge Arms* (42 Cambridge Road, Kingston; 01-546 0937) currently boasts two of the best international players amongst its regulars.

Buy your darts from *Lillywhites* (Piccadilly Circus) or *Stablers*, the fishing (q.v.) experts, wear a silk shirt (q.v.) from *Turnbull & Asser* with an Old Etonian cravat, allow a sly smile to play upon your features in the manner of Paul Newman, and you'll soon put those pot-bellied beer-swilling northerners in their place.

Best darts venue: the *Sussex*.

Delicatessens/Grocers

The first issue each month of *The Grocer* gives a list of wholesale prices of groceries, enabling you to judge what you *ought* to be paying. By pretending to be a grocer yourself – *Alternative London* suggests that you should have your own letterhead printed which must be cheating – you can buy wholesale at the Cash and Carry outlets.

Assuming that you don't buy in bulk, you have the choice of supermarkets – see under that heading – grocers or delicatessens. Grocers such as *Cullens* (many branches) offer courteous service and a spot of gossip. But many of the traditional grocer shops have been squeezed out by the Asian shopkeepers, who open on Sundays and late into the evenings, and try hard to please.

Still surviving are two civilised Italian grocers in the Italian quarter of Clerkenwell: *Gazzano's* (169 Farringdon Rd, EC1; 01-837 1586) and *Terroni's* (138 Clerkenwell Rd, EC1; 01-837 1712).

In the West End the sad loss of *Jacksons* of Piccadilly has left the posh people the choice of *Harrods Food Hall* or *Fortnum's*. *Harrods* stock everything. You can, for example, get wild rice there (£6 for ¾ lb) which is, so far as I know, unobtainable elsewhere in London. The service is slow, ingratiating, and can be eccentric. Once I saw a salesman in *Harrods* fruit department take off his white jacket, put up his fists and challenge a difficult customer to 'come outside' with him. *Fortnum's* with its tail-coated assistants and hampers for all occasions stocks whatever is out of season, out of fashion, or outa sight. It's amusing trying to buy Heinz baked beans there and it is, as you would expect, *expensive*. *Partridges* (132 Sloane Street, SW1 and a branch at 11 Melcombe Street,

NW1; 01-730 0651) is where sloane rangers buy their ham; they eat it cut very thin while watching Coronation Street and insulting the au pair.

For delicatessens there is no better place to start than Old Compton Street, not that *Lina Stores* (18 Brewer Street, W1; 01-437 6482) or *G. Parmigiani Figli* (43 Frith Street, W1; 01-437 4728) are actually *in* OC Street, but both are *of* it. They are excellent for pasta, parmesan, mozzarella, olive oil, and such, and one can commute between them comparing prices. Amongst French delis, one could do worse than *Délices des Gascognes* (3 Hillgate Street, W8; 01-221 4151) with their bisques and terrines, *Hobbs & Co* (3 Garrick Street, WC2; 01-240 5653) and *Justin de Blank* (42 Elizabeth Street, SW1; 01-730 0605). In south London *O. Bellusci* (39 South Lambeth Road, SW8; 01-582 9766) is an oasis of delights and *La Ciocciara* (54 Garratt Lane, SW18; 01-874 9529) specialises in homemade pasta. *The Richmond Hill Delicatessen* (22 Richmond Hill; 01-940 3952) is open every day except Christmas Day until 7 p.m. and is first rate for cheese and wine. Whether or not *Rogg* (137 Cannon Street Road, E1; 01-488 3386) is open on Christmas Day I can't tell you – more likely to close on Yom Kippur – but it *is* open from 7 a.m. on Sundays. Pickled herrings, bagels, gefilte fish, and excellent smoked salmon are amongst their treats. There is also *L'Herbier de Provence* (341 Fulham Road, SW10; 01-352 0012) which should also feature under Cosmetics (q.v.), for besides herbs and spices of a multitudinous variety they stock essential oils, dried flowers and beauty products. The people who serve you are charming and smell delightful as does the whole establishment. See also *Take-Away*.

Best grocer: *Harrods Food Hall.*
Worst grocer: Anywhere with space invaders in it.

Discos

The London club scene is currently run by impresarios in their early twenties who have discovered a formula which suits the mood of the early eighties. But be warned. It is quite possible that the clubs mentioned below may no longer be operating by the time you read these words. Some close because they fail, others because they succeed; one of the many paradoxes in the present London scene.

Phil Sallon, who dresses mainly in sable, James Lebon, ex-punk, ex-hair dresser, Gary Vincent, son of the great John Mayall, and Perry Haynes, ex-young businessman of the year, are typical of these young impresarios. What they frequently do is take over an established club for a single thematic night. The guests may be required to wear yellow, or to be David Bowie lookalikes, or to be going down on the Titanic (like Linda Lovelace's grandma), and these evenings usually sell out by word of mouth. Reggae toasting and rapping (improvised speaking against a recorded beat) are the latest vogue. The greatest rappers in town are the elegant Grandmaster Flash, the brilliant Simon Super-Ace, and the droll Clint Eastwood and General Saint, a Jamaican double-act.

Up and coming bands perform at pubs (*see* events magazines or Nicolson's *London Pub Guide*, compiled by Judy Allen). The best rock pub just now is the *Greyhound* (175 Fulham Palace Road, W6; 01-385 0526). The sound system and the air conditioning are both good and the man who does the mixing knows his knobs.

Some of the principal clubs in and around London:

The Camden Palace, now known as *The Palace* (1a Camden Road, NW1; 01-387 0428). Formerly the *Music Machine*, this club has one of the most sophisticated sound and lighting systems in London and also the largest video screen upon which are projected a variety of promotional films. A continuing success story it is becoming benignly tacky.

Le Beat Route (17 Greek Street, W1; 01-734 1470). Used to be the home of the New Romantics and the Rockabillies (remember?), this venue is a large low basement for would-be trendies who can't quite afford the real thing – but then who can? Drinks 25p (sic) on Wednesdays.

Dingwall's (Camden Lock, Chalk Farm Road, NW1; 01-267 4967). Don't arrive too early or you will feel like Kafka's K awaiting his trial. Interesting artists with some emphasis on Blues. I saw Helen Shapiro there recently. Fun. But the atmosphere is somewhat decrepit.

Foobert's (18 Foubert's Place, W1; 01-734 3630). The new Sallon Salon featuring anything from hard funk to early 70s bubble-gum. Disc jockeys are Marine Boy and Flipper. Food is free when (as frequently) they forget to ask you for money.

The Fridge (390 Brixton Road, SW9; 01-737 1477). Done up like a fridge, this is known as 'Europe's only thermal disco'. The owner Andy Czekowski promises that things will be unpredictable and predictably they usually are.

Gossips (69 Dean Street, W1). Clammy and sweaty and trendy and therefore crowded this place specialises in jazz-funk and reggae. Try and catch the fashionable DJ, Steve Walsh.

Gulliver's (11 Down Street, W1; 01-499 0760). Wall to wall mirrors. Electronically avant-garde. Not for the arthritic, the impoverished, or the spotty.

Heaven (Under the Arches, Villiers Street, WC2; 01-839 3892). Gay men only except for Tuesdays. A splendid dance floor for 1000 people, a more intimate bar for when things get serious, videos, pool tables. And so on. Boy George is good value; also Amanda Lear. Europe's largest gay disco.

Rock Garden (corner of King Street and James St, Covent Garden, WC2; 01-240 3961). A rather good restaurant upstairs. Downstairs is the music (avant-garde pop) and a sweaty, ear-bursting ambience with frightful atmospherics.

Spats (37 Oxford Street, W1; 01-437 7945). Exclusively gay males. Open Fridays and Saturdays. An underground air-conditioned sauna – sort of – with good music and Tricky Dicky at the controls.

Stringfellow's (16-19 Upper St Martin's Lane, WC2; 01-240 5534). Was trendily elite, with black suede walls and a glass dance floor, but has been getting kinda rough. Expensive.

Sol y Sombra (74 Charlotte St, W1; 01-580 7719). Scruffily informal and modestly priced, but has played host to some of the better bands.

Xenon (196 Piccadilly, W1; 01-734 9344/5). Gained a great deal of free publicity when it incorporated real lions and tigers into its interior decor. A deplorable trend. Now merely cocktails, fountains and a space-age disco.

Besides the above keep an eye open for concerts at the various colleges, universities and polys. The bands are often worth hearing, and the charge is minimal.

Best Disco: (Camden) *Palace*.

Doctors etc

The best gynaecologist in London is *Bridgett Mason*, 25 Weymouth St, W1; 01-631 1583.

The best osteopath is *Neil Mann*, 8 Becmead Avenue, SW16; 01-769 3267.

The best VD Clinic is *James Pringle House* (attached to the Middlesex Hospital) in Charlotte Street where the best consultant is *Dr Duncan Catterall*.

The safest test of psychiatrists is to check whether they bite their fingernails.

The worst doctor in London was the one who took me in for a routine cartilage operation and released me from hospital with a probable lung embolism. Wild horses wouldn't drag his name out of me unless, as Ben Travers put it in *Thark*, there were an awful lot of them.

Dogs

In the porch of *St George's*, Hanover Square (John James, 1724) stand two fine pointers in bronze. They are said to be by Landseer. Either side of the *Battersea Dogs' Home* (4 Battersea Park Road, SW8; 01-622 4454 and *do* buy your dogs there) two shaggy-haired somethings hold up their paws in supplication. In St Pancras Gardens, NW1 a stone retriever waits for you to scratch his chilly ears. Outside *The Greyhound* (151 Greyhound Lane, SW16) stands a white greyhound, tail permanently frozen in mid-twitch.

If you have a friend who likes dogs, propose to him/her in *St Pancras Gardens*, marry him/her in *St George's*, Hanover Square, buy him/her a dog at *Battersea* – guaranteed distemper-free – and go to celebrate with the hair of the dog down Greyhound Lane.

Best London dogs: *St George's pointers.*
Worst London dogs: *those like mine that shit on the pavement.*

Dog Tracks

One evening at the *White City* I offered my usual generous prize to whomsoever could come up with the best anagram of

GREYHOUND. To my amazed delight the winner produced 'HEY DOG, RUN!' and the second 'HEY, RUN DOG!'.

The best dog-track for food is *Wimbledon*; the best for odds are *Hackney* and the *White City* (occasionally 33/1 in a six dog race and very occasionally 66/1) where the food is basic but the service friendly, *Walthamstow* is becoming fashionable, but the best for atmosphere is *Catford* where all the south London villains go with their jewel-encrusted fancy-women. Until recently *Catford* was the only London track to stage 8-dog races. Now sadly they conform. But you may still tickle the ears of the dogs after the races.

Two hints when dining at a dog-track:

(a) Book early, especially for the big meetings, and reserve a table opposite the winning post. Far more exciting and can be profitable.

(b) Place your bets yourself. If you wait for the ladies from the tote to get your bets on for you, you will risk not getting on.

Best dog track: *Catford*.

Domes

There is a fine pair of domes (one with a clock, one with a compass) on the Queen Mary and King William blocks of the *Royal Naval College*, Greenwich. They are by Wren who knew about domes. *St Mary Abchurch* (Abchurch Yard near Cannon Street) is a Wren church and has a magnificent painted dome attributed to both Sir James Thornhill and William Snow. There are three rather half-hearted domes on the *National Gallery* (William Wilkins) in Trafalgar Square. I always enjoy the demi-dome (sliced open like an orange) on *Bush House*, looking north up Kingsway; illuminated at night it makes a bright show. The dome which was added to *Brompton Oratory* in 1896 (George Sherrin trying to improve on Herbert Gribble) is a powerful landmark at least, and you could say the same about the domes on *Harrods*, which are best studied from the Chairman's dining room at the IBA. (Name-dropping!) *The Alexandra Hotel*, Clapham South Side (opposite the tube) has one of the most endearing domes in London, a bosom-shaped protuberance with a wrought iron nipple.

The delightful dome roof of the *Diorama*, one of the earliest London cinemas in Camden Town, is at risk. Greycoates Estates have received planning permission from the Crown Commissioners to turn the place into an office complex. If they remove the dome they will have me to reckon with.

But when you get right down to it (or up to it) there are only two serious domes in London: *St Paul's* and the *British Museum Reading Room*. Like the whole structure, the dome of *St Paul's* is a double miracle. That it was built at all is the first miracle; that it survived the Blitz the second. Almost enough to make you believe in a benevolent God. As for the dome of the *Reading Room*, Thackeray put it best:

> I have seen all sorts of domes of Peter's and Paul's, Sophia, Pantheon – what not? – and have been struck by none of them so much as by that catholic dome in Bloomsbury, under which our million volumes are housed. What peace, what love, what truth, what beauty, what happiness for all, what generous kindness for you and me, are here spread out! It seems to me I cannot sit down in that place without a heart full of grateful reverence. I own to have said my grace at the table, and to have thanked Heaven for this my English birthright, freely to partake of those bountiful books, and to spread the truth I find there.

Best dome: *St Paul's.*
Worst domes: *National Gallery.*

Drinking Clubs

> Blessed are the rich
> Who can afford the clubs
> Where they go on drinking
> When the poor have left the pubs
>
> Nicolas Bentley

The two best drinking clubs in London are *Tatty Bogle's* (11 Kingly Court, Kingly Street, W1; 01-734 4475) and *Macready's* (17 Mercer Street, WC2; 01-836 8281). I was going to tell you why but memory plays tricks. As my mother once said to my father: 'You must be drunk – your face is all blurred.'

Embassies

It is not generally known that 3 St James's Street, a fine edifice with a façade of five arched windows, the home of Berry Brothers and Rudd, wine merchants (q.v.), was once the embassy of the

Republic of Texas; well it was. But now Texans have to muck in like everyone else under the eagle eye in Grosvenor Square.

The *Indian Embassy* (Sir Herbert Baker, 1930) has an extremely pretty interior decorated by Indian artists and a reading room open to the public (Aldwych, WC2; 01-836 8484). The *Chinese Embassy* (110 Westcombe Park Road, SE3), despite being a listed building, is the most ramshackle, the *Icelandic Embassy* (1 Eaton Terrace, SW1) the friendliest. The *Czech Embassy* (25 Kensington Palace Gardens, W8) is disconcertingly close to the *Russian* (18 Kensington Palace Gardens, W8) and has hidden cameras clearly visible everywhere. At one of the Far Eastern embassies (I can't remember which but it was in Tufnell Park) I mistook the ambassador for the gardener; most embarrassing. The *Bulgarian Embassy*, they say, is entirely staffed by spies. As you might predict, it is not listed in the phone book.

Best embassy: *Indian.*
Worst embassy: *Italian.*

Emergency Services

The best emergency information service is the *Daily Telegraph Information Service*. Recently at dinner the conversation turned to the wettest and driest months of the year. A quick call to 01-353 4242 and all was resolved (see under Weather).

Problem (01-828 8181), *Universal Aunts* (01-730 9834) and *SOS Services* (01-458 3258) pride themselves on getting you out of a hole in a hurry. Once when Binkie Beaumont was on his way to our place to hear the songs of the new musical we hoped he would present in the West End, the pianist discovered that humidity had affected the action of the piano. The notes kept sticking. Panic! *Problem* Ltd were roused and, despite it being a Sunday, swiftly sent round a little man with a tin of talc. Hey presto!

Universal Aunts is the oldest established of these organisations; staid and reliable especially in such matters as needlework and au pairs. *SOS Services*, who liaise with UA on occasions, is the latest of these organisations to get going (July 1982), but can put you in touch with experts in more or less any field in your London postal area. Curtains re-lined with your own material, stuffed ferrets, hired greenhouses; no problem.

If you've been busted, or have urgent need of legal advice, or emotional rescue try *Release* (01-289 1123 or 01-603 8654 for

24-hour emergencies). If you're contemplating suicide ('Death is nature's way of telling you to slow down', said a graffiti I saw recently) it has to be the *Samaritans* (01-283 3400), who have many local branches (see phone books).

There is little doubt in my mind, or in that of any rational person, as to the worst emergency services in London – see below.

Best emergency service: *Samaritans.*
Worst emergency services: *London electricity and gas boards.*

English Restaurants

From the popularity of old recipe books and old recipes it is now accepted that traditional English cooking is a great deal more imaginative than meat and two veg and apple pie and custard. Try *Dan's* (119 Sydney Street, SW3; 01-352 2178), *Drakes* (2a Pond Place, SW3; 01-629 9933), the *English House* (3 Milner Street, SW3; 01-584 3002), *Fingal's* (690 Fulham Road, SW6; 01-736 1195), *Reflections* (85 King's Road, SW3; 01-352 1008), *September* (457 Fulham Road, SW10; 01-352 0206), or the *Tate Gallery Restaurant* (Millbank, SW1; 01-834 6754). None of these is cheap, but in each of them you should find something unusual to delight your taste buds. In sequence you might find Wiltshire pink trout, suckling pig, collops of venison with juniper berries, roast wild duck with fresh fruit salad, lamb and apricot pie, carpetbag steak (steak and oysters), or Hindle Wakes (a medieval Lancashire chicken dish). *Walton's* (121 Walton St, SW3; 01-584 0204) is international cuisine as well as English. A small agreeable place which does the best omelettes in town.

If what you are after is something rather more basic, good solid red meat or steak and kidney pudding or marmalade tart, then any of the following should please: *Aunties* (126 Cleveland Street, W1; 01-387 3226), the *Baron of Beef* (Gutter Lane, Gresham Street, EC2; 01-606 9415), the *City Gates* (Great Eastern Hotel, Liverpool Street, EC2; 01-283 4363) – the best carvery in London but crowded – the *Hungry Horse* (196 Fulham Road, SW10; 01-352 7757) and *Porters* (17 Henrietta Street, WC2; 01-836 6466). The specialities at these are: beef in Guinness, roast sirloin, freshly carved joints, marvellous puddings, and homemade pies with real ale respectively.

I have particular fondness for *Maggie Jones* (6 Old Court Place, W8; 01-937 6462) which is wittily named after one of the neighbours and enhanced with music from a wind-up gramophone. I was present at the launching party many years ago, and so feel myself to have the status of a godfather where Maggie Jones is concerned. *The Quality Chop House* (94 Farringdon Road, EC1 – no telephone) is a surviving working men's cafe complete with mahogany pews and sauce bottles. The food is excellent and the tea complements it perfectly. But my favourite English restaurant is *The Refectory* (6 Church Walk, Richmond; 01-940 6264), where the food is unusual and succulent, the English wines – elderflower, gooseberry etc – are not easily obtained elsewhere, and the Old Parish Rooms in which or outside of which you sit are a delight. It's friendly and not expensive, but closes early.

I am no longer very keen on the historic *Rules* in Maiden Lane, WC2 or the antique *Simpson's-in-the-Strand*. Standards have fallen at both. *Locket's* (Marsham Court, Marsham Street, SW1; 01-834 9552) is within 8 minutes of the House of Commons and the division bell rings to remind MPs to vote. The food and service are undistinguished. *Wilton's* in Bury Street and the *Guinea* (30 Bruton Place, W1; 01-629 5613) are exorbitantly expensive. And as for the mediaeval banquets held nightly in the *Tudor Rooms* (80 St Martin's Lane, WC2; 01-240 3978) what can I say without risk of being put in the stocks (yes, they really do that!)? I just don't believe 'Merrie England' was like this, and the food was surely better.

Best English restaurant: *The Refectory*.

Epitaphs

In *Alperton Cemetery*, Clifford Road, Wembley there is, beneath a carving of a 1928 schoolboy, neat and tidy in his uniform, the following epitaph:

> With a kindly smile and a wave of his hand he has wandered into a better land.

Equally cheerful is the charming goodbye to Isabella David who died in 1954 and lies in *Brompton Cemetery*, Old Brompton Road:

> Have a good sleep, dear.

The intellectual equivalent of such healthy matter-of-factness is the memorial in *Highgate Cemetery* to Professor Clifford, the Atheist. He sums up his life thus:

> I was not and was conceived.
> I loved, and did a little work.
> I am not, and grieve not.

As for Susan Dunford in *Pinner Cemetery*, under a life-sized red granite armchair, 1950s vintage, we read that she 'left her chair vacant'. It is hard not to feel admiration for those content to leave this vale of tears with so little fuss or bother. But there are those who are remembered more effusively. David Nieto (1654-1728) lies in the *Old Sephardic Cemetery*, Mile End Road, east London and this sometime rabbi at the Bevis Marks Synagogue is remembered thus:

> Sublime theologian, profound sage, distinguished physician, famous astronomer, sweet poet, elegant preacher, subtle logician, ingenious mathematician, fluent rhetorician, pleasant author, expert in languages, learned in history.

A saint obviously. Mary Page, buried in *Bunhill Fields*, City Road, EC1 was another:

> Here lies Dame Mary Page relict of Sir Gregory Page Bart. She departed this life March 11th 1728 in the 56th year of her age. In 67 months she was tap'd 66 times had taken away 240 gallons of water without ever repining at her case or ever fearing the operation.

Most affecting, of course, are the epitaphs on children's graves and, in some of the poorer cemeteries these make up a tragically high percentage of the total. In the *Jewish Cemetery*, Kingsbury Road, N1, for example, during the first ten years (1843-1853) of burials, forty-two deaths are recorded, of which seven are still-births, and the average age of the remaining thirty-five is only thirty-three years.

Frequently the epitaphs contain awful warnings. The following dire example from the cemetery in *Church Road, Mitcham*, is all too explicit:

> Mary, Susan and Eliza Atwood . . . who were poisoned by eating fungous vegetables mistaken for champignons on the 11th day of October 1808 and died at the ages of 14, 7, and 5 years within a few hours of each other in excruciating circumstances. The Father, Mother and now, alas, an only child, partakers of the same meal, have survived with debilitated constitutions and to lament so dreadful a calumny. This monument is erected to perpetuate the fatal event as an awful caution to others, let it be too a solemn warning that in our

most grateful enjoyments even in our necessary food may lurk deadly poison . . .

The ultimate in Victorian morbidity, written to commemorate 17-year-old Louisa Waklein who died in 1840 and lies in *Kensal Green Cemetery*, the following was carved:

> She is mine and I must have her
> The coffin must be her bridal bed
> The winding sheet must wrap her head
> The whispering winds must o'er her sigh
>
> For soon in the grave the maid must lie
> The worm it will riot
> On heavenly diet
> When death has deflowered her eye.

Finally a non-existent epitaph. Derek Bentley (1934-53) was wrongly executed for the murder of a policeman. His father wished to have the phrase: 'A victim of English justice' inscribed on his tombstone, but permission was refused. I wonder whose decision that was, and whether it kept him/her awake at night.

Best epitaph: *Professor Clifford* (see above).

PS Much of the above information comes from Hugh Meller's marvellous book *London Cemeteries* (Avebury Publishing)

Estate Agents

It must be pleasant to be an estate agent. Somebody comes in and tells you they wish to sell their house; you put a photograph of it in the window; somebody else comes in and says they want to buy it; you take anything up to 3% commission on what may be £100,000.

Well of course this is a simplification, and there is nothing to stop the owner selling his/her house privately and keeping the commission; but it is a curious business. The agent is paid by the seller whom he/she may never meet. But the agent may show the potential purchaser round thirty houses, and never receive a penny piece from him/her.

The concept of the House Shop – the seller pays a fee to have details of his house put up in the shop – has recently gained credence. The latest is *The London Property Centre* (17/23 Southampton Row, WC1; 01-404 0235), and it saves potential purchasers a good deal of foot-slogging.

As I write the range of house prices in London is from £13,000 (Lower Road, SE15) to £3 million (Kensington), and estate agents' commissions from 1% to 3% with an additional charge for advertising. In the suburbs 2% is par for the course. The London operation ranges from a small office like *Alan Fisher*, with a staff of four, all in Alan Fisher T-shirts, based in Kennington to *Chesterton's* of Kensington. *Alan Fisher* claims to move forty houses a month; *Chesterton's* sell 36% of their houses to foreign purchasers (Far East 18%, America 12½%, Nigeria 12%), while being prepared to eat sheep's testicles or sleep with Eskimos' wives while concluding a deal.

Not having bought or sold a house for over ten years my advice on estate agents is based on hearsay, but I have received glowing accounts of the following: *Raymond Bushell, Strutt and Parker, Sturt and Tivendale, Stocker & Roberts* (of Blackheath), *Pye* (of Wimbledon Village) and *John D. Wood*. Less happy reports have reached me concerning *Dutch and Dutch, Gascoigne Pees, May & Co, Ruck and Ruck, Bernard Thorpe & Partners, Benham & Reeves, Stickley and Kent*. I must emphasise that I cannot personally substantiate these remarks. More reports please!

Fancy Dress

It is a craze. By being someone else for a night you can Be Yourself. That's the theory, and there are plenty of practitioners to support it.

The traditional suppliers are *Morris Angel & Son* (119 Shaftesbury Avenue, WC2; 01-836 5678) and *Berman's & Nathan's* (18 Irving Street, WC2; 01-839 1651), who deal principally with theatres and television and film companies. As a result they have massive stocks.

Barnum's (67 Hammersmith Road, W14; 01-602 1211) lists in its catalogue seventeen different kinds of comic moustaches and eighteen different beards. They will hire out anything from a false nose to a marquee. Almost next door at the *Carnival Store* (95 Hammersmith Road, W14), Mr Stephanides worked hard to turn me into a monk or a monkey; at £10 to hire and £10 deposit it seemed like a cheap transformation. *Escapade* (150 Camden High Street, NW1; 01-485 7384) makes a similar charge.

Both *C. and W. May* (9 Garrick Street, WC2; 01-836 5993) and *Mardi Gras* (54 Browning Road, Manor Park, E12; 01-472 2012) will design and make a costume to meet your private requirements, while at *Call to Arms* (79 Upper Street, N1; 01-359 0501) they specialise in matters military. The most bizarrely intriguing of these emporia is *Theatre Zoo* (28 New Row, WC2; 01-836 3150). They will hire out costumes and wigs perfectly efficiently, but their real love is masks, false feet and hands and fantastical animal costumes. It is not easy to walk past their crowded window without breaking your stride. I append some other recommended suppliers:

The Costume Studio (227 Eversholt Street, NW1; 01-388 4481); *Fancy Dress Shop* (24 Hartfield Crescent, SW19; 01-540 4868); *Fantasy Studios* (22 Coronet Street, N1; 01-739 1948); *Joker* (97 Chiswick High Road, W4; 01-995 4118); *Nite-Out Fancy Dress* (52 Beulah Road, E17; 01-520 1542); and *West End Costumes* (43 Compton Close, NW1; 01-387 5343).

For children: *Anthea Moore Ede* (16 Victoria Grove, W8; 01-584 8826) is the place to go.

Best fancy dress: (for grotesquerie) *Theatre Zoo;* and (for comprehensive range) *Berman's & Nathan's.*

Fanlights

In early Georgian London a shell-hood was provided above the door of the more substantial houses. It gave a Sheraton elegance to the house entrance and some protection from the weather. Later this feature was replaced by the fanlight, although some Edwardian architects re-introduced the shell-hood. An expert can date a house by the patterns of the glazing bars in the fanlights, but it's a rather barren accomplishment. The earliest, though, is at *36 Bedford Row*, just east of Red Lion Square. It is the work of Nicholas Barbon. *Islington* is where most of the better examples may be found, Duncan Terrace, Bewdley Street, Canonbury Square, Barnsbury Street, Cloudesley Road and Colebrooke Row in particular. Despite the ponderous claims of the vast fanlight at *Waterloo Station*, with the names of our First World War allies in the cartouches around the arch, and the unexpected lunette of the Last Judgement in the gate of *St Giles-in-the-Fields*, I prefer the confident swirls of *1 Ripplevale Grove*, N1 or *3 Lincoln's Inn Fields*. I love the things; really I should start a fan club . . .

Best fanlight: *1 Ripplevale Grove*, N1.

Farms

There are eight non-commercial farms in London. They are open to visitors. These are: *The City Farm*, Grafton Road, NW5; *Freightliners*, Sheringham Road, N7; *Hackney City Farm*, Leslie Road, E5; *Mudchute Community Farm*, Manchester Road, E14; *Spitalfields Farm*, Buxton Street, E1; *Stepping Stones*, Ben Jonson Road, E1; *Surrey Docks Farm*, Gulliver Street, E14 and the *Vauxhall City Farm*, St Oswald's Place, SE11. *The City Farm* in Grafton Road is close by the headquarters of InterAction, Ed Berman's Community empire which runs the City Farms Advisory Service and produces a newsletter. The address for both of these is 15 Wilkin Street, NW5 (01-403 0881). *The City Farm* itself is a pleasantly mucky place where the kids can even sit on the pigs if they wish to or the pigs on the children; the same probably applies at the other farms.

Petersham Farm, Petersham, Surrey, is rather different. A small working farm-cum-garden-centre on the banks of the Thames, where children are invited to attend such arcane mysteries as the milking of a cow. Recently it changed ownership and bought a goat. Goat's milk may now be purchased there.

Ferries

> Ahoy! And Oho, and it's who for the ferry?
> (The briar's in bud and the sun going down:)
> And I'll row ye so quick and I'll row ye so steady,
> And 'tis but a penny to Twickenham Town.

Twickenham Ferry by T. J. H. Marzials (1850-1920)

The ancient *Twickenham Ferry* still operates, though not if the weather is inclement (for Ham House 7-12, 2-sunset). Sandy Scott, the ferryman, uses an outboard motor these days, but will pull on the oars for special occasions. Since the ferry links Ham House (1610, built by Sir Thomas Vavasour) and its marvellous furniture with Marble Hill House (the Palladian villa built for George II's mistress) and James Gibbs's exciting Octagon Room (in Orleans House), this ferry is a perfect adjunct to a warm summer's afternoon out.

The *Woolwich Free Ferry*, rapidly approaching its centenary, carries over three thousand vehicles and twice as many passengers across the Thames each day between 8 a.m. and 8 p.m.

Although the paddle-steamers were replaced by diesel power in 1963, this remains an agreeable way of crossing the river.

Best ferry: *Twickenham.*

Fish and Chips

What is remarkable about the *Sea Shell* (33-35 Lisson Grove, NW1; 01-723 8703) is not just that it serves the best fish and chips in London, but that it does so cheaply, has done so for a long time, and should continue to do so. The problems attaching to success – crowds and queues and the temptation to take things easy – have been avoided, and the fish, served with a commendable lack of frills, are as big and crisp and succulent as ever, while the fish cakes, the size of small cannon-balls, delectably peppery, and made entirely of fresh white fish are the best forty pence worth of nourishment in London. The *Sea Shell* has two adjacent establishments; one for take-away customers and one for nobs, who sit amongst nets and chianti bottles, happily gregarious, for the success of the *Sea Shell* often means that tables are shared. The proprietors will even fry your own fish for you at Passover.

There is another *Sea Shell* fish restaurant under the same management at 392 Kingsland Road, Hackney, E8 (01-254 6152).

Other establishments that serve take-away fish and chips and may be securely recommended include: *Something Fishy* of Elmers End, *The Rock & Sole Plaice* (sic), 47 Endell Street, WC2 (01-836 3785), *John's Fish Bar* of Thornton Heath, *Belle's Fish and Chips* of Bromley South, *Redfords* of Golders Green Road and the fish and chip bar on the corner of Harrow High Street and Weald Lane.

Geale's (2 Farmer Street, W8; 01-727 7969), who cook their fish in beef dripping, no longer serve take-away, but their fish are delicious. So too is their apple crumble.

I have *not* enjoyed my fish and chips at *Berni Inns*, nor at the branches of *The Hungry Fishermen* (Thurloe Street, Victoria Street, and a very crowded branch in Oxford Street). For grander establishments see under Fish Restaurants.

Best fish and chips: *The Sea Shell.*

Fishing

The Thames is rich in barbel, flounders and smelt upstream of *Vauxhall Bridge* and particularly during the winter months when the boat traffic is diminished. You may even find the occasional trout, but 'Thames trouting', as it is known, is a specialist art. Pike, carp and bream may be found in *Pen Ponds* in Richmond Park, and particularly large carp enjoy themselves in the warm water from the power station at *Canbury Gardens*, Kingston. The largest tench ever caught in Great Britain weighed 11lbs and was landed from a pit at *Wraysbury*, but it was probably diseased and filled with fluid, so it was not permitted to stand as a record.

George Bennet (Leisure Sport) at 53-55 High Street, Feltham, Middlesex (01-890 1313) can let you have a season ticket to streams and gravel pits in the area, while you can get your Calpac Season ticket (£5.75) to nineteen local waters from *Stabler's* (350-352 Garratt Lane, SW18; 01-874 4683). *Stabler's*, opposite Earlsfield Station, and established almost 100 years, has a fine selection of rods, guns, darts, penknives and wellies. I am happy to say it also displays an urgent warning against discarding lead shot, which has been killing swans. Also recommended are *Kennington's* (195 Kennington Lane, SE11; 01-582 3540) and, inevitably, *Farlow's* of Pall Mall (01-839 2423), who is to fishing what Purdey's (57 South Audley Street, W1; 01-499 1801) is to guns.

The *Thames Waters Angling Guide* and Bill Howes's *Fishing for Londoners* are the law and the prophets for anglers in London, while the *Angling Times* is more useful for those with things to buy and sell than for those with fish to catch. The *Thames Water Authority* (New River Head Laboratories, 177 Rosebery Avenue, EC1; 01-837 3300) can be helpful. Their trout fisheries are at *Barns Elms Reservoir*, Merthyr Terrace, SW13 (01-748 3423) and it is to the TWA that information and inquiries about pollution should be addressed.

Best fishing: *Canbury Gardens*, Kingston.
Worst fishing: *Haydens Road Effluent.*

Stop Press: A very large carp has just been sighted in the lake in front of the Palm House at Kew Gardens by Jane Heslop, who retreated alarmed in some haste.

Fishmongers

Fishmongers tend to come in shoals. There are several around the old Billingsgate Market and in Kingston Market, and two excellent fishmongers in Camden Town.

The best in London by a short fin is *Steve Hatt* (88 Essex Road,

N1; 01-226 3963). He will sell you live lobsters, oysters, eels and salmon from the River Tay. He smokes his own – haddock, trout and mackerel, that is – and behind his counter he keeps a box of fishheads and fishy unmentionables for sleek and pampered cats.

R. Rowe and Sons (243 Camden High Street, NW1; 01-485 4676 and five other branches) stock over fifty varieties of fish. There ought to be a competition – haddock at fifty yards – between him and John Truman at *La Maree* (76 Sloane Avenue, SW3; 01-589 8067), who enjoys a challenge and stocks crab, lobster, langoustine, oysters, scallops, clams and dressed salmon. *Richards Ltd* (11 Brewer Street, W1; 01-437 1358) could well have monk fish, octopi and sea urchins as well as more plebeian fish. *Ashdown Ltd* in Leadenhall Market, EC3 (01-626 0178) has salt water tanks in its basements, so nobody's fish is fresher. On Sunday mornings *Bob White* (1 Kennington Lane, SE11; 01-735 1931) sells shellfish of all kinds, but it would be sacrilege to go to anyone but *Tubby Isaacs* (Goulston Street, E1) for jellied eels. The present Tubby is brother-in-law of the original Tubby.

On Friday mornings the fishcart from Grimsby anchors at *Flask Walk*, Hampstead, while the displays in *Harrods Food Hall* are scaly creations of great glory, and change daily.

Also strongly recommended: *R. E. Wright & Sons* (10a Warwick Way, SW1; 01-834 7702), where the Minister of Agriculture and Fish gets his; *J. Mist & Sons* (254 Battersea Park Road, SW11; 01-228 6784), who smoke their own cod and haddock; *Talby's* (263 Camden High Street, NW1; 01-485 5000) sells splendid salmon trout in season; *Treadwells* (94 Chippenham Road, W9; 01-286 9267); *J. F. Blagden* (64 Paddington Street, W1; 01-935 8321) and – notably – *Portch Brothers* (405 King's Road, Chiswick, SW10; 01-352 4464 and Upper Richmond Road West, SW14) are all deeply committed to matters fishy. The best smoked salmon in London comes from *Barnett's* of Frying Pan Alley, E1. But at *S. Baron* (Assembly Passage, Stepney, E1) you can buy smoked salmon in 'cocktail piles' at £1.15 per half pound.

Best fishmonger: *Steve Hatt.*
Worst fishmonger: *Anywhere that stocks tins of peaches.*

Fish Restaurants

When the success of this book (see under Clairvoyants) has made me rich, I shall have the following lunch twice a week: grilled Dover sole served with the newest of Jersey potatoes and branch spinach, followed by a generous portion of fresh raspberries and wild strawberries with coffee from Higgins and a Bendicks bittermint chocolate. Old-fashioned fish restaurants at which you can order just such a sole are numerous (though Dover soles no longer come from Dover); there is the *Wheeler's* chain, all twelve branches, which cook Dover sole in twenty-five ways, but recent experiences at *Wheeler's* have not been entirely reassuring; there is *Manzi's* (1-2 Leicester Street, WC2; 01-437 4864), which has a somewhat pretentious Cabin Room upstairs, and a much-to-be-preferred fast service restaurant below. Here you will eat economically and well without being pampered; there is *Bentley's* (11 Swallow Street, W1; 01-734 4756) founded sixty-eight years ago by a barrow-boy/actor and little changed; and there is *Sweeting's* (39 Queen Victoria Street, EC2; 01-248 3062) which buys its fish in Billingsgate Market and sells it cheerfully. *Sheekey's* (29 St Martin's Court, WC2; 01-836 4118) is an attractive and lively old-fashioned restaurant, particularly after a show. We enjoyed artichokes stuffed with mushrooms as a starter, but my sole was more like a tiddler, there was too much salt in the hollandaise, and they refused to let me have two half portions of new and hash brown potatoes instead of a single portion of either. Rotters. In this category too I should mention *Geale's* and the *Sea Shells*, which I have described under Fish and Chips.

Moving up-market brings me to the French fish restaurants of the *Le Suquet* group, including *Le Suquet* itself (104 Draycott Avenue, SW3; 01-581 1785), *La Croisette* (168 Ifield Road, SW10; 01-373 3694), and *Poissonerie de l'Avenue* (82 Sloane Avenue, SW3; 01-589 5774 next to *La Maree*, the fishmongers, who supplies it). All are excellent, though they tend rather to Fulham chic; the last-named being my favourite.

Finally *Grahame's Sea Fare*, 38 Poland Street, W1 (01-437 0975) which is unusual, being a kosher fish restaurant (which means of course large portions and no shell-fish). The food is fresh, the service maternal, and business brisk, though last orders are 8.45 p.m. Latkes, sweet and sour halibut and lemon tea betray its middle-European origins, but you could travel a lot further than middle-Europe and fare a lot worse.

Best fish restaurant: *Poissonerie de L'Avenue.*

Florists

Should you see an aged crone with a basket of flowers on her arm shouting 'Vilets – luvly vilets!' in Covent Garden, she will be filming for American TV. But despite the market itself moving south of the river some good florists remain. *Alberts* (1 Betterton Street, WC2; 01-240 0450) and *Ellen Keeley* (4 Shorts Gardens, WC2; 01-836 2375) are two; the latter used to make barrows for the bummarees too.

Constance Spry (74 Marylebone Lane, W1; 01-499 7201) runs a school for flower arrangers at 53 Marylebone Lane; the shop is an excellent advertisement for the school. *Felton's* (5 Cheapside, EC2; 01-236 7261 and two branches), *Moyses Stevens* (Lansdowne House, Berkeley Square, W1; 01-493 8171) and *Flower Power* (94 Holland Park Avenue, W11; 01-229 8788) are all excellent but not cheap. Indeed flowers in the centre of London can't – and shouldn't – be cheap.

My favourite flower seller is the gentleman who sits outside the Spanish Embassy in Belgrave Square and has done so, year in year out, for as long as I can recall. Franco, Juan Carlos, the Socialists, he has seen them come and seen them go to the scent of roses and jonquils in the spring.

Best florist: *Constance Spry.*
Worst florist: Those who set up their stalls at the approaches to hospitals and cemeteries. Who about to bury a relative will hassle over a bunch of chrysanths? Be warned.

PS The most beautiful display of flowers in London – and what's more they never fade – may be seen in the *Marianne North Gallery* at Kew. Here 832 pictures of flowers, all drawn by Marianne on her world travels, testify to the brilliance and dedication of this brave and remarkable, untrained artist.

Foot-scrapers

The wittiest foot-scraper may be found outside the Foreign and Commonwealth Office in *Downing Street*. I'm sure there is a great deal of protocol as to who uses the thing and who brings the mud in from St James's Park. This scraper is in wrought iron, although most of them are cast. There are other interesting scrapers at *28 Meadway*, NW11 (a street full of interesting survivals), where a horse stands on top of the actual scraper, at *30 Chester Street*, SW1 (like a pair of squatting toads) and at *36A Elvaston Place*, SW7 (hemispheric, double-ended with bulging finials). Outside the other St Paul's (*The Ridgeway*, NW7) you can scrape your feet on dolphins' tails, and at *12 Blenheim Road*, NW8 on dragon's wings. But the best, which appears to be quite ancient has a white face mask, a bit like a silver hallmark above the scraper; its expression is of someone who has seen it all and yet somehow survived. Wipe your feet on that! It is at . . .

Best foot-scraper: *2 Cheyne Row*, SW3.

Fountains and Drinking Fountains

Perhaps because of its climate London is not rich in fountains. We cannot compare with Paris or Rome or even New York, where some of the newer architects are releasing water down the sides of their buildings in refreshing cascades. The forest of fountains at the *Barbican* looks magnificent when you sit in the sun, enjoying the occasional splashes which dry on your cheeks within seconds, as you shade your eyes to stare at the arch of rainbows – the real purpose of hoisting spouts of water into the air, I think.

But when the skies are grey and the rain is heavier than the water from the fountains, it all seems pointless. I shall not choose the *Barbican*; nor the *Trafalgar Square* fountains, which explode into action every morning when Big Ben strikes ten, although the Lutyens additions – merpeople and porpoises – are really quite fine; nor the fountains in the waterlily pond in *Queen Mary's Gardens*, Regent's Park, exotic as those are with their brazen ladies and gentlemen and fish; nor the pleasant fountains at the northern end of the *Serpentine*; nor the *Victims of Yalta* fountain opposite the Victoria and Albert Museum; nor *Brent Cross*, nor *Gray's-in-the-Mews Antiques Market* (an indoor fountain), nor *Marble Arch*.

I shall note in passing the fountain in the lobby of *Fontana Books* – of *course*! – (useful for cooling the brows of contentious authors) and the fountain at the north end of *Lamb's Conduit Street*, whose marble lady pours out a vial of tears most pathetically and settle instead upon the charming little stone fountain – a single modest spout arising from a beautifully carved and weather-worn basin – in the centre of the *Little Cloisters*, in the precincts of Westminster Abbey. Once upon a time these cloisters formed part of the Monks Infirmary; if one were ill, there can have been no sweeter place to moisten one's fever.

The first Metropolitan Drinking Fountain was squirted at the public in 1859. It may be seen outside the *Church of the Holy Sepulchre*, Holborn Viaduct. 'Replace the cup', it demands of guilty and innocent alike. The one at *Spaniards End*, NW3, is

reminiscent of the Pierian spring at Delphi, which Keats suggested you should drink deep of if you needed inspiration. (It did less for me than for Keats.) Outside *Queen Mary College*, Mile End Road, is a miniature temple, so grand that it seems a waste merely to drink water there, and the drinking fountains in *Birdcage Walk*, SW1 are embellished with what appear to be nude gardeners. Delightful is the drinking fountain in *Victoria Tower Gardens* upon which is carved in relief three leaping dolphins, but then I have a thing about dolphins.
(See also under Horse Troughs.)

Best fountain: *Little Cloisters*, Westminster Abbey.
Best drinking fountain: *Queen Mary College*, Mile End Road, E1.
Worst drinking fountain: *Deptford Playground*, Watson Street, SE8.

Free Entertainment

London can be free. You need not pay rent, rates, nor hotel bills by joining a squat. You may eat free by cadging from market traders at the end of the day or by pocketing a hotel key and returning to eat meals there (but I would not recommend you doing anything so disreputable). It is also possible to eat free at press conferences (see under Canteens) or big exhibitions such as the *Ideal Home* – take a paper bag. Use skips to furnish your flat, or have an arrangement at the municipal dumps; it's surprising what you can find there if you have transport. To look respectable have your hair cut free as a model for one of the hairdressing schools, such as *Vidal Sassoon* or *Crimpers*.

Cultural activities may be enjoyed by starting your own magazine and informing the press officers of the various theatres, cinemas and publishers accordingly (printed letter headings helps). You will then receive free tickets and review copies of books, which you can sell after reviewing. You might even become a press baron, God help you.

It is always possible by mingling with the crowds outside a London theatre to get in free to see the second half of a London play, and, by turning up at a pop venue at 3 p.m. on the day the band is scheduled to appear you should be able to walk in and listen to them balancing their sound. Ice-skaters have to practise before the big competitions; one can usually sneak into the rinks and watch. There are free exhibitions of art, free 'platform' plays and recitals at the *National Theatre* and the *Barbican*, while at the *Commonwealth Institute* in Holland Park, there are free showings of films and free exhibitions, often of exceptional interest. Along the *Bayswater Road* and in *Piccadilly* at weekends there are free art exhibitions but be warned if you are tempted to buy, for the 'artists' are often merely agents for unscrupulous wholesalers. Anyway the commercial art galleries are always free. Try *Cork Street* for the best of modern art, and *Bond Street*.

At the *Piazza* in Covent Garden – a huge success – and on the Portico of the *Inigo Jones's Actors' Church* there, street performances of all kinds are given, including Punch and Judy shows. The best time to watch these splendid gipsies is Saturday afternoons (see also Buskers).

Viewing at auctions is a favourite activity of mine, but it doesn't always turn out free. Read the *Telegraph* on Mondays or *The Times* on Tuesdays for details of upcoming sales.

The *Parks* are free and in many of them there are free concerts of military music. A visit to the *Law Courts* is not only free but extremely instructive. Currently the liveliest entertainment may be pursued at the *Knightsbridge Crown Court*.

For those of a mechanical bent you can watch the planes taking off and landing at *Heathrow*. Those of us who live in west London would not consider that an afternoon well spent. On the last Sunday of every month there is a parade of custom cars from *Chelsea Bridge* along the King's Road, and CND marches are not only free, but may do some good, apart from enabling you to catch up on hits of the 60s. Obviously *Speakers' Corner* (Hyde Park at Marble Arch on Sundays) is free; it may change your life. So may the *Notting Hill Carnival*!

Most museums are free, although special exhibitions may not be. A week at the *Victoria and Albert* would scarcely be enough to see all there is to be seen.

At the *BBC's Maida Vale Recording Studios* and at the *Paris Studio* in Lower Regent Street it is possible to enjoy quiz shows, comedies, concerts, poetry, and panel games in great comfort and entirely free. Write to the BBC Ticket Unit, BBC, London W1A 4WW.

The flowers in London are free, but the *Bluebell Wood* in Kew will cost 10p on top of your 15p admittance – a bargain in May. In February the crocuses around *Hyde Park Corner* are exceptional, so later in the year are the roses in *Regent's Park* and the azaleas in *Queen Isabella's Garden* (Richmond Park). Some like the *Changing of the Guard*; I am perfectly happy with them the way they are.

The best free entertainment I ever enjoyed in London was the firework display in *Hyde Park* on the occasion of the last Royal Wedding. The pyrotechnics were impressive (though not a patch on those fired from the Venice Lagoon every summer), but the good humour of the multifarious crowds and the sense of holiday was astonishing.

French Restaurants

If I favour the *vieux jeu* as against the *nouvelle cuisine*, then it's because anyone – well almost anyone – can run a successful restaurant for a few weeks or months. I have tried many of these new places and liked them well enough, but it's the ones I cut my wisdom teeth on in the late fifties that I return to with the greatest pleasure.

The first French restaurant I ever ventured into without a grown-up was *L'Epicure* (28 Frith Street, W1; 01-437 2829), and I continued to patronise it throughout the sixties and seventies. Often Harold Wilson was there, a clever man in affairs of food as in much else, for the service in this typical old Soho restaurant was always discreet, friendly and respectful. The food, often flambéed in front of you, was always what it purported to be; it was there I learned how to diane steak. Then there was the *Chanterelle* (119 Old Brompton Road, SW7; 01-373 5522), where one was always made to feel important even if one wasn't. And the *Chanterelle* always *smelled* so good. It has changed ownership since those days, and is now run by Fergus Provan, whose cooking incorporates such ingredients as salsify, chestnuts, sorrel and sweetbreads. His salmon en croute is best. One mystery: in one of three leading restaurant guides the *Chanterelle* is categorised as a 'luxury' restaurant; another calls its prices 'moderate'; while the third calls them 'lower-middle'. It does a set lunch at £4.50; a slap-up dinner with wine will be about £25 a head.

I used to be taken to *A l'Ecu de France* (111 Jermyn Street, SW1; 01-930 2837) by a friendly publisher in the days when publishers were friendly. It was always expensive but it used to be entirely dependable. The meat was succulent, the service was formal, and the food, it seemed, *mattered*. Not so on a recent visit. Last orders were advertised as 11.30 p.m. and, arriving at 10.45 we were quickly made aware that we could well hold up the proceedings (by which I mean the waiter's bedtime). The chariot of desserts, which had always been such an eye-catching feature of the *Ecu*, looked as though the wolves had been at it. We felt unloved.

In the days of sexy Tory MPs and Lady Docker, the best of all French restaurants, I think, was *Daphne's* (112 Draycott Avenue, SW3; 01-589 4257). The tables were always a bit close together so that once, when my companion had spent the evening explaining to me that Laurence Olivier had been dreadfully over-the-top in *Othello*, we were rather stunned to be greeted by none other as he rose to leave from the next table. Despite the sad death of Daphne *elle-même*, Daphne who would always show you upstairs to her sitting room where a fire blazed to wait while your table was prepared and to study the menu, very little has changed; the mousse of smoked salmon on tiny rectangles of buttery toast certainly hasn't, and the invitation to inspect the kitchens still holds good. Daphne's is not cheap, but a special occasion does feel special there.

But a private survey I conducted confirmed what I suspected. That for the grand occasion almost everyone would like to be taken to the *Connaught* (Carlos Place, W1; 01-499 7070). I use the passive tense because it *is* very expensive. At his best Michel Bourdin, the chef, is superb – just try the light hollandaise sauce served with the turbot – but a reliable friend reports that the marron in her meringue mousse desert tasted 'as though it came from a bottle'.

Au Jardin des Gourmets: Established 1931. Very attractive, with attentive service, a set menu at £9.50 or a highbrow à la carte, including such delicacies as sliced breast of duck in red wine with pink peppercorns. (5 Greek Street, Soho Square, W1; 01-437 1816).

Brasserie St Quentin: Busy, noisy, smart, women without men welcomed (not always the case), downstairs less fun, the paté of three vegetables *elegant*. (243 Brompton Road, SW3; 01-589 8005).

Les Halles: An authentic-seeming brasserie, perhaps because it's run by Mr Conrad from the language school next door – he also runs the wine bar. The tarte au calvados is scrumptious. (57 Theobalds Road, WC1; 01-242 6761.)

L'Etoile: Only deserves a mention for its hors d'oeuvre trolley, the best in London (30 Charlotte Street, W1; 01-636 7189).

Ma Cuisine: (113 Walton Street, SW3; 01-584 7585). In this street of restaurants (and magistrates courts alas) this one is the hottest ticket in town. Booking a table is like being elected to the Royal Society – worth it if you can. But the tables are too close together. Leave room for the mousse brûlée.

Au Bon Accueil: Heartily recommended for reliable French cooking without formality (27 Elystan Street, SW3; 01-589 3718).

La Tante Claire: One of the restaurants in London most seriously dedicated to the gastronomic arts. M. Koffman presides over the kitchen; Madame Koffman is front of house manager. Their way with scallops is unique. Very expensive and should be. (68 Royal Hospital Road, SW3; 01-352 6045.)

Didier: One of the prettiest and most intimate restaurants in London, but the Welsh dresser leaves little room for customers. Rather a fragile menu (too much of which can be prepared in advance) but the parsnip purée and the house wine justify a visit. Good value but closed at weekends (5 Warwick Place, W9; 01-286 7484).

Au Provençal: Improbably situated at the entrance to Herne Hill Station, this imaginative and modestly priced restaurant coped remarkably well with my niece's 18th-birthday dinner and her effervescent friends. (295 Railton Road, SE24; 01-274 9163).

Lichfields: My favourite place for the grand occasion. The chef, Stephen Bull, concentrates on a limited menu, but everything is supremely well cooked. The cheese gougères brought to you while you order melt in the mouth. Eat these and leave, pleading faintness. Lunch at a very reasonable prix fixe. (Lichfield Terrace, Sheen Road, Richmond, Surrey; 01-940 5236).

La Poule Au Pot: The producer of my first (and only) West End play used to manage this charming restaurant, which survives virtually unchanged after more than twenty years. Mustard imaginatively employed in the cooking. Friendly and welcoming (231 Ebury Street, SW1; 01-730 7763).

Langan's Brasserie: Its fashionable reputation has lasted longer than such fashions usually do principally because the two rooms are ebulliently decorated and the manager, Richard Shepherd, and his staff know their onions. The vegetables and pastries especially recommended (Stratton Street, W1; 01-493 6437).

Best French restaurants: *Lichfields, Ma Cuisine, La Tante Claire,* and *Daphne's;* (more modestly) *La Poule au Pot.*

Friezes

Since the *Elgin Marbles* in the British Museum are 'generally agreed to be the finest in the world' (*The New Penguin Guide to London*) and 'generally held to be the greatest ever executed' (*The Blue Guide to London*), it would be churlish and contrary of me to prefer any other friezes, so I won't; but the frieze on the pediment of *Liberty's* store, overlooking Regent Street, with its massive Britannia (1924), and Nash's flamboyant Wedgwoody frieze on the pediment at the top of *Cumberland House* in Regent's Park, are worth more than a cursory glance.

A notable high camp mosaic frieze of peacocks and cockatoos by Walter Crane in the Arab Hall of *Leighton House* (Holland Park Road, free admission) is not to be missed. The house with its delightfully secluded garden is a hymn to late Victorian culture. A curiosity is the frieze running along the *ABC Cinema* in Shaftesbury Avenue. Gladiators, actors, camels, bacchanalians, all in a sort of Eric Gill neo-Hellenic profusion; or confusion. They say that Eric Gill did his carvings on Broadcasting House up a ladder in a monk's robe without underpants. People *are* bitchy.

Our beloved poet laureate recommends that one should always look *above* the shop fronts in London; if you do so you will certainly discover many treasures – if you live long enough . . .

Best Frieze: *Elgin Marbles.*

Gambling Clubs

In this age of dogmatism and dole queues, the atmosphere of a gambling club seems anachronistic. Indeed almost all the big money men are Arabs, Africans, Americans and Japanese, and the clubs at which they play cater accordingly. American roulette has taken over from the French variety, which is altogether more sedate, and blackjack and punto banco are increasingly popular. Craps, which offers the gambler in search of a genuine even money chance the best opportunity (by betting 'Don't Come'), is not played in the posh places, being regarded as noisy and undignified. Sky Masterson played, you will recall, in a New York drain. But the most comprehensive change has been in the running of the clubs. The Gaming Board inspectors have been responsible for such a tightening up of the regulations that it's as if the dice have to provide three referees before being thrown.

The beaux arts splendour of the *Ritz Casino* ('the last fling of a great age' – Betjeman) is all very well, but the handsomest house currently being gambled in is 20 Curzon Street, W1, the new *Crockford's Club*. Here is Horace Walpole writing about it in 1786: 'I was at Lady Macartney's last night. They have got a charming house in Curzon Street. It was Lord Carteret's and all antiqued and grotesqued by Adam, with an additional room in the court four score feet long, then dedicated to orgies, and now to books.' No orgies now, but a blackjack table with stakes from £100 to £1000 and American roulette at up to £200 en plein. The club is in the same ownership as the *International*, Berkeley Square, and offers two bars, a French restaurant and a Chinese restaurant. Outside the obsequious figure of Crockford, the hump-backed fishmonger from Temple Bar, invites you in. The gambling is conducted in English (which is naff) and instead of green the baize is vomit-coloured. The croupiers are tactful and cheerful.

The other two major gambling empires in London are *Pleasurama* (Ritz, Casanova, Palm Beach and Golden Nugget) and *Trident* (Claremont, Victoria Sporting Club). *Aspinall's* still has considerable cachet, for John Aspinall has style. He ran the Clermont Club to subsidise his zoos, for he loves animals even more than gamblers.

Best casino: *Crockford's*. (But it's been running less than a year.)

Garages

To understand why most garages are so disastrously bad, it is necessary to read *Zen and the Art of Motorcycle Maintenance* in which the problem is improbably set in its philosophical context. The author offers one useful hint. Any garage mechanic who works to music is likely to be less committed to his work than one who works in silence. Furthermore you should look at the condition of the tools scattered around (or hopefully *not* scattered around) the workshop. A more prosaic reason for the appalling standards of most British garages is that the Motor Agents Association has persistently done so little to improve things, and that the motoring associations seem keener on selling life insurance and semi-literate magazines than in securing the health of their members' cars.

But to be positive. The following garages have done good work in the past, and so may be expected to continue to do good work in the future. *Carpoint* (69 Borough Road, SE1; 01-403 1314), *R. A. Creamer & Son Ltd* (Drayson Mews, W8; 01-937 1275), *Daleham Garage* (19 Daleham Mews, NW3; 01-435 9136), *R. E. King* (1 Baynes Mews, NW3; 01-435 7096) (specifically for bodywork) and, more grandly, *Normand's* of Abbey Road, NW10 (01-965 7757). *Kenning's* (12 Berkeley Square, W1; 01-499 3434 and branches) from whom I bought my last car, were straight and efficient, but I had a tough time with their insurance department and the guarantee did not live up to its promise. *Morris Stapleton Motors* of 4 Kendrick Place, SW1 (01-589 5259) have the prettiest showroom, for it is choc-full of the prettiest cars, Morgans, lined up in colourful array. *Motorists' World* in White Hart Lane, Twickenham is open twenty-four hours per day, and offers, besides spares, videos and refreshments.

For the rest it is as well to anticipate the worst and avoid it by taking evening classes in car maintenance, or change to renting your cars. For repairs Renault and Volvo agents seem especially expensive.

On the street where I live is *Tiger Motors*, whose proprietor, Derek, takes a concerned interest in all of us. On cold winter mornings he will drop everything to jump start our cars, and if any of us had to undertake at short notice a lengthy car journey, Derek *will not allow us* to leave without first checking our brakes. Furthermore a domestic crisis was avoided when he pumped up my daughter's space-hopper. A hero of our time.

Best garage: *Tiger Motors*, Alexandra Road, East Twickenham.
Most improbable garage: 'The Chinese Garage' (*Park Langley Garage*, Wickham Road, Beckenham – built in pagoda-style).

Garden Centres

As a child, when I travelled west, either by car or by train on the Great Western Railway, the view I most looked forward to was *Waterford's Floral Mile*. The idea of *a mile* of flowers stimulated the mind of this would-be plutocrat. There were no such things as garden centres then. Plants came from nurseries, and seeds, gnomes and trellis work from Mr Chalk, the hardware man.

Now, in the age of the patio garden and the hatchback, we have garden centres. Of these the most celebrated is *The Clifton Nurseries*, which has expanded into three centres (Little Venice, 5a Clifton Villas, Warwick Avenue, W9; 01-286 9888; The

Collonnades, Bishop's Bridge Road, W2; 01-402 9834 and 16 Russell Street, Covent Garden, WC2; 01-379 6878). There are many who swear by the firm, but others have complained to me that it is too expensive and that at the Little Venice branch 'they were amazingly rude on several visits'.

The Earl's Court Road is an improbable venue for a garden centre, but *Russell's* at No 80 (01-937 0481) is recommended and not just for koolabar cuttings; while the *Parkhill Garden Nursery*, 84 Parkhill Road, NW3 (01-485 5985) is as polite and helpful as others are – reportedly – rude. Both the *Croxted Road Garden Centre*, SE24 (01-674 4366) and *Cramphorne's* in Keston are a bit 'rich' (as they say in the markets); the latter is reported to have refused to change defective goods.

The cheapest places to buy plants and such are the street markets at *Columbia Road*, Bethnal Green (strongly recommended) and *East Street*, Walworth Road, SE17; also, predictably, the *New Covent Garden* flower market at Seven Dials, where the wholesalers will 'see you're all right'. The *Petersham Garden Centre* at Petersham Farm, 143 Petersham Road, Surrey (01-940 5230) is a delight. *Sutton's*, of course, is the place for seeds (33 Catherine Street, WC2; 01-836 0619), just as *Garden Crafts* (158 New King's Road, SW6; 01-736 1615) is the place for garden statuary – some of their stock has to be seen to be believed. However, as a regular garden centre, *Syon Park*, Brentford (01-568 0134) is the place. You push a huge trolley around the spacious grounds which contain all you can reasonably expect, and pay at the check out with plastic money, if you're lucky enough to have any. You can combine your visit with a trip (I think it's the appropriate word) around the Butterfly House (see under Butterflies). But it's not particularly cheap.

Best garden centres: *Petersham* (for charm), *Syon Park* (for choice), *Columbia Road Market* (for value).

Gardens

God Almighty first planted a garden; and, indeed, it is the purest of human pleasures; it is the greatest refreshment to the spirits of man; without which buildings and palaces are but gross handy-works; and a man shall ever see that, when ages grow to civility and elegance, man comes to build stately sooner than to garden finely: as if gardening were the greater perfection.

Francis Bacon

Kew is of course unique. The Royal Botanic Gardens were laid out in 1751 by William Chambers, tutor to the Prince of Wales, and fastidious author of the splendid *Treatise of Civil Architecture*. Dominating the gardens is the Palm House (Decimus Burton), a mere 362 feet long by 100 feet wide by 66 feet high at the centre. But dimensions can do no justice to the most beautiful glasshouse in existence. Despite the claims of the Pagoda, the flagstaff on Victory Hill, the Bluebell Wood in early May and other vernal delights, *Kew Gardens* are not primarily frivolous. Many – possibly even most – of the 240,000 plants in existence are grown and studied at *Kew*, and since one tenth of these are under threat in our polluted world, one can appreciate the importance of the place. There is too the Queen's Garden behind the Palace, an endearing replica of a 17th-century garden in which only 17th-century flowers are permitted to grow, and the museums of botanical specimens, and the Temperate House, altogether less flamboyant than the Palm House but just as useful. And the pinetum, the herbarium in the library (over a million specimens), the azalea garden and many other delights. Open all the year round except Christmas Day and May Day, *Kew* charges adults 15p admittance, an extraordinary bargain.

Older than *Kew* by nearly a hundred years is the *Chelsea Physic Garden* contained within a triangle of less than four acres bounded by the Chelsea Embankment, the Royal Hospital Road and Swan Walk. 'Physic' in the sense of pertaining to things natural, for, by the philosophy of Paracelsus, every plant in the world had curative properties if the right antidote could be brought into opposition with its contrasting ailment. So the garden, founded by and for the Worshipful Company of Apothecaries, once dominated by the four great cedars of Lebanon which were planted in 1673, contained as wide a variety of species as could be brought together, and, under the ownership of the tubercular but munificent Dr Hans Sloane, it flourished. By 1795 specimens of over 3,700 varieties had been presented to the Royal Academy; Philip Miller, the greatest botanical horticulturalist of the age, had 'raised the reputation of the Chelsea Garden so much that it excels all the gardens of Europe' (Peter Collinson, a contemporary botanist).

Today the cedars have gone and the garden is no longer administered by the apothecaries, but it still flourishes (admission by appointment). From it cotton seeds were sent to the new colony of Georgia, and specimens were used as models at the Chelsea Porcelain factory just down the road. It sent Chinese bananas to

Fiji and Samoa, tea to India and rubber to Brazil, and even in this century it has proved invaluable, for the Madagascan periwinkle has become invaluable in cancer research and Professor F. G. Gregory's work on photo-periodism and vernalisation has helped alleviate starvation throughout the world.

And the white marble statue of old Sloane looks benevolently out over the peaceful order beds, the flowering shrubs, the heathers and rare trees, amongst which are the largest olive tree in Britain, and the finest example of a 'Willow Pattern Tree' (*Koelreuteria Paniculata*). An amiable and secluded paradise, soon to be made more available to the public.

Buckingham Palace possesses thirty-nine acres of generally 'natural' garden in the centre of London. If you have been to a garden party there you will not quickly forget the herbaceous border which is over 500 feet long, nor the imposing Waterloo Vase set amidst the shrubbery, nor the summerhouse. Over 100,000 crocuses have been planted and more than a hundred varieties of rhododendron. The list is almost endless.

It must not be inferred that these are the only memorable gardens in London. There is *Queen Mary's Gardens* in Regent's Park with its unforgettable roses; there are the formal sunken gardens of tulips and pleached limes in the grounds of *Kensington Palace*; and there are the gardens at *Hampton Court* – Dutch in influence thanks to William of Orange. These may be viewed through clairvoyées (ornamental grilles in brick piers) but there is something a bit *civic* about the Pond Garden, the Sunk Garden and the reproduction Knot Garden – too many lobelias and begonias amidst the fine old brick. The *Rembrandt Gardens* in Little Venice is an oasis amidst the concrete desert and *Richmond Terrace Gardens*, whose mysterious statuary and huge chestnut trees seem about to tumble into the Thames, are intriguing. In Richmond Park *Queen Isabella's Garden* is justly celebrated for its azaleas. The *Cutty Sark Gardens* in Greenwich and *Geffrye's Garden* in Shoreditch are full of charm, while the gardens attached to the gutted remains of *St Anne's*, Soho, *St Ethelburga-the-Virgin-Within-Bishopsgate* (see Churches), *St George's*, Mount Street (beautifully tended), the *Actors' Church* in Covent Garden, and *St John's*, Downshire Hill, NW3 are a few of the pleasantest church gardens in London.

And what about the gardens of *Lambeth Palace*, alight with daffodils, what about the *Inns of Court* (a wistaria and a fig tree flourish still in Lincoln's Inn) and *Victoria Embankment Gardens* with that sassy old camel? And what about *Beverley Nichols' garden*

(Sudbrook Cottage, Ham Common, which used to be open on Sundays in May to the public and all that a cottage garden should be – he planted everything himself except the copper beech)?

And what about all those private gardens, bird-bedecked, deck-chaired, and pleasuresome?

Best garden: *Chelsea Physic Garden.*
Worst garden: *Chalcot Square Garden.*

Further reading: *The Gardener's London* by Dawn MacLeod (Duckworth).

Gates

Amongst many wrought-iron gates the following are early 18th century and splendid: *Old Abney House*, Church Street, Stoke Newington; *44 Vicarage Crescent*, Battersea; and the *Old Burial Grounds*, Dulwich Village. Better still though are the gates to the garden at *Burgh House*, Well Walk, NW3.

There is a fine pair of late 17th-century gates which have been admiringly restored by the enlightened borough council of Enfield. What is curious about them (the gates not the borough council) is that they lead nowhere. Once they led to Gough Park, but the big house went, and the New River, which ran through the park, was taken away too. The fine original gates of the *Cremorne Pleasure Gardens* – the last of these pleasure gardens to close – were removed to a brewery in Tetcott Road, Chelsea.

Magnificent iron gates by the great Frenchman, Jean Tijou, he of the Tijou Screen at Hampton Court, open upon the South Choir Aisle in *St Paul's*. There's not much to praise about *Buckingham Palace*, except maybe the mews, the gardens, the stamp collection, the welcome given to intruders . . . and the gates. These have agreeable cherubs on them, if you like cherubs, and were the gift of the Dominions in 1906, when we still had dominion.

The gates into *Queen Mary's Gardens* in Regents Park, and those which open onto *Holland Park* from Kensington High Street are ornate to the point of vulgarity ('keep vulgarity for the bedroom', says a character in one of Joe Orton's plays) and I prefer the simple rusticity of the tottering gates which give into *Dulwich Park*. In fact, though it's a bit late in the day to admit it, I'm not sure I much care for wrought-iron gates at all. You may admire us, they seem to be saying, but we are here to *Keep You Out*. For this reason, but also because they're grand, I nominate as best in London the gates which lead nowhere.

The gateway into *Lambeth Palace* of russet Tudor brick is very pleasing.

Best gates: *Gough Park*, Enfield.
Worst gates: *Wormwood Scrubs Prison.*

Ghosts

> I am the ghost of Shadwell Stair.
> Along the wharves by the water-house,
> And through that dripping slaughter-house.
> I am the shadow that walks there.

from *Shadwell Stair* by Wilfred Owen (1893-1918)

I believe (though I can't prove it) that London is more cluttered with psychic phenomena than anywhere in the world. Many of these ghosts congregate around such places as Tyburn Hill, the old London hospitals, Jack the Ripper country in the East End, and, of course, the Tower of London.

Most London theatres have their ghosts, notably the *Theatre Royal*, Drury Lane (the fourth theatre on the site), where a slim young man dressed in grey, with a white wig and carrying a tricorn hat occupies the first seat of the fourth row of the upper circle. Moving along the gangway at the back of the circle he disappears into the wall near the Royal Box. Unusually for a ghost, he only appears in daylight hours and his presence during rehearsals or at the start of a run augurs well for the success of the show.

The *British Museum* is haunted by a Priestess of the Temple of Amen-Ra, a malevolent spirit which drives dogs mad and, according to Thurston Hopkins, the ghost hunter, has been responsible for the deaths of at least thirteen people. The coffin lid which is supposed to exercise these fatal powers is Exhibit No 22542 and may be found in the second Egyptian Room, labelled: 'Mummy Cover from Thebes XXIst Dynasty. About 1050 BC. Presented by A. F. Wheeler 1889.'

The *Tower of London*, where tortures and wallings-up and executions have taken place for a thousand years, contains many ghosts. The princes haunt the White Tower where they met their end. Headless women are almost commonplace while St Thomas

Beckett, Henry Percy, Anne Boleyn, Sir Walter Raleigh, Guido Fawkes and a huge bear are just a few amongst many spectral celebrities. More intriguingly in 1817 a cylindrical tube containing a blue and white fluid attacked the wife of the Keeper of the Crown Jewels.

The Grey Lady of *St Thomas's*, an amiable middle-aged lady in a grey uniform, appears in a sympathetic guise and Block 8 to those who are soon to die. She is only seen from mid-calf upwards, a detail attributed to the raising of the level of the floors when the hospital was rebuilt.

The nastiest ghost haunts, or haunted since there have been no sightings for many years, *No 50 Berkeley Square*, now occupied by Maggs Brothers, antiquarian booksellers. Whether the ghost is a child who had been frightened to death, or a young girl who threw herself from the window to escape her lascivious uncle's advances, or merely a gang of counterfeiters pretending to be a ghost, is not clear, but the walls of the house are said to be 'saturated with electric horror supernaturally fatal to body and mind'.

The *BBC* has a ghost in Langham Place, a limping butler with an empty tray, and at *Vine Street Police Station* there is a ghost of a police sergeant who committed suicide in one of the cells. There was a haunted jacket worn by actresses at the *Duke of York Theatre* which grew tighter and tighter the more it was worn, and a ghostly bus, driverless and without any visible conductor, which careered through *North Kensington*, forcing motorists off the road, but, since the junction of St Marks Road and Cambridge Gardens was made safer, the ghost bus has apparently stayed in its garage – along with the 137.

The most improbable London ghost haunts *Pond Square*, Highgate. In March 1626 Francis Bacon, riding in his carriage through Highgate, ordered his coachman to stop by the pond and buy a chicken from a farm. This done, the coachman was instructed to kill, pluck and clean the bird, thereafter stuffing it with snow, more snow being packed tightly around it. This early experiment in refrigeration proved fatal not only to the bird but also to the 65-year-old scientist, who was overcome with excitement. It is not Bacon however who haunts *Pond Square*, but the bald chicken which flaps its wings and turns in frenzied circles.

In conclusion I feel obliged to mention the *Westminster Abbey* ghost, one Father Benedictus, a Benedictine monk. Tall, thin, sallow and contemptuous, he walks an inch above the ground between five and six in the evening, and talks in Elizabethan English.

For more ghosts see *Haunted London* by Peter Underwood (Harrap).

Best ghost: *The Man in Grey*, the Theatre Royal, Drury Lane.
Worst ghost: *The High Priestess of Amen-Ra*, British Museum.

Golf

> A caddy at St Andrews named Lang Willie was teaching one of the professors of the University the noble game. The professor was not a promising pupil. Willie fairly got out of patience and said to him: "Ye see, Professor, as long as ye are learning thae lads at the College Latin and Greek it is easy work, but when ye come to play ye maun hae a heid!"
>
> *The Oxford Dictionary of Quotations*

Any true golfer will tell you that a golf course should either be a links with its bracing air, its sea vistas, its romantic associations – *Troon* is perfection – or a downs, with its springy turf, its heather, and its wide horizons. Park courses, even at their best (*Augusta National, Georgia*), are effeminate, and London courses, created on the clay of the London basin, tend to be dull, flat and soggy. There are fair courses around London: *Sunningdale* and *Wentworth* (très snob) to the south west; *Temple* to the east, breathtakingly beautifully especially in autumn and easy so long as you keep well to the right of the ninth fairway; *Moor Park* and *Sandy Lodge* to the north west. *Walton Heath* is high, wide, heathery and handsome; probably as good as any.

Within the Greater London area, *Highgate* is pleasant, and the *Royal Mid-Surrey* at Richmond, though flat, is on gravel as well as clay, and boasts partridges, pheasants, herons, swans and kestrels; birdies are no problem here.

Public courses are not necessarily inferior, but *Beckenham Place Park* is far too heavily golfed upon, with 88,000 green fees a year. Golf should not be like this; one should have space around one, room to brace one's shoulders and let fly. Read Patrick Hamilton's wonderful novel: *Hangover Square*. That says it better than I can.

The cheapest golf in London, indeed at £2 a round the cheapest golf in South East England, has been available on the public courses in *Richmond Park*, but the Government intends to sell the franchises so that will be that.

Best golf course (in or near London): *Walton Heath.*

Greek Restaurants

Bitter Lemons (98 Lillie Road, SW6; 01-381 1069) is my favourite Greek restaurant in London. On my last visit we were joined by the proprietor's large and friendly dog and later by his small and friendly daughter, who had come downstairs in her nightie. This is the sort of thing that tends to happen in Greek, Turkish and Cypriot restaurants. Oh, and the food's excellent.

It is to the eternal credit of the *Dionysus Taverna* (13 Heath Street, NW3; 01-794 2862) restaurant that when I arrived alone at 9 p.m. on a Saturday night, and they had two tables left – both for four – they invited me in. They fed me kleftiko with vast quantities of rice, potatoes and peas off nasty bone china. One could do worse.

The *Anemos* (32-34 Charlotte Street, W1; 01-636 2289) is all to do with dancing on the table, smashing your bouzouki over the head of Anthony Quinn, and throwing food. Try that sort of thing at the old-established *Beoty's* (79 St Martin's Lane, WC2; 01-836 8768) and you will regret it. This formal and classy place is quite expensive and the waiters expect to be called 'Waiter'. A good deal better than the *Elysée* (13 Percy Street, W1; 01-636 4804) which was once so fashionable. The *Marmara* (166 Evelyn Street, SE8; 01-692 5557) is probably the only place in Deptford where you can eat Turkish-style stuffed vine leaves. Not as lively as heretofore, it stays open late, and the food is palatable. The oddest Turkish restaurant in London is the *Gallipoli*, which stands in the courtyard of Bishopsgate Church (where Keats was baptised) looking like something dreamed up by a demented designer of cigarette advertisements. Once it was a Turkish bath, vintage 1895; today belly dancers wiggle and squirm as you tackle your biryan Gallipoli. Quite an experience (01-588 1922).

Some of the best Greek food in London is to be sampled at the *White Tower* (1 Percy Street, W1; 01-636 8141), but it costs. Expect to pay £30 a head. The menu informs you that Aubergine Imam Bayaldi commemorates an Imam who ate so many aubergines that he bayalded. Nasty.

My two other recommendations are for the *Salamis Taverna* on Richmond Hill (86 Hill Rise; 01-940 7557). This has gods disporting themselves on the ceiling and a sensationally good kleftiko (casserole of lamb). And *Kalamaras* (76-78 Inverness Terrace, W2; 01-727 9122) and another restaurant of the same name in the same street (No 66; 01-727 9122) are informal, delightful and nourishing establishments – the former a touch posher than the latter.

Demestica (white or red) is an excellent Greek plonk. Sea bass is the best Greek fish. And the *Greek Food Centre* (12 Inverness Street, NW1 – there's a coincidence! – 01-485 6544) is where to buy all middle-eastern comestibles. A splendid shop.

Best Greek Restaurant: *Bitter Lemons.*

Greengrocers

Between 1961 and 1971 the number of greengrocers in London declined by 27%. The statistic is remarkable, though no more remarkable than the fact that I carry it in my head, and sad. One of the survivors is *Robert Bruce* (19 James Street, WC2; 01-240 0194), close by the site of the old Covent Garden fruit and vegetable market. The others have moved out, but *Bruce* seems to have flourished, and there is virtually nothing of a vegetabular kind which you cannot get from him. Such delicacies as samphire, and the rarer kinds of dried mushroom are to him as everyday as sprouts, but he stocks your regular apples and oranges too. When I worked in Floral Street he would always sell off cheaply any perishables at the end of the day; he probably still does.

The most amusing places to buy fruit and vegetables are the street markets, and *Berwick Street Market* in particular. Two greengrocers within my immediate neighbourhood which I can unhesitatingly recommend are the splendid *Peter Childs* (8 Lichfield Terrace, Sheen Road, Richmond; 01-940 2934) and *A. C. Bush* (376 Richmond Road, Twickenham; 01-892 4042). The latter is not only an excellent supplier of whatever is in season and much that isn't, but he has been rash enough in the past to cash my cheques when things got desperate. The grocer may be a wicked man * but nobody could dislike a greengrocer; could they?

Best greengrocer: *Robert Bruce.*

*He keeps a lady in a cage,
Most cruelly all day,
And makes her count and calls her Miss
Until she fades away. G. K. Chesterton

Hairdressers

For me the idea of sitting passively in front of a mirror under bright lights is equivalent to the trauma of a Dorian Gray facing his aged portrait for the first time. What I need from a hairdresser is dim lights, discretion, and silence. Those unisex establishments that blast your ear-drums with their idea of music, gossip mischievously about their famous clients, offer you cups of coffee and then cut your hair into them, are to be avoided like herpes.

The posh ones for men are *George F. Trumper's* (9 Curzon Street, W1; 01-499 1850), as solid and tweedy as it sounds, and *Joshua and Daniel Galvin* (69-71 Park Road, NW1; 01-724 2341), where, if Daniel gives you just a haircut you won't get away with it under £20, and you will probably be persuaded to have an avocado wax, or something equally exotic. For a short back and sides you need only pay £1.60 and it need only take ten minutes if you patronise one of the small Greek Cypriot establishments that abound in the Camden Town area of London, in Islington and in other inner suburbs. An excellent example is *George Papas's* establishment in Cowcross Street, EC1. Here you can even get a shave or a friction rub and a discreet packet of hum ha.

On the subject of women's hairdressers I cannot write with first-hand authority. But Fiona Byrne at the *Cut & Colour Salon* in Streatham (Streatleigh Parade, 12 Streatham High Road, SW16; 01-969 5151), won first prize in a nationwide contest, and, if you wish to be grand, *Leonard* (6 Upper Grosvenor Street, W1; 01-499 7409) is where to mingle with those celebrities who wish to be mingled with. *Vidal Sassoon* (60 South Molton Street, W1; 01-491 8848) you will already know about – and if you're male ask for Trevor – and *Hugh & Alan* (161 Ebury Street, SW1; 01-730 2196 and at the Hyde Park Hotel) are currently and deservedly in *Vogue* as well as in vogue. *Splinters* (27 Maddox Street, W1; 01-493 5169) is a large – it employs a staff of 40 – and smart establishment catering principally to clients who are black and female. Winston Isaacs, who runs it, is ambitious and influential.

Any of those mentioned could qualify as the best depending on your sex and your preference.

Hamburgers

Although it should be a simple matter to serve a hamburger successfully it obviously ain't. There are more failures than successes. Amongst the former *Casey Jones's*, *Huckleberry's*, *Maxwell's*, *Wendyburgers*, and *Wimpys* have been noted. At *Strikes* (it used to be called Strikes, 1926, until less cynical councils prevailed) the hamburgers are too expensive to be enjoyable. At *Tramps* they are acceptable but the orange drinks taste of soap. *McDonalds* are quick and cheap but crowded and consequently tend to get grubby (evidence the Oxford Street branch between noon and 1.30 p.m.). Besides on my last visit to a *McDonalds* (Wimbledon) they had run out of hats, badges and pencils, which was partly what the children had come for. All one wants is sesame seeds on the buns, a good selection of relishes, crisp salad, and meaty meat, but it's not that easy. At *The Hard Rock Cafe* (150 Old Park Lane, W1; 01-629 0382) the charcoal grilled hamburgers are fine when you get them, but the wait is tiresome and the noise is excessive. I can also recommend *Benson's* (39 St Barnabas Street, Ranelagh Grove, SW1; 01-730 2572), the *Burger King* (Coventry Street, W1, and Victoria Street, SW1), the *New York Cafe* (60 Old Brompton Road, SW7; 01-584 4028), *Fay Schneider* (7 New College Parade, NW3; 01-722 7116) for her schneiderburgers, *Smiles* (16 Jermyn Street, SW1; 01-734 7334) for its turkey burgers, and the *Zanzibar* (30 Great Queen Street, WC2) where flash buggers hang out, but the monarch of them all is *Macarthurs* with branches at Sheen, Barnes and Turnham Green (opening a restaurant in Turnham Green is condemning yourself to a lifetime of bad jokes). Consistently over more than five years *Macarthurs* have proved their hamburgers to be the best, their milk shakes the thickest, their bills the most reasonable, their music the gentlest, and their tables the least crowded together. You also get an avalanche of peppermint eggs when you leave.

Best hamburgers: *Macarthurs* (Sheen branch).

Hats

The bowler was invented by *Lock* of St James's (6 James's Street, SW1; 01-930 8874) to please a certain William Coke who kept losing his tall hats when hunting. *Lock* asked a Mr Beaulieu to come up with a design; hence the *bowler*. *Lock* flourishes while the bowler is at risk. *Bates* (21a Jermyn Street, W1; 01-734 2722) also sounds like a hatter and, estimably, is. At *George Malyard* (137 Lavender Hill, SW11; 01-223 8292) they will make a hat to your specifications; they also sell that best of hats, the panama. For a fedora go to *Herbert Johnson* (13 Old Burlington Street, W1;

01-439 7397); they serve ladies hats in the basement, which they could never do at *David Shilling* (36 Marylebone High Street, W1; 01-486 6456), for they would never get them up the stairs. *David Shilling*, of course, is the milliner whose hats at Royal Ascot, as worn by his mother, do everything except frighten the horses. Such brave vulgarity can only be applauded; needless to say the hats on sale in Marylebone High Street are somewhat less eccentric. But to be safely hatted a lady would probably go to *Simone Mirman* (9 Chesham Place, SW1; 01-235 2656). The best wearers of hats in London are Lady Diana Cooper, George Melly and Michael Kustow.

Best men's hats: *Lock.*
Best women's hats: *Simone Mirman.*

Hills

Some love to roll down Greenwich Hill,
 For this thing, and for that;
And some prefer sweet Marble Hill,
 Though sure 'tis somewhat flat!
Yet Marble Hill and Greenwich Hill,
 If Kitty Clive can tell,
From Strawberry Hill, from Strawberry Hill
 Will never bear the bell!

William Pulteney

Most London hills are 'somewhat flat'. *Corn-*, *Craven-*, and *St Andrews* are three examples. *Notting Hill* is really quite sharp as a view from the water tower will prove.

Primrose Hill rises to 206 feet above the Trinity high watermark of the Thames, and is a real hill, as the kiteflyers will testify. It used to be a forest filled with wolves and was originally called *Greenberry Hill*, supposedly from the names of three murderers, Green, Berry and Hill, executed there in 1678, but possibly innocent. Lurid murders also feature in *Muswell Hill* (350 feet high), which was once a place of pilgrimage for those with scrofula. The steepest may well be *Mill Hill*, although Nightingale Lane which runs aslant *Richmond Hill*, is alarmingly steep for a short distance and *Highgate Hill* was steep enough to send a tramcar crashing fatally down in 1906. *Crooms Hill*, Greenwich, is decidedly picturesque, and so is *Forty Hill* in Enfield, at least if you can get off the main road. *Holly Hill* and *Golders Hill* deserve to be better known, but for charm and literary associations I shall not look further than *Downshire Hill*, NW3 where Keats lived. If you prefer C. Day Lewis to Keats, then you should prefer *Crooms Hill*.

The nastiest hill is either *Shooters Hill* or *Denmark Hill* although it's not the fault of the hill.

Best hill: *Downshire Hill.*
Worst hill: *Denmark Hill.*

Horses

At *Deptford Playground* in Watson Street, SE8 is Bonny Bright Eyes, bridle long since gone, eyes blind, jutting under-lip, a survivor. A more cheerful sight is the blinkered dray above the door of *Ye Olde Spotted Horse* in Putney High Street. There is a flying horse on a drainpipe in the Inner Temple, and the following brazen gentlemen are amongst those who ride horses for eternity through London: Prince Albert, Charles I, Richard I, George IV, St George, Edward VII, whose horse seems fractious, and Field Marshal Earl Roberts. Boadicea's fine pair strut and prance at *Westminster Bridge*, but for the real thing visit *Clapham Common* during the Greater London Horse Show.

Recommended riding stables:

(a) Smart
Civil Service Riding Club, c/o the Royal Mews (01-930 7232)
Ross Nye, 8 Bathurst Mews, W2 (01-262 3791)
Lilo Blum, 32 Grosvenor Crescent Mews, SW1 (01-235 6846)
Stag Lodge School of Equitation, Robin Hood Gate, Richmond Park, W14 (01-546 9863)
Snaresbrook Riding School, 67 Hollybush Hill, E11 (01-989 3256)

(b) Children, newcomers, nervous riders, those with handicaps
City Farm, 1 Cressfield Close, Grafton Road, NW5 (01-485 4585)
Willow Tree Riding Establishment, Ronver Road, SE12 (01-857 6438)
Lea Bridge Riding Centre, Myddelton House, Bulls Cross, Enfield, Middlesex (0992 717711)

Best live horses: *Royal Mews* (where else?).
Best dead horses: *Boadicea's.*

Horse Troughs

At the Cornhill end of the passage which runs behind the Royal Exchange a fountain commemorates in suitable fashion (a nude bronze girl inside a red granite base) the 1911 Jubilee of the Metropolitan Drinking Fountain and Horse Trough Association, whose portentous name may be found on horse troughs throughout London. But sadly there's no longer much call for horse troughs, and those who still operate by horse make their own arrangements. Some years ago the MDFAHTA gave all its troughs and fountains to the local authorities and its records to the London Museum – they now only operate abroad – and the Chairman, Mr Randall (Crayford 528062) was unable to direct me to any water trough which still contains water. Flowers are what the local authorities fill them with, so flowers are what we must have. But many of the old troughs bear poignant witness to the tremendous work of the association. There's a typical trough in *Spencer Park*, SW18 and another, like a stone cot, at *Meadway*, NW11; *Albany Street*, NW1, has a fine example of a long double trough and you may have spotted others. My favourite with delightfully intertwining wrought-iron griffins stands outside the *Star and Garter Home* at the Richmond Gate entrance to Richmond Park. The one in *Chalk Farm Road*, NW1, is decrepit.

Best trough: *Richmond Gate.*

Hostels

There are five recognised youth hostels in London, besides the YMs and the YWs. These are:

Carter Lane (36 Carter Lane, EC4; 01-236 4965) was once home and school for St Paul's choirboys. The vibrations of their singing still hang in the air. Usefully central.

Earl's Court (38 Bolton Gardens, SW5; 01-373 7083). A lively area for insomniacs and peripatetics. This hostel has direct access from Heathrow by Piccadilly Line underground to Earls Court. Closed between 10 a.m. and 3 p.m.

Hampstead Heath (4 Wellgarth Road, NW11; 01-458 9054 and 7196). This former nursing college has a pleasant games room and something often frowned upon in youth hostels, a television.

Highgate (84 Highgate West Hill, N6; 01-340 1831). A Georgian house conveniently close to Kenwood and Keats House. This hostel is closed between 10 a.m. and 5 p.m.

Holland House (Holland Walk, W8; 01-937 0748). Incorporating part of a fine Jacobean pile (see Theatres-Open Air), Holland House is ideal if you wish to visit the Kensington Museums or the Commonwealth Institute.

If you don't qualify for youth hostels, you have problems. There are the *Church Army hostels* (HQ 01-903 3763) which charge a rent of between £4 and £5 a night, but permit no alcohol, no smoking, and lock the front doors at 11 p.m. Privacy scarcely exists. There is *Arlington House* (Arlington St, SW1; 01-493 3094) with over 1000 beds, ten bathrooms, two televisions and two one-armed bandits. A year ago the staff walked out and picketed the place, considering a weekly wage of around £25 per week (including cubicles and food) inadequate.

Rented accommodation at £50 a week for a self-contained flat is out of the reach of many flat-hunters. Numerous squats, such as the famous Tolmers Square community, have been demolished, and the relief organisations such as *Alone in London* (Euston Square, NW1; 01-387 5470), *Centrepoint in Soho*, a night shelter for the under-25s at 25 Oxford Street, W1; the *Catholic Housing Aid Society* (189a Old Brompton Road SW5; 01-373 4961) and *Stopover House* (65 Bell Green, Lewisham, SE26; 01-659 5060), are finding it hard to cope.

The best hostel for students is probably *Jerome House* (19 Harrington Gardens, SW7; 01-370 3145) but, if you can run to it, the best hostel in London has to be the *Albany* (between Piccadilly and Vigo Street) which was originally 'residential chambers for bachelor gentlemen'.

Best Hostel: *Albany*.

Hotels (most and least expensive)

The most expensive hotels in London at the time of writing are *Blake's*, 33 Roland Gardens, SW7, maximum £214*; the *Sheraton Park Tower*, maximum £121.90*; the *Ritz*, maximum £120.70*; the *Inn on the Park*, maximum £116.70; the *Hyde Park Hotel*, maximum £108; the *Connaught*, maximum £104*; *Grosvenor House*, maximum £102.50; the *Churchill*, maximum £101.48;

Brown's, maximum £100.50. All these prices are for a double room with bed and breakfast; those starred exclude service. The *Athenaeum*, maximum £110.24, is redeemed by its wide selection of malt whiskies.

A respectable bed and breakfast double room at less than £10 may still be found. The following are recommended. The *White House* (Mrs Mark), 242 Norwood Road, West Norwood, SE27 (01-670 3607) – £9-£10; *London Budget Accommodation*, 169 Sutherland Avenue, W9 (01-289 0787) – £9; *Mrs Miles*, 37 Brewster Gardens, W10 (01-969 7024) – £6-£8; *Westpoint Hotel*, 170 Sussex Gardens, W2 (01-402 0281) – £7.50; *Sass House*, 11 Craven Terrace, W2 – £7.50; and *Londoner Lodge*, 62 Lauderdale Mansion, Lauderdale Road, W9 (01-286 7067) – £4.50.

When the *Berkeley Hotel* moved from Piccadilly to Wilton Place, the management, sensitive to their clients' conservatism, took with them the wall panels, the chandeliers, the fireplaces, the bedroom furniture, the light brackets, and the entire Lutyens writing room. It also clings to the old-fashioned way of doing things, such as cleaning your shoes if you leave them outside your room. Alan Whicker describes it thus: 'A well-run country house in the heart of London, a delicious Omelette Arnold Bennett pleasantly and swiftly served on Wedgwood in your room, where the decor will be tasteful and charming with every comfort to hand.' Were it not for the possibility of meeting Alan Whicker early in the morning I would have few reservations about recommending the *Berkeley*.

The *Ritz*, Piccadilly, designed in the grand beaux arts style by Mowes and Davis, is experiencing a revolution. The huge baths have gone and weekend packages (£75 for 2 nights) are in. There are tea dances on Sundays at 4.30 followed by musical evenings. The new chef, Michael Quinn, has replaced the massive Escoffier-inspired menu with something simpler. For £10.50 you can have a starter and a pudding, but it's too soon to say whether the new regime is succeeding.

The *Savoy* is for theatrical snobs, but it's architecturally fascinating too. Built by D'Oyly Carte some years after the theatre, it was Europe's first fire-proofed building. It had 'ascending rooms' (lifts), seventy bathrooms, and speaking tubes on every floor. Escoffier was the chef, Strauss led the orchestra, Pavlova danced in the cabaret. Sir Henry Irving, Sarah Bernhardt, and Elaine Stritch have all taken up residence there; Arnold Bennett based *Imperial Palace* on it. A remarkable institution. The Riverside Suite is the one to book when entertaining film stars discreetly.

William Claridge and James Brown were both butlers who became celebrated hoteliers, and both hotels have survived for well over a century. *Claridge's* is opulent, has a magnificent entrance hall, and caters for minor royalty; they have never permitted dancing or cabarets. *Brown's* is cosier, comfortable and courteous.

Of the six large hotels in Park Lane, the grandest is the *Dorchester*, now Arab-owned. The frontage on Park Lane is uninspired to say the least, and the food has been mediocre recently. Unless you book the Oliver Messel Suite which is not unlike Kew Gardens, I should suggest you try elsewhere. The *Basil Street Hotel* and the *Capital Hotel*, also in Basil Street, are a better bet than any of the Park Lane bunch, while the prettiest hotels in London are the creeper-lined *Brook Hotel* in Stamford Brook and *Durrants* (George Street, W1; 01-935 8131). At Durrants you will receive excellent personal service; it is well placed for the Wallace Collection.

The best valet service in town has always been at the *Connaught*. The *Sandringham Hotel* (3 Holford Road, NW3; 01-435 1569) is a pleasant modestly priced family hotel with notably large towels and breakfasts. The *Portobello* (22 Stanley Gardens, W11) is eccentric, chatty and fun. The restaurant is open 24 hours a day. Also recommended the *Stafford*, the *Montcalm*, and amongst the cheaper ones the *Wilbraham* in Wilbraham Place and the *Half Moon Hotel* (10 Earls Court Square, SW5; 01-373 9956). The *Great Eastern Hotel*, Bishopsgate (the hotel for Liverpool Street Station travellers) has a magnificent dining room copied from the Palais Soubise in Paris.

I have had discouraging reports about the *Clarendon* (Montpelier Row, SE3), the *Mayfair Hotel*, the *Sheraton Skyline* near Heathrow, where a bottle of whisky ordered through room service set a friend back £38, the *Penta Hotel* in Cromwell Road, the *Bloomsbury* hotels in general and the *Russell Square* hotels in particular. The *Imperial* must be one of the ugliest post-war edifices in London.

Best hotel: *Durrants.*
To be avoided: *Those which expect you to make your own coffee.*

See *The Good Hotel Guide* edited by Hilary Rubinstein.

Houses

(a) Big

I shall narrow the contestants down to five finalists, *Kenwood, Ham House, Fenton House, Queen's House*, Greenwich, and *Chiswick House*. I shall listen politely to those who press the claims of *Osterley Park* (very fine), *Winfield House, Leighton House* (see Friezes), *Apsley House* (on a traffic island and renovated), and the fine Adam houses, of which *Chandos House* (Cavendish Square) and the *Courtauld Institute*, Portman Square, have survived without being mauled. I should like to consider the amazing *Strawberry Hill*, and – but no, no, to the short list.

Kenwood House, a well-proportioned 18th-century mansion in Highgate (only just, it's almost Hampstead) is bigger but no better than many other houses of a similar period, but it is so beautifully renovated to its original Adam magnificence by the curator, John Jacobs, and it is so prettily situated, that it commands respect. So do the treasures of the Iveagh Bequest, which are housed there. Any house would look its best when it can display upon its walls a Rembrandt self-portrait and one of the finest Vermeers.

Ham House is Jacobean and magnificent. It was enlarged by the Duke and Duchess of Lauderdale in the 1670s; they were a flamboyant couple and ensured that only the finest craftsmen were employed to paint the ceilings, panel the walls and parquet the floors. Silver-mounted fire implements were the ultimate status symbol and, as with *Kenwood, Ham* has been wonderfully restored with much of the original furniture – including superb chairs – still in place. It is an annexe to the V and A. To arrive in style avoid the crowded Petersham Road, with some very fine Georgian houses along it, and take the ferry from Twickenham.

Fenton House in the Grove, Hampstead Heath, is almost as old as *Ham House*, and almost as magnificent. Where *Ham House* boasts a stone figure of Father Thames in its forecourt, *Fenton House* contains within its enclosed garden a statuette of a shepherdess being courted by a shepherd, who is shamefully unbuttoned. The house is notable too for its collection of musical instruments, pride of place going to a harpsichord played upon by Handel. *Fenton House* is not grandiose like the other houses in this section, but charming. The architect is not known – at least to me.

Queen's House, Greenwich. Designed by Inigo Jones (1616-1635) *Queen's House* is framed by Wren's Queen Mary and King William blocks, so that one gets a strange perspective on this symmetrical house, which appears as a retiring child hanging back between its two parents. Wonderfully preserved, it contains the haunted Tulip Staircase (not open to the public) where the Reverend Hardy and his wife took a photograph of one (perhaps two) ghosts. Canaletto painted the vista in 1755 from the north bank of the Thames, and it has scarcely changed in two and a quarter centuries.

Chiswick House. Of the five this is the only one which is neglected. Yet it is a Palladian villa of substantial reputation; it was built by the Earl of Burlington as a museum for his works of art and as a place to entertain friends in; so it has no bedrooms. The Inigo Jones gateway is there, of which Pope wrote:

> Oh gate, how cam'st thou here?
>   I was brought from Chelsea last year,
> Battered with wind and weather:
>   Inigo Jones put me together,
> Sir Hans Sloane
>   Let me alone,
> Burlington brought me here.

I almost prefer its shabbiness to *Marble Hill House's* shiny sleekness, for the latter, started in the same year as Chiswick House (1725), is splendid and the curators very kind, but Chiswick has a soul.

Best big house: *Ham House.*
Worst big house: *Knightsbridge Barracks* (Sir Basil Spence).

(b) Small (see also under Cottages)

Those who argue that Nash was senile when he came to design *Buckingham Palace* in 1824 conveniently forget that in the following year he was responsible for the delightful houses known as *Park Villages East* and *West* (we have lost half of *Park Village East* but *Park Village West* survives). These like the equally attractive houses on the *Bedford Park*, Chiswick estate – the first 'garden suburb', inspired by Jonathan T. Carr, cloth merchant, designed by E. W. Godwin and Norman Shaw in the 1870s – are all distinctive but complementary. Nash's designs were completed after his death by his pupil, James Pennethorne.

There are other such estates. The Georgian houses in *Bloomsbury*, the Victorian houses in *Primrose Hill*, *de Beauvoir Square* (neo-Jacobean with ornate Flemish gables), the back streets of *Chelsea*, miniature delights like *Hasker Street*, and the studios known as the *Italian Village* off the Fulham Road, all are agreeable to look at and happy to live in. *Holly Lodge Gardens*, off Highgate West Hill, is a sinister development of some eight or nine Gothic houses straight out of Hammer films. The stairs creak and mad axemen are a commonplace. Individual houses of distinction include 2 *Harley Street, Kelmscott House* (William Morris's place in Hammersmith Mall), *Pond Cottage*, Dulwich, *Numbers 6 and 8 Rugby Street*, WC1, and the house which above all others I should like to live in, *The Wick*, at the top of Richmond Hill. Maybe the owner – it used to be Sir John Mills – is reading these plaintive words . . .

Best small(ish) house: *The Wick.*
Worst small house: the automatic lavatories recently imported from France.

Ice Cream

The claims of the Soda Fountain at *Fortnum and Mason's* cannot be ignored but there has emerged recently plenty of competition to the sodas and frappés, shake floats and ice creams of this upper-crust haven. At the Crock Pot on the fourth floor of *Peter Jones* (Sloane Square, SW3; 01-730 3434) you may sample something called King's Road, a confection of chocolate ripple and mint ice cream with walnuts, marshmallows and chocolate sauce. Surviving that you might stagger southwards to *Santa Croce* (112 Cheyne Walk, SW10; 01-352 7534) where they specialise in a chocolate covered ice cream in the shape of an apple and filled with strega.

Marine Ices (8 Haverstock Hill, NW3; 01-485 8898) has been much enlarged and is now open seven days a week from 10 a.m. to 11 p.m. Their products are entirely without artificial additives, and their flavours include such provocative novelties as marsala, mango and walnut. Vesuvius, which is vanilla chocolate and marsala ice cream with crushed meringue, cherries and sponge soaked in marsala, is a memorable way of parting with £1.70.

Nor should the claims of the *Regent Milk Bar* (362 Edgware Road, W2; 01-723 8669) be overlooked. Eaten amidst basic neon-lit 40s decor (green and yellow striped counter, chromium chairs) its gelati do something to redeem a glum area of London and its black coffee is splendid. One can also depend upon *Lessiter's* (Finchley Road, NW3 and branches) while in the mass market *Baskin and Robbins* are much better than *Dayville*; *Loseley* ices, though limited in flavours and often sold in theatres before they have been properly defrosted, are *dairy* ice creams, and it shows. *Marks & Spencer* rum and raisin ice cream at £1.75 a litre is excellent.

The best Sorbets in London are undoubtedly those at *La Maison des Sorbets* (140 Battersea Park Road, SW11; 01-720 8983/4) where Julian Tomkins, master sorbetier, pulps fruit from the nearby New Covent Garden Market into unforgettable confections and serves them in *timbalines* or a *nougatine* box of assorted and contrasting colours.

Best ice creams: *Marine Ices/La Maison des Sorbets.*
Worst ice creams: Those bought from vans outside tourist spots, especially Madame Tussauds.

Indian Restaurants

Of all the addictions that afflict Londoners in the late 20th century – drink, drugs, alcohol, sex, Channel 4 – Indian food is the most damaging. We will lie, cheat, steal, or prostitute ourselves for a spoonful of bhendi bhaji. Like many addictions it can never be entirely cured; once the rogan josh has entered the bloodstream, all that remains is a wretched fifty years of tikka and musallam, hanging about Euston Street corners, weeping sag-flavoured tears. The nearest thing to a curry-eaters anonymous is *The Curry Club* (PO Box 7, Haslemere, Surrey; 0428-2452).

My favourite Indian restaurant in London is *The Last Days of the Raj* (22 Drury Lane, WC2; 01-836 1628), a cooperative restaurant, clean, elegant, popular, and less expensive than an equivalent French restaurant. A shami kebab or a prawn puree followed by a meat thali or a murgh musallam and a frinee (ground rice with milk, pistachios, and flavoured with rosewater) will cost £11 a head inclusive.

The Westbourne Grove curry houses are also strongly recommended. Notably: *Khan's* (Numbers 13/15; 01-727 5420) with its emphasis on Muglai dishes from the north of the sub-continent; the *Standard* (Number 23; 01-727 4818), quick, efficient, reliable and inexpensive; the *Diwana Bhel Poori House* (Number 50; 01-221 0721 with another branch at 121 Drummond Street, NW1; 01-387 5556) for Gujerati vegetarian food, delicious and sustaining; try the Deluxe Dosa, a crispy savoury pancake, and the Shrikhand (whipped cream with lemon and cardamom); no licence and inexpensive; and the *Baba Bhel Poori House* (Number 118; 01-221 7502) with a similar vegetarian menu.

Many other recommendations, so the briefest details of the best of the rest (with a warning always to check the bill):

Agra (135 Whitfield Street, W1; 01-387 4828). Good tandooris.

Aziz (116 King Street, W6; 01-748 1826). Large portions, sitar music. Combine with the Lyric, Hammersmith.

Bangla Desh Cuisine (327 West End Lane, NW6; 01-435 3327).

Bullock Cart (77 Heath Street, NW3; 01-435 3602).

Diwan-I-Am (161 Whitfield Street, W1; 01-387 0293).

Gaylord (79 Mortimer Street, W1; 01-580 3615) Popular with BBC people.

Light of India (284 King Street, W6; 01-741 1903). Tandoori. An alternative to the Aziz above.

Mandeer (21 Hanway Place, off Tottenham Court Road, W1; 01-323 0660). Self-service lunches in the Ravi Shankar Hall; dinner downstairs. Vegetarian. Sitar music.

Memsahib (22 Upper Richmond Road, East Putney, SW15; 01-874 3593). 'Food from the Indian sub-continent; customers from wherever we can find them'. A confession: I haven't tried Memsahib yet, but the advertising is irresistibly witty.

Rama Sita (6 Clarendon Road, W11; 01-737 9359). Indian nouvelle cuisine. Adventurous, expensive, erratic.

Shahbhag (70 Rosslyn Hill, NW3; 01-435 1077).

Tandoori (153 Fulham Road, SW3; 01-589 7617), and of course,

Veeraswamy's (99-101 Regent Street, W1; 01-734 1401). The daddy of them all. Very pukka, very camp, not cheap. Mulligatawny.

Best Indian Restaurant: *Last Days of the Raj.*

Italian Restaurants

Bertorelli's, Bianchi's and *San Frediano*, how many bowls of pasta, bottles of Barolo, oranges in caramel and zuppa inglese do those names recall? That they've survived is proof of their quality; one could travel further and fare worse.

Bertorelli's in Shepherd's Bush was where I used to eat with Peter Luke when we both worked on the BBC Wednesday Plays. Veal peperonata and a bottle of Verdicchio was what we ordered, and the wine always came marvellously chilled and cloudy with condensation. The service was motherly and the food nourishing. Then one day it was pulled down for a vast shopping complex which nobody much uses. *Bertorelli's* now has a branch in Charlotte Street and one in Covent Garden. Damask tablecloths, menus in duplicated purple ink, amiable chaos – little has changed. The new Notting Hill *Bertorelli's* is not of the same family and is worryingly upmarket.

For years *Bianchi's* (21a Frith Street, W1; 01-437 5194) was run by Elena (Salvoni); indeed for many it *was* Elena. Then that tireless lady moved to another establishment across the road and it was thought that would be that; but *Bianchi's* has survived, and upstairs the same old journalists and writers bitch about their agents, while the publishers dine with their investment advisers at the *Gay Hussar* up the road. The food? Well, it's traditional London Italian – perfectly adequate – but that's not really what one goes to *Bianchi's* for.

The *San Frediano* (62 Fulham Road, SW3; 01-584 8375) is the most recent of the three, and looks like what it is, a smart sixties trattoria; soups and pastas, liver and wild duck, an excellent house chianti, all testify to the continuing success of this old favourite.

Also worthy of note:

The Pizza Express Chain. Well-cooked pizzas and pastas and well-played music (usually jazz) reflect the style of the owner, who did more than most in the successful Save Piccadilly campaign.

Il Pollo Sorpresa (3 Heath Street, NW3; 01-435 0024) is currently enjoying a huge popularity. It is certainly jolly, but my spaghetti carbonara – the best test of an Italian restaurant – was a sad disappointment. Avoid that and you should be O.K.

La Casalinga (64 St John's Wood High Street; 01-722 5959). Regular visits from a large and noisy section of my family have never given rise to a hint of impatience, no matter how curious our demands. The food is quickly served and extremely good, especially the starters which change daily.

La Bussola (42/49 St Martin's Lane, WC2; 01-240 1148). Light, airy, well organised and with a tantalising cold buffet, this is a confident recommendation.

Next door is the huge plebeian *Laguna 50* (50 St Martin's Lane, WC2; 01-836 0960) where the spaghetti carbonara is just like Mamma made. A casual friendly place.

Il Girasole (126 Fulham Road, SW3; 01-370 6656) offers the second best hors d'oeuvre in London, also excellent tortellini and osso bucco (don't forget the marrow) and cheese. Girasole means 'sunflower', which turns with the sun.

Cecconi's (5a Burlington Gardens, W1; 01-434 1509) is simply one of the best and most expensive Italian restaurants in town. Jackets and ties are required and the pasta is homemade. Posh people.

Santa Croce (112 Cheyne Walk, SW10; 01-352 7534). One sits at tables covered with lemon yellow cloths in one of the prettiest restaurants in London. There was not enough salt in the spinach and I was pursued relentlessly with a giant pepperpot, but Santa Croce is charming.

The Spaghetti House chain and the *Tavola Calda* restaurants suffer sadly from their nasty piped music, and I have never eaten well at *Paradiso E Inferno* (389, Strand). The Italian restaurants in the neighbourhood of Leicester Square are the ones to be avoided.

Best Italian restaurant: *Cecconi's.*

Japanese Food

Although I dislike eating raw fish in particular and Japanese food in general, I am prepared to concede that the Japanese have been around a great deal longer than I have and have achieved rather more culturally. That being so, the problem is to find a Japanese restaurant sympathetic to my shortcomings. I had heard that the *Ajimura* (51-53 Shelton Street, WC2; 01-240 0178), run as it is by four English nippophiles, could be the answer, but it was not on the night I was there. The diner is given an illustrated recipe card to take away and study, but I ate nothing which tempted me to try to repeat the experience at home. The set lunch at £5 must be good value, unless it is horrid. A new restaurant, the *123* (27 Davies Street, W1; 01-499 3911) – the name refers to the use of chopsticks – is another place aiming to initiate and convert. Set menus at lunch (£6.90 and £8.90) and at dinner (£16.90 and

£17.50) include classic dishes, such as sashimi, tempura and yakitoni (skewered chicken and onion grilled in a teniyaki sauce), with sake at £1.90 for a small flask. All my information suggests that the *Hiroko* at the Kensington Hilton (179 Holland Park Avenue, W8; 01-603 5003) under the direction of Mr Shoji will complete my conversion so that is where I shall go next. I shall have to earn some money first, for the *Hiroko* is expensive, but, as a friend says, the *Hiroko* 'stuns you with another culture', and I'm anxious to be stunned.

Seaweeds imported from Japan and other Japanese delicacies such as sake, rice cakes and green tea may be ordered or purchased from *Sunwheel Mail Order*, 196 Old Street, EC1V 9BP (01-250 1708); they also have a restaurant at 3 Chalk Farm Rd, NW1 (01-267 8116). Reports please, as they say.

Jazz

The *Pizza on the Park* (11 Knightsbridge, SW1; 01-235 5550) and the *Pizza Express* (10 Dean Street, W1; 01-439 8722) are admirably committed to good cheap food and good cool music. There is even a Pizza Express All-Star Jazz Band. Pizza Express concentrates on groups, P on the P on visiting musicians, often from overseas. But there is only one *Ronnie Scott's*.

It was the crazed and scintillating Sonny Rollins; it was Blossom Dearie with her smokey-sweet voice and immaculate technique; it was cherubic George Melly like an evil-minded putto; it was, above and beyond the rest, Roland Kirk RIP, blind and with a mouthful of saxophones, driving himself and his musicians to new heights of joy and new depths of pain; it was all these and more; it was *Ronnie's*, and still is. Ronnie's jokes ('My girl-friend is so dumb she thinks Moby Dick is a venereal disease') about the generous nature of the waitresses, about the misanthropy of the chef, get no better with the passing years – just more familiar, as do the faces of the regulars, Spike Milligan, John Le Mesurier, David Spanier and Suzy Menkes, and those boring people who will keep tapping out the rhythms with their knives and forks. The bouncer/maître d' is departed and we mourn him, the prices are high and we grumble about it, but at least *Ronnie's* has survived – just.

Other jazz venues in London include:

The Canteen (4 Great Queen Street, WC2; 01-405 6598). An

up-market wine bar with mainstream jazz nightly, except Sundays.

100 Club (100 Oxford Street, W1; 01-636 0933). Ebullient and old-fashioned with emphasis on Dixieland and Blues, though not exclusively so. Don't miss the visits of Bo Diddley and Ken Colyer.

The Bull's Head (373 Lonsdale Road, SW13; 01-876 5241). Every night of the week. The best jazz pub at the moment. Music free.

Dixie Strand Jazz Cafe (75 The Strand, WC2; 01-240 1321). Traditional and Dixieland Jazz.

Seven Dials Jazz Club (27 Shelton Street, WC2). Thursdays 8.30 p.m. Exciting modern groups.

Prince of Orange (118 Lower Road, Rotherhithe, SE16; 01-237 9181). A wide-ranging and imaginative programme of music with lunchtime concerts at week-ends. Music free.

Also live concerts in the BBC Jazz Club series may be enjoyed free at *Studio 3*, Maida Vale (for details see Free Entertainment). And free, if you dine there, is the jazz piano playing at *Kettners* (29 Romilly Street, W1; 01-434 1214), now risen from the ashes as a pizza place.

The four best jazz record and cassette shops in London are *Dobell's* (21 Tower Street, WC2; 01-240 1354), *Mole Jazz* (374 Gray's Inn Road, WC1; 01-278 8623), *James Asman's Jazz Centre* (23a New Row, St Martin's Lane, WC2; 01-240 1380) and *Honest Jon's* (278 Portobello Road, W10; 01-969 9822).

Best jazz: *Ronnie Scott's.*
Worst jazz: Anywhere where they play 'When the Saints . . .' by request. Even worse if it's *not* by request!

See also under Pubs with Entertainment.

Kiosks/News stands

According to New York folklore, when your first night is over you repair to Lindy's where you await the early editions in which you will read whether the butchers of Broadway have chopped your play into gobbets and fed it to the crows. Well, it wouldn't work here. You *can* buy the early editions in *Fleet Street* (and sometimes at the main line stations too) and, while they may carry the evening racing results, they don't carry the theatre reviews.

When Londoners had a choice of evening papers the fun of it was whether the news vendor could guess right; were you a *Star*, or *News*, or *Standard* man? But some of the newspaper sellers still feel free to comment. According to a friend, the vendor at West Hampstead tube 'always smirks when you buy *Spare Rib*'. Leaving aside hotel lobbies, which don't count, the classy place to buy your paper is the small but charming kiosk next to Sotheby's in *New Bond Street* (you can even get the *Burlington Magazine* there!) or the Crown Passage bookstall in *St James's*. But there is also a kiosk in *Kingsway* with an awning and above it a signboard announcing that 'The Times, TES, TLS, THES on sale here'. *Very* classy.

The kiosk at *South Ken* tube is good, while the one at *Bank* tube is bad. In *Leicester Square* is a theatre kiosk, where you can buy half-price tickets for West End shows that have not sold out on the day of performance. This kiosk is reminiscent of the tent in which Olivier's Richard III passed such a troubled night before the battle of Bosworth Field. Almost as though he was waiting for the reviews in the first editions . . .

Best kiosk: *New Bond Street.*
Worst kiosk: *Piccadilly Circus.*

Kite Flying

The most traditional places in London for kite flying are *Parliament Hill* and *Kensington Gardens. Parliament Hill* has to be the more promising. *Primrose Hill, Blackheath Common* and *Hampstead Heath* have their adherents, but you can tell that *Streatham Common* is unsuitable by the kite tails flapping in the trees.

I can recommend three specialist kite shops.

(a) The Kite & Balloon Company (613 Garratt Lane, SW18; 01-946 9562) runs a kite hospital and also sells vast helium-filled balloons.

(b) Mitsukiku (90 Regent Street, W1; 01-437 5582).

(c) The Kite Store (69 Neal Street, WC2; 01-836 1666).

Best kite flying: *Parliament Hill.*
Worst kite flying: *Park Lane.*

Kosher Food

Having enjoyed an excellent salt beef sandwich – the beef spread thick with lashings of mustard and the bread an authentic rye – at the inappropriately named *Continental Bar* (30 Charing Cross Road, WC2; 01-836 4233), I asked for a latke.

'Where's your membership card?' flashed back Gaby, from behind the counter. It is improbable that Gaby is one of the Chosen, and his bar prides itself, besides its salt beef, on falafel, shawarma and kebabs, none of which is traditional Jewish food. (In fact the Palestinians took Israel to the UN for adopting falafel which belonged by rights to the Arabs.) But he serves a falafel every bit as good as his salt beef on rye.

Although there are those who pray by *Reuben's* (20a Baker Street, W1; 01-935 5945 and 486 7079), the doyen of kosher restaurants has to be – since the sad demise of *Isow's* – *Bloom's*. Morris Bloom opened his first restaurant in Brick Lane in 1920 and, his talents appreciated by immigrants nostalgic for gedempte meatballs and lockshen, for stuffed kishka and kneidlach, never looked back. Within ten years he had opened a kosher food factory, and in 1960 his son, Sidney, inaugurated a canning department so that *Bloom's* food, supervised by a rabbi and a religious adviser every day, may be eaten nationwide. The two London branches (90 Whitechapel High Street, E1; 01-247 6001 and 130 Golders Green Road, NW11; 01-455 1338) serve predictable and hugely sustaining food which may either be eaten at a table (slow) or directly from the serving counter, which is a great place to eavesdrop.

The best kosher fish restaurant is *Grahame's Seafare* (38 Poland Street, W1; 01-437 3788), while *Harry Morgan's* (31 St John's Wood High Street, NW8; 01-722 1869) has the unusual habit of serving all the courses simultaneously, but the food is more elegant than *Bloom's*. The old-fashioned *Cosmo* (5 Northways Parade, NW3; 01-722 2627) is great for breakfast.

The Nosh Bar (42 Great Windmill Street, W1; 01-437 9518) is – how shall I put it? – *basic*, but its position, squeezed between record exchanges and blue movie-houses, ensures that it's never dull. I also warm to a place called *Cohen & Wong* ('from Salt Beef to Won Ton Soup' at 39 Panton Street, WC1 (01-839 6876).

Best kosher food: *Bloom's* for atmosphere; *The Continental Bar* and *Harry Morgan's* for food.

Lavatories

Somewhere in Wandsworth exists a public lavatory containing one of the kindest women in the world. She sits in a little room with an electric fire and a radio and once she solved one of those insoluble problems which afflict fathers with young daughters. I have seen neither her nor her lavatory since.

Certain general rules may be followed when taken short in London. Department stores are a better bet than underground stations; cinemas and theatres are grim, especially during the intermissions; London clubs have lavatories which are awe-inspiring in their magnificence. (Kipling remarked that whenever he went to the lavatory in the Athenaeum he expected to find a bishop on his back kicking his legs in the air like a black beetle.) Hotels are the safest option. *Durrants* (George Street, W1) is the best for men with marble surfaces and Pears soap (if you happen to be a man with marble surfaces).

The ladies' lavatory at *Paddington Station* is the home of the largest cat in London. The walls are covered in fan mail. Over the labatory at St Pancras is 'GENTLEMEN' beautifully carved in Lombardic lettering; an architecturally distinguished loo. Other stations are less interesting, and *Richmond, Westminster* and *King's Cross* are disgraceful.

The ladies at *Fortnums* oozes old-fashioned elegance, but *Selfridges* ladies, which used to be, is now just run-of-the-mill. The public lavatory in *Fleet Street* is for men only, and it's no use unaccompanied ladies seeking relief in *El Vinos*. The lavatories at the *National Film Theatre* are very limited, so whip your bladder over to the *National Theatre*. Six young ladies of my acquaintance tell me that *Oxford Walk*, though always free, is a bit 'yukky'; they add that *Piccadilly Circus* is 'always locked'.

Besides those mentioned above, I can recommend: *The Greenwich Pier* ladies (spotless), *Sydney Street*, Chelsea, the *Royal Academy*, the *RAC Club*, Beckenham High Street, *Harvey Nichols*, the *Law Courts*, *Queensway* (just opened, nice railings), *Harrods*, and the ladies toilets in *Cambridge Gardens*, East Twickenham which have carpets and pictures on the walls. The *Anchor* pub on Bankside and the early Victorian *Union Jack* pub in Union Street have surviving outside urinals.

I cannot recommend the *Aldwych Theatre*, Kingsland Road, E8, or *Mortlake Green*. Almost all London schools have vile lavatories.

A constipated generation will surely result. What a false economy!

I recently had cause to use one of the French designed automatic lavatories, so far available in *Hammersmith, Leicester Square, Shepherds Bush* and *Soho Square*. For my 10p I had fifteen minutes of privacy (one can imagine what these loos will principally be used for), hygienically cleaned pans and seats, a rather low bowl, which helps children and recalcitrant bowel movements, and a selection of Hawaiian guitar music which, if things are touch and go, would certainly militate against going! There are no public lavatories in Belgravia.

Best lavatory: *Royal Box*, Covent Garden.
Worst lavatories: *Too numerous to specify.*

Learned Societies

The *Aetherius Society* is a metaphysical organisation which believes that Jesus is alive and well and living on Mars. *La College de Pataphysique* (President Alfred Jarry) exists for the study of improbable solutions, so do not expect to find it in the phone book. There are societies for the *Friends of Reptiles*, for the *Friends of Bulgaria* (if you can befriend Bulgaria you can befriend anything), for the *Industrious Poor*, for *Foreigners in Distress*, for the *Scientific Study of Anomalous Phenomena* (everything from marine monsters to metal bending) and for *Public Lighting Engineers*.

The *Knights of the Round Table* swear that every word of Mallory's *Morte d' Arthur* is literally true, while the most exclusive society in London has only two members, Jean Campbell, Beaverbrook's grand-daughter and Andy Garnett. Neither has a navel.

Moving up the intellectual scale there exists an *Anarcho-Syndicalist Association* (I wonder how they elect their president), the portentous *Institute for Strategic Studies*, and the estimable *Linnaean Society* at Burlington House, to whom Darwin first read *The Origin of Species*. The *London Society for the Study of Religion* does excellent work, and the *Society of Genealogists* (37 Harrington Gardens, SW7; 01-373 7054) has the biggest selection of books on genealogy in the world, and is open to non-members during the daytime.

However there can be no doubt about the best and worst in this category:

Best learned society: *The Royal Society.*
Worst learned society: *The Society for the Conversion of the Jews.*

Libraries

The *Reading Room* of the British Museum is unique. If the quintessential dust of all the learned men and women who have studied there hangs in the air, it must also be the place most likely to impose inspiration on its students. But getting a reader's ticket is not easy, since you have to show that what you need is not readily available at more plebeian libraries, and, once you have your ticket, getting the book or books you need is a lengthy and elaborate procedure. This is a library to be used when you are entering upon a prolonged course of study, but never casually.

The *London Library* (14 St James's Square, SW1; 01-930 7705) is a registered charity run by a committee of members of the library and dedicated to accumulating standard and authoritative works in the humanities. With over a million volumes, almost all of which are on free access, the annual membership fee of £60 (tax deductible and, if you genuinely can't pay, the Trust may be able to help) is truly a bargain. A grand and generous-hearted institution.

The *Colindale Newspaper Library* – actually a branch of the British Library, which is a part of the British Museum – contains the National Collection of Newspapers, provincial from 1700, London from 1800. It is not easy to find, and, once found, is profoundly eccentric. The book of rules states: 'Persons under 21 years of age are not normally admitted. In the interest of the preservation of the collections admission is not granted for the purpose of researching into football match results and horse and greyhound racing, or for competing for prizes.' Other conditions make it something of an obstacle race before you can actually sit down in front of the research material you are after, and no sooner have you done so than at the early hour of 4.45 p.m. a warning bell is rung and the newspapers are cleared from the room. Nonetheless it is a priceless establishment, and the only one of its kind in the country.

Other useful and agreeable libraries in London include the *Keats Library* at Keats Grove, NW3, where a particular effort is made to engage the imagination of children, *Dr Williams Theological Library*, Gordon Square, WC1, the *Fulham Public Library*, which a writer friend claims to have 'the best research

123

facilities in the world', the *Westminster Reference Library*, St Martin's Street, WC2, with a first-rate collection of books on art, cinema and the theatre, the *Financial Times Library*, the *Swiss Cottage Library* (airy and pleasant to work in), and *Sutton Central Library*, St Christopher's Way, Sutton, Surrey, where there is a coffee bar, a story-telling pit for children, study carrels with typewriters to hire, an exhibition area, and even, if you're lucky, a tame author to bait.

Among the less successful libraries in London one has to include *Streatham Public Library*, the *Bishopsgate Institute*, and *Richmond*, which is not peaceful.

Best library: *The London Library*.

Lions and Eagles

London is a-prowl with sculpted lions. The bronze ones in Trafalgar Square, designed by Landseer and erected around *Nelson's Column* as an afterthought in 1868, are 20 feet long and 11 feet high; splendid creatures, except that their paws are those of cats, not lions. Fine stone lions guard the Lion Gates at *Hampton Court, Syon Park* and *Kew*. The haughtiest lion preens itself hugely at the *British Museum*. The fiercest lion is rampant on the wall of *White Lion Street* with his date (1714), and the most bewildered lion stares out at a noisy world from *19 Durand Gardens*, SW9. The royalest of lions wears one crown and clutches another on the top of *Palace Gate* at the entrance to Kensington Gardens. Another fine stone lion (by Coade, and rescued from the old Lion Brewery) guards *County Hall*. Stucco lions prowl moodily around the roofs and gables of terraced houses in *Parson's Green*, hundreds of them, and there is even a composition lion called Flora to be found on Flora's Lawn at *Syon Park*. It was made by the props department at Shepperton Studios. *St Peter's Square*, Hammersmith, boasts quite a variety of lions and eagles as well as a sad church designed by a bridge builder. The greatest London eagle, however, must be the bald American one which spreads its wings to a span of 35 feet on the roof of the *American Embassy*. Made from gilded aluminium, its head is turned the opposite way to the official American eagle, as though turning a blind eye to all those intended immigrants who sidle up to the immigration officers looking as though they've got ice-picks in their back-packs.

Other fine eagles sit atop the gatepost of *Oakfield Park School*, SE21, hover over *Counter Court*, Southwark, prepare for take-off from the top of the *RAF Monument* (Victoria Embankment) and glare disapprovingly from *118 Clapham Common West Side*, SW11. A lion with eagle's wings supports the frieze of the *De Vere Hotel*, De Vere Gardens, W8 and another plays with a ball on the *Holborn Viaduct*.

Best lion: guarding the tomb of George Wombwell, the lion-tamer, in Highgate Cemetery.
Best eagle: *US Embassy.*
Worst lions and eagles: Those held in captivity in London Zoo.

PS For further information see *Lion Hunting In London* by Frank J. Mannheim.

Litter Bins

The best litter bin in London is a huge squatting toad with an open mouth in *Battersea Park*. Children cannot resist feeding it with rubbish. The Lewisham shopping precinct has other litter-beasts besides toads.

Very horrid are the yellow plastic litter bins in *Trafalgar Square*. But the worst litter bin in London is a big round pebble-dash thing in *St Botolph Street*, EC3. It's not so much the thing itself as where it is. Which recalls to mind the story told me by the poet P. J. Kavanagh, who was paying a sentimental visit to Dove Cottage, home of Wordsworth in the Lake District. He was standing in awe in the poetic bedroom, when the curator crept up behind him and startled him out of his mellifluous reverie with the words: 'Sobers is out!'

Best litter bin: *Battersea Park.*
Worst litter bin: *St Botolph Street.*

London Clubs

A member of the *Guards Club* was asked his reactions to playing host to the *Savile*. 'They were quite decent little fellows. No trouble. Make their own trousers, of course.'

I find the institution of London clubs faintly absurd, although they keep a lot of eccentrics off the streets and the reading stands provided for solitary diners are a delight. The only club I would wish to join would be the *Garrick*, but it is undeniable that many of the established clubs are architectural treasures. *Barry's* two Italianate clubs, the *Travellers'* and the *Reform*, are most impressive, while the *Athenaeum* and the *United Service Club* ('The Senior') provide an elevated and dignified framework to Waterloo Place. So far as members are concerned bishops and fellows of the Royal Society join the *Athenaeum*, actors and publishers the *Garrick*, diplomats, politicians, and spies, *Brooks's*, the *Travellers'*, *Boodle's* or *White's*. The *Savile* is literary and academic, the *Reform* is snobbish (candidates for membership have to acknowledge the Reform Act of 1832), the *RAC* has the best facilities but little else, the *Turf Club* the most dukes, the *Carlton* the top tories, and the *Junior Carlton* the ones who would like to be top tories.

According to the late Ian Fleming, at *White's* the members 'gassed too much' so he lunched at *Boodle's* because he 'liked dull clubs'. *Brooks's* he described as 'like a duke's house – with the duke lying dead upstairs'.

For women the *University Women's Club*, formed in 1883, provided 'facilities for intercourse' for university educated women. It also provided lavatories which were not readily available for women at the end of the last century. This club, which has been in Audley Square since 1921, still flourishes, and just as well, since almost all the men's clubs, with the notable exception of the *Army and Navy*, are inimical to women; the worst in this respect is the *Naval and Military*, otherwise known as the In and Out, whose marvellous entrance in Piccadilly is for men only.

All in all most traditional London clubs provide dull food, better wine, boring company, a smoky atmosphere, and seats it is almost impossible to rise from after marmalade sponge. But they *do* provide cheap accommodation (once you're a member), excellent cellars of wine, telex machines, and sometimes squash courts and swimming pools.

See also Gambling Clubs.

Best London club: the *Garrick*.

Magistrates Courts

The most enlightened magistrates courts in London at present – although much depends upon who is sitting – are *Marylebone* (especially Mr Romain), *Hampstead* and *Bow Street*; the most severe are *Highgate, Highbury Corner,* and *South Western.* Highgate refuses 46% of legal aid applications; Hampstead 6%. I got costs against the police at *Marlborough Street,* was discharged from *Greenwich,* where my evidence confused everybody present, myself included, at the end of a tiring week, and was treated very civilly at *Petty Sessions* in Walton Street. Mr Mark Romer, sitting at *Clerkenwell,* recently gaoled a man for seven days for whispering in court, which seems excessive.

Best magistrates court: *Marylebone.*

Mews

'Mews' derives from 'Mew', meaning to cage or coop, hence it meant a stabling built around an open space, and specifically the *Royal Stables* built at Charing Cross in the 14th century. So a mews that has retained its original function should be preferred, and the *Royal Mews* at Buckingham Palace, which is open between 2 and 4 on Wednesdays and Thursdays, except, of course, during Ascot week, is.

Of those mews which have been prettified and gone residential, *Albion Mews,* W2, is a typical example – pretty houses and flower tubs on granite setts – while *Clabon Mews,* SW1, *Elizabeth Mews,* off Englands Lane, *Belsize Park Mews* in Belsize Park and *Chelsea Mews* in Chelsea all have their supporters. *Portman Mews South, Clarges Mews,* and *Headford Place,* SW1, are all minor disaster areas, while *St George's Mews,* NW1, urgently needs a wash and brush up.

Hays Mews, W1, is notable for a pub with the improbable name: 'I am the Only Running Footman'. An explicatory painting is on view over the fireplace in the bar.

Best mews: *Royal Mews,* Buckingham Palace.
Worst mews: *Portman Mews South.*

Mexican Food

There is some confusion at the flamboyant *Texas Lone Star Saloon* (154 Gloucester Road, SW7; 01-370 5625) as to whether it is a Texan or Mexican establishment, and frankly does it matter? This Tex/Mex place is so deeply committed to cheering everyone up – country music, pre-recorded tapes by the ubiquitous Tim

Rice, gun-totting cowboys on the TV – that one may not notice that the food is really rather good in a macho way – spare ribs, chilli, frankfurters and T-bone steaks. It's no place to take your Red Indian friends.

At the *Pacifico* (Langley Street, Covent Garden, WC2; 01-379 7728), which is cheerful, clean, noisy and a bit silly, the menu is genuinely Mexican, which is to say that almost every dish consists of corn, beans and chilli contained in pancakes of differing shapes and sizes. Four of us ate sopa de elote (sweetcorn soup), quesadilla, quesada, enchillado el burrito (I don't *think* it was mule) which, with coffee, an almost undrinkable sangria and wine to take the taste away, came to £30, or £7.50 a head. Cocktails are also served and the atmosphere is described accurately as 'Cantina'.

La Cucaracha (12 Greek Street, W1; 01-734 2253) is elegantly up-market. Although Mancha Manteles de Cerdo ('The Pork that Stains the Tablecloth') was 'off', there are many authentic Mexican alternatives. The extremely hot appetiser makes the Dos Equis (imported beer) almost essential, and, if only the tortillas had been crisper and the guitar-player in tune, I could have recommended it unreservedly.

But a less happy evening was spent at *El Mexicano* (62 Lower Sloane Street, SW1; 01-730 4637) and its adjoining *Taverna* (01-730 1110). On a previous visit a booked table had been taken by other diners and we were turned away into the night (I can't recall whether it was snowing or whether we were carrying a newly born baby, but it's possible).

Best Mexican restaurant: *La Cucaracha* (for food). *Texas Lone Star Saloon* (for exuberance). *Pacifico* (for atmosphere).

Milestones

Why do so many milestones feature *Hounslow* and *Uxbridge* (not places that one often wants to visit)? And what is the signification of the mysterious stone on *Haverstock Hill*, outside No 79, which reads: '4 Miles From The Post Office 45' North.'? I'm fond of milestones with pointing fingers such as the one at *No 1 Kensington Gore*. Here the fingers appear to be pointing at one another. There is a fine carved obelisk on *Richmond Bridge* marking the spot where tolls used to be exacted. It bears highly informative legends on three of its sides and on the east facet it says: 'The First

Stone of this Bridge was Laid 23 August 1774 and Finished December 1777.' It's more like reading a novel than a milestone. More succinct is the one in front of the Old Grammar School, *Dulwich*: 'V Miles from the Treasury, V Miles from Standard Corner.'

The handsomest milestone is the one in *Harmsworth Park*, SE7. In fine bold script (the same as is used in the corners of the penny reds) it says: 'One Mile From Palace Yard Westminster Hall', and there's no arguing with that.

Best milestone: *Harmsworth Park.*

Model Boats

Whitestone Pond, *Hampstead*, on a fine spring Sunday is the place for model boats. Here it was that Shelley used to sail paper boats for Leigh Hunt's children. A flag pole nearby marks the highest point of Hampstead Heath (440 feet) which may be why the model boats sail so bravely there. Easily second best is the Round Pond at *Blackheath*, followed by the Round Pond, *Kensington Gardens* (not so windy, but classy Harrods boats), and the pond at *Clapham Common.*

Best for model boats: *Whitestone Pond.*
Worst for model boats: *The Quaggy*, Lewisham.

Modern and Commercial Buildings

Most modern London buildings appal by their dreariness rather than by their spitefulness. It's the mean, cheese-paring style of office block, the disheartening greyness of the high rise accommodation that makes the shoulders droop and the spirit wilt. *State House* (corner of Red Lion Street and High Holborn) is an example. Under the name of the architects on the foundation stone graffiti artists write: 'Ought to be ashamed of themselves'. Consider too the *Department of the Environment*, 2 Marsham Street, SW1, which should be setting us all such a good example; the *Shell Centre*, SE1; the *Inn on the Park*; the dreadful *Sunley House* in the Upper Richmond Road by Putney High Street; the *Polytechnic of Central London* in Marylebone Road ('architectural Marxism', I've heard it called); almost any of the commercial buildings along the North Circular Road. Then they have the gall (Trafalgar House do) to pull down the *Firestone Building* – one of the very few amusing commercial buildings in west London.

But let me name some of the good ones to cheer myself up. There's the headquarters of the *Hogg Robinson Group* (9 Crutched Friars, EC3) which is composed of gold or bronze reflecting mirror glass and is very beautiful. *Wool House* in Carlton House Terrace, SW1 is tactfully deferential to the adjacent Pall Mall clubs. The *Natural History Museum* extension is a generous solution to a taxing problem, while the extension to the *Covent Garden Opera House* is such a brilliant pastiche that it's almost impossible to tell where the old ends and the new begins. The *Daily Express Building* in Fleet Street is an art deco gem, and the interior details are splendid; running your hands along the banisters may be enough to restore your fading virility. The *Michelin Building* (Brompton Road, SW7) is a well-known treasure – though ominously deserted at the moment – by François Espinasse (1905). It features the exterior tile panels by Gilardoni Fils et Cie of Paris which record with wit and charm the early history of motoring. The *Michelin Building* may be at risk; the *Battersea Power Station* (Sir Giles Gilbert Scott, 1929-35 completed 1944-46) certainly is. Wandsworth Council has plans to use it for waste disposal. Huh. The *HMSO* building in Seven Dials is energetic in blue and silver, while the new *Covent Garden Market* next door is imaginative but ugly. Both have an engaging Lego flavour to them.

With some buildings it's almost impossible to separate the architecture from the symbolism. *Centrepoint* (St Giles Circus), designed in 1965 by Richard Seifert & Partners, seemed not unsuccessful until the scandal of its continued emptiness while the homeless lived in railway waiting rooms soured us to its merits. Latterly it is used to house both the young homeless and the Confederation of British Industries; the symbolism continues to intrigue. Also designed by Seifert is the *NatWest Building* in Threadneedle Street, EC2. At over 600 feet this is the tallest building in Britain, but what's the use of that when only NatWest executives and possibly their friends and fancy women are allowed to go to the top?

On a more domestic level the house which Michael Hopkins built for himself in *Downshire Hill*, NW3 from steel and glass and determination for less than £20,000 is a triumphant example of the new complementing the old. In *Blackheath*, 10, Blackheath Park is a house of a great beauty designed by Leslie Bilsby of Span. It consists of three conjoined pentagons in stone and black glass with steps and a ramp inviting you up to the front door.

The best estates are *Crown Reach*, the new Wates development in Grosvenor Road, SW1 (next to Vauxhall Bridge); its four houses and fifty-six apartments advance and recede in witty perspective around the central lift shaft. *Brooklands Park*, Blackheath is pretty good too. The worst is the four tower block development at the corner of *Adelaide Road* and *Fellows Road* which cast a derisive shadow over a vast acreage of residential north London.

Best modern building: *The Daily Express.*
Worst modern building: *Polytechnic of Central London.* Also *59/67 Portland Place* (see under Architecture).

I recommend: *Modern Buildings in London* by Ian Nairn (London Transport).

Most Confusing Street

John Street becomes *Doughty Street* becomes *Mecklenburgh Street* becomes *Mecklenburgh Square* all within 500 yards. Within half a mile *Southampton Place* becomes *Russell Square* becomes *Woburn Place* becomes *Tavistock Square* becomes *Upper Woburn Place* becomes *Eversholt Street*.

As for the house numbers in *Holland Park Avenue* it would take the patience of a water-diviner to sort them out.

The least confusing street? *The Inner Circle, Regent's Park*.

Museums

The Victoria and Albert for its superb collections of glass and ceramics, and general Victoriana. Its identification service (01-589 6371 for details) is extremely useful, although wisely the V and A won't value items brought in. The size and scope of the museum ('fine and applied arts of all countries and periods') is so immense that several visits are called for.

The Museum of Childhood, Bethnal Green. This branch of the V and A, saved from imminent closure by Paul Channon, is charmingly cheerful. It is over-crowded with a collection valued at nine millions, but doesn't *feel* over-crowded. The dolls' houses are terrific.

The London Planetarium for its Zeiss star projector. Its astronomical programmes are inspirational, and its laser lights concerts remarkable. *Madame Tussauds*, to which it is linked, is something of a disaster these days.

The Kew Bridge Pumping Station, Green Dragon Lane, Brentford, for its five giant beam engines, which demonstrate the majesty of machinery. Lovingly restored by amateur well-wishers.

The London Dungeons for their showmanship. You may not care to see hangings, drawings and quarterings, boilings to death, amputations, devil worship, human sacrifice, leprosy and syphilis (get all that at home), but you have to admire the panache with which it is presented. It's usually the boys who faint.

The Wallace Collection, Manchester Square, for its completeness. The majority of the treasures were collected by the third and fourth Marquesses of Hertford and are lodged where they belong in Hertford House, so it doesn't seem like a museum. Wonderful French furniture and European pictures, many of which are familiar old friends.

The British Museum for its Print Room, its Elgin Marbles, its ghosts, and much much more. Wear stout shoes.

The Museum of Mankind, Burlington Street, for its anthropological exhibits. This is a particularly well-maintained museum with an unusual care for detail. They even spray the exhibits daily with the authentic odour.

The Geological Museum for its astonishing range of minerals and fossils, of precious and ornamental stones, its wonderful reference library, and its piece of moonrock, brought back on Apollo 16 and thought to be nearly four million years old.

The Hornby Museum, Forest Hill, for its participatory events for children. Apart from its remarkable clock it has little of significance in its permanent collection.

The Natural History Museum for its exuberant architectural façade, and its fifty million exhibits including souvenirs from Captain Cook, Captain Scott and Charles Darwin. Dinosaurs and whales, scorpions and tarantulas. Essential but overheated.

The Geffrye Museum, Kingsland Road, Shoreditch, for its furnished rooms, each representing a period of British history.

The Courtauld Institute Galleries, Woburn Square (don't go to the

Institute itself in Portman Square by mistake, as I did) for its superb impressionist and post impressionist pictures.

Ham House, Ham, Surrey, for its beautifully restored rooms (it dates from 1670) and its lovely furniture.

Apsley House, 1 Piccadilly, also restored, for its Wellingtonia, for the Waterloo Gallery, 90 feet long, for the Waterloo Vase, and for many fine pictures.

The National Maritime Museum and Library, Romney Road, Greenwich, for its comprehensive collection of nautical antiques, and don't miss the Barge House.

Sir John Soane's Museum, 13 Lincoln's Inn Fields, WC2. The house and museum of a small country builder, who made good. After his wife's death in 1815 and being disappointed in his two sons, he turned to collecting. Besides the stunning Hogarths (*The Election* and *The Rake's Progress*), the Sarcophagus of Seti I in alabaster with hieroglyphics is an astonishing relic. Open Tuesdays and Thursdays; free admission; charming and knowledgeable assistants.

Patrick Cook's Bakelite Museum (by telephone appointment only at 01-691 2240). A unique display of the products of the inventor Dr Leo Baekeland; in Greenwich.

But I can't recommend *The Black Museum*, New Scotland Yard, Victoria Street. This is not like the London Dungeons, for the exhibits here are not reconstructions. Death masks, murder weapons, victims' remains and other stomach-churning trouvailles make it no place for the faint of heart.

Best Museum: *The Victoria and Albert.*
Worst Museum: *The Black Museum*, New Scotland Yard.

The splendid guide: *Museums and Galleries in London*, edited by Malcolm Rogers, lists in lively fashion and spread over 370 pages, some 160 London museums. Essential really.

Music Halls

On my 18th birthday I went to see Max Miller on what must have been his final tour. He looked as old and tired as the nudes who shared the bill with him, but wore more rouge than they did. If this was music hall it deserved to die.

Most of what passes for music hall in London today is geared more to tourists than to aficionados, but an old style music hall is promoted on the first Tuesday of every month at the *Notre Dame Theatre*, Leicester Square, by the British Music Hall Society (membership £5 annually, quarterly magazine *Call Boy* free to members).

The tourists can choose between the Abadaba Company at *The Pindar of Wakefield* (3-8 Gray's Inn Road, WC1; 01-837 7769) and the *Players Theatre*, once Gatti's Music Hall, under the arches at Charing Cross (01-839 5080). The Players has been going the longest and its performers are more experienced in such matters as soubrette singing, but the Abadaba remains relentlessly cheerful. Note that it only gives performances from Thursdays to Saturdays inclusive. Neither of these two companies is cheap.

Numerous pubs offer old time music of various kinds while the *Prince of Wales* (73 Dalling Road, W6; 01-748 1236) can seat 300 people in its upstairs lounge where Black and White Minstrel shows may be seen at weekends. A few of the London Borough Councils organise music hall evenings for what they choose to call their senior citizens. On these occasions the performers are often as venerable as the audience, but everyone seems happy enough. The *Lewisham Town Hall* is a regular venue.

Ah but Collins burnt down, the old Met was redeveloped, and the Empire became a cinema. I actually *saw* Albert Chevalier (at a Butlins!) perform but the very best was Lily Morris singing, 'Don't Have Any More Mrs Moore'.

Best music hall: *Players Theatre*.

Night Clubs

There are few classy night clubs remaining. *Annabel's* (44 Berkeley Square, W1; 01-629 3558) is unique. Discreet, classy, expensive. Michael White's brave conversion of the *Piccadilly Theatre* into a cabaret/night club featuring the fantastic revue 'Y' deserves to succeed, while Paul Raymond's *La Vie En Rose* (at Windmill St, W1; 01-437 6312) on the site of the lamented Windmill Theatre features a curious floor-show appropriately named 'Bizarre'.

Finally there is *The Talk of London* (Drury Lane; 01-831 8863), the most conventional of the bunch.

Here follows a list of some of the rest of the night clubs:

L'Hirondelle, Swallow Street, W1 (01-734 1511). Two floor shows a night, two bands, hostesses, set menus, and someone to park your car for you.

Chaplins, 9 Swallow Street, W1 (01-734 7447). 'Theatre' in the round, a cabaret at midnight, a duo to dance to, and compliant hostesses.

Miranda, 9 Kingly Street, W1 (01-437 6695). Dancing, striptease, and hostesses. If your constitution can stand it, Miranda also does lunches.

New Georgian Club, 4 Mill Street, W1 (01-629 2042). Good food, average cabaret and hostesses. The old Georgian Club was more fun.

The Bristol Suite, 14 Bruton Place, W1 (01-499 1938). You need to be proposed for membership here. Sort of antique French decor and sort of new-to-it-hostesses.

The Office, 16-17 Avery Row, W1 (01-499 6728). Strictly members only. Rude cabaret at midnight, steaks, and hostesses on two floors (the club not the hostesses).

Gaslight Club, 4 Duke of York Street, SW1 (01-930 1648). Hostesses in Regency corsets, a topless bar, striptease, hostesses, live musicians (well . . .), and a clientele of wide-eyed hicks from the sticks. Grim.

Director's Lodge, 13 Mason's Yard, Duke Street, SW1 (01-930 2540). Expensive and up-market with champagne and topless waitresses (a dangerous combination).

Venus Room Club, 46 Old Compton Street, W1 (01-437 1020). The Venus Rooms have been there as long as any of us, and have never been what you might call smart or sophisticated. Intriguing and cheap.

Studio Valbonne, 62 Kingly Street, W1 (01-439 7242). The mixture as before.

Tudor Club, 12 Denham Street, W1 (01-437 3180). A juke-box, topless waitresses and not much else. This is one of those addresses where various clubs seem to open and close with confusing rapidity.

Twilight Room, (122 Charing Cross Road, W1 (01-836 2179). A large establishment, quite respectable, with average prices, and no more than usually bored hostesses. No membership required.

Champers International, 5a Stratford Place, W1 (01-408 2492). Live music, and topless waitresses in an intimate environment.

Then there are the discreet private clubs. A telephone call is necessary to establish *just* what to expect at any of the following:

The New Maddox, 21 Kingly Street, W1 (01-437 3421).
Old Spot Club, 23a Conduit Street, W1 (01-629 4088).
Little House Club, 10 Shepherd's Market, W1 (01-499 4212).
Napoleon's Club, Lancashire Court, W1 (01-493 3075). Gay.
Mazurka Club, 4 Denman Street, W1 (01-437 3547).

A word of warning. Many of these clubs pass like ships in the night. Check with a phone call before you commit yourself to going on board.

Best Night Club: *Annabel's.*
Worst Night Club: Too many to choose.
See also under Cabarets.

Obelisks

The obelisk was originally the Egyptian sun-worshipping symbol and stood for eternal life. Which makes the black *Katyn Memorial* obelisk in Gunnersbury Cemetery all the more poignant. This was erected in memory of 14,500 Polish prisoners of war who disappeared in 1940. Other cemeteries contain fine obelisks, particularly that to Sir Richard Mayne in *Kensal Green*, and the example erected by the Society of Friends in the *Great Northern Cemetery*, Brunswick Park.

Cleopatra's Needle, which dates from 1450 BC, was first erected in Heliopolis where it was one of a pair. It finally reached London in 1878 after being twice abandoned in the Bay of Biscay. The 186 tons of pink granite were cleaned in 1979 with money donated by a kindly Arab who preferred to remain anonymous. But it is so badly sited on the Embankment that few Londoners notice it. It has nothing to do with Cleopatra.

Near the Imperial War Museum is the *Brass Crosby Obelisk*. Crosby (1725-1793) was a friend of Wilkes and a staunch libertarian; his monument is beautifully proportioned as befits such a rational man.

Best obelisk: *Brass Crosby.*

Worst obelisk: *The Metropolitan Board of Works Obelisk* (junction of City Road, Old Street and East Road, EC1) which has a ball on top.

Opera

In Britain in 1982 there were over a million visits to the opera and more than £23 million was given in grants to opera companies by the Arts Council, a large proportion of it to the two main London houses. A top ticket for a top show at *Covent Garden* is £35 and at least half that at the *Coliseum*. But it is possible to go cheaply, even to *Covent Garden*, by queueing at the Floral Street box office on the day of performance, and a seat in the Slips, where the acoustics are as good as anywhere in the hall, will only set you back £2. The problem is that the vast sums expended (Domingo gets £8,000 a night) raise expectations too high, since many productions at *Covent Garden* and the *Coliseum* strike me as old-fashioned, even tawdry. A production may stay in the repertoire for many seasons, receiving only a handful of performances each season, so that the costumes and sets get to resemble something bought cheap at the bring and buy sale. *Covent Garden's* recent record of new productions hardly exists.

Besides the two main companies, David Freeman's *Opera Factory* (a branch of the English National Opera operation) applies many of the techniques of contemporary theatre to opera production with stimulating results. Harrison Birtwhistle's 'Punch and Judy ' was staggering. *Kent Opera*, which tours the south east and sometimes makes it to *Sadler's Wells* (a bad house to play in) concentrates on small scale productions with great musical sophistication. Visits to London by the *Welsh National Opera* have been more successful than those by the *Scottish Opera*. D'Oyly Carte, temporarily defunct, deserved (but refused) to die. I saw their last production of 'The Mikado' at a matinée, and not only two of the principals were absent but so too was the conductor! Productions by *Opera Bouffe* at the French Institute and by the *Singers Company* should be sought out, but there is more imagination in modern musicals, especially when Hal Prince is involved, than in modern opera productions.

Best opera: *Covent Garden* (but only at their best).

Orchestras

The *London Philharmonic Orchestra* recently celebrated its jubilee year with pomp and circumstance. Since 1932 it has played under six principal conductors, Beecham, of course, and Van Beinum, Boult, bless him, Pritchard, Haitink and Solti. It's a sign of the times that to the LPO's regular sponsors have been added three new names, Mars Bars, McDonald's Restaurants and Prudential Assurance. But there is no evidence that the orchestra's increased dependence on commercial sponsorship has affected its high artistic standards or its programming. Don't miss it when the LPO tackles Mahler.

The *Royal Philharmonic Orchestra* is in a stronger financial situation, thanks to the astonishing and deplorable success of its 'Hooked on Classics' recordings, the first album of which sold more than six million copies. Can six million people be wrong? You bet your sweet bippy they can. Was the RPO ill-advised therefore to undertake such a cynical project? Emphatically no. On New Year's Day 1983 it played its hits at the Orange Bowl American Football Final in Miami Beach, an event which was beamed to a breathless world by satellite. The RPO is indeed a star and the pressure on the regular conductors – Walter Weller, the new principal, Antal Dorati and Yuri Temirkanov – to maintain standards will increase. Recently the GLC has promoted a series of concerts in works canteens; let's hope that such a scheme is more successful than Centre 42 was in the sixties.

The *London Symphony Orchestra*, not too happily installed at the Barbican, is also an extrovert organisation and plays that way. ('Pops in Space' is *their* bid for the big time). Although Abbado is principal conductor, the orchestra is dependent on the Davis clan, Sir Colin and Andrew conducting and Michael, the exemplary leader. From time to time Previn visits; also the rebarbative (do I mean that?) Henze. Frank Zappa hired the orchestra to play his compositions at the Albert Hall, and you may rent any of these big orchestras, possibly using American Express.

The *BBC Symphony Orchestra* is the mainstay of the Proms, and always strong in its woodwind section. If none of these orchestras ever quite attains the nobility of, say, the *Berlin Philharmonic* at its best, they are all musicianly and committed.

Amongst the smaller groups, the *Academy of St Martin's in the Field* is outstanding, and the *Amadeus String Quartet* is, simply, the best in the world; which is more than can be said for the *London Mozart Players* or the *Dagenham Girl Pipers*.

Best orchestra: *depends on who is conducting.*

Organs

The best classical organ is the one in the *Festival Hall*. The *Albert Hall* instrument is still the original one and has been well-described as 'the second coming in Panavision'. It has 9,999 pipes, is excellent for French music, and may soon wear out the way old organs do. The Father Willis organ which will figure in the rebuilt *Alexandra Palace* should be worth the wait. A decorative gem is the Renatus Harris Organ in the Church of *St Sepulchre Without Newgate*. Both Wesleys certainly played it, and Handel and Mendelssohn probably did. It was built in 1677 and carries Charles II's monogram. Even more spectacular is the Whitehall Organ, removed to *St James's*, Piccadilly. For playing on, the new organ at *St Paul's Girls' School* is strongly recommended.

A fine collection of organs, including the only self-playing Wurlitzer in Europe, may be enjoyed (and played) at the *National Musical Museum* (368 High Street, Brentford, Middx; 01-560 8108). Also there is a grand selection of pianos and over 30,000 music rolls. Open Sats and Suns 2-5 p.m. April-October.

The best cinema organ used to be at the Granada, *Tooting*, but now it's eyes down for a full house. Autres temps, autres moeurs . . .

Best organ: the *Festival Hall*.

Palaces

Excluding Palaces of Justice and Palais de Danse there still exist a surprising number of palaces in London. The *Crystal Palace* is just a football team and a memory, the *Kennington Palace* is just a plaque on the wall; all that remains of *Whitehall Palace* is the (marvellous) Banqueting House, and all that remains of the *Palace of Sheen* (renamed Richmond Palace by Henry VII, the Earl of Richmond) is the gateway and a quantity of bricks, but that still leaves at least seven palaces more or less complete (or eight if you count *Greenwich* as a palace which I don't), viz *Kensington, Fulham,*

Lambeth, Westminster, Buckingham, St James's and *Hampton Court*.

I am not alone in finding *Buckingham Palace* displeasing; everyone always has. Poor old John Nash. It could not have been easy working for George IV, and, after the king's death, the design was taken away from Nash and given to Edward Blore, although his work too was substantially altered in 1913 by Sir Aston Webb. But the Mews is nice.

Each of the others has something to recommend it. *Kensington Palace* has its ornate Cupola Room, decorated by Kent, and the state bedroom, in which Victoria passed so much of her lonely childhood (her toys and the cradle she slept in are on view). *Fulham Palace*, where the bishops of London bishopped, has a pleasant public garden in what once was the moat, but it is becoming an embarrassment to the local authority. *Lambeth* has fig trees and a wonderful hammerbeam roof, and the *Palace of Westminster* has the cheapest beer in London. *St James's Palace*, built to Holbein's designs on the site of a leper hospital, has a splendid clock tower, and *Hampton Court*, well *Hampton Court* apart from the maze and the gardens and the orangery and the tennis courts and the wrought iron and the letter box, has chimneys like sticks of liquorice as created by a paranoid schizophrenic.

Best palace: *Lambeth.*
Worst palace: *Buckingham.*

Parking Meters

> Now the parking meters picket and pick the Georgian locks and invisible
> Meters tall as the yellowing trees docket and dock our history,
> Though Charles James Fox unconcerned in a bath towel sits on his arse in Bloomsbury Square
> While plane tree leaves flop gently down and lodge in his sculptured hair.
>
> from *October in Bloomsbury* by Louis Macneice (1907-1963)

I have just been clamped and it is not pleasant. Expensive (£29.50 plus a £10 parking fine which they try to make you pay at the time though you need not), time consuming, and humiliating. Nonetheless it is effective and conditions in the West End, and particularly in those areas, such as Bond Street, in which the clamp patrols operate, have improved.

140

In meter areas there are various devices which have proved successful in the battle against fines. The rottennest of these is the removal of a ticket from a nearby car and the putting of it on your car's windscreen. Notices such as 'Wife Having Baby – Sorry' or 'Delivering Double Bass to Chief Constable' are often treated with the contempt they deserve by the wardens, who are known in Paris, incidentally, as the Periwinkles, from the distinctive colour of their uniforms. The friendliest London periwinkle is the smiling lady in *Long Acre* who used to operate outside Harvey's Auction Rooms before they removed to Neal Street. It was always a pleasure doing business with her. There used to be a dead ringer for Marilyn Monroe operating in *Hammersmith Broadway* where they could keep an eye on her from the upstairs window of the Hammersmith Police Station. Where is she now? An equally pretty periwinkle operates at the *South Ken* end of the *Old Brompton Road*, but she has no humanity in her deep-frozen heart. If you do get ticketed it is unwise to pay the fine at once. A high percentage of parking tickets get permanently gummed up in the bureaucratic works.

You are most likely to get away with it in *St John's Wood, Finsbury Circus,* and *Rugby Street*, WC1. The riskiest areas are *Lincoln's Inn Fields, Pelham Street, Richmond Green, Essex Street* (disastrous), *Bond Street* (horrific), *Mayfair,* and *Doughty Street*, WC1, where Dickens lived. Here hoards of traffic wardens duck out of sight whenever they see a motorist likely to park illegally; what ensues thereafter makes the Alamo seem like coffee-time at the Mothers' Union.

Best parking meters: (least attended) *St John's Wood.*
Worst parking meters: (most attended) *Essex Street*, WC2.

Parks

If you call *Epping Forest* a park, then at 5,600 acres it is easily the largest in the Greater London area. Thereafter in diminishing dimensions we find *Richmond Park* (2469 acres), *Wimbledon* and *Putney Common* (1178 acres), and *Hampstead Heath*, including *Kenwood* and *Parliament Hill Fields* (800 acres). The smallest are *Highgate Woods* (70 acres), *Green Park* (53 acres) and *Waterlow Park* (26 acres), but there are also the tiddlers such as the *David Copperfield Gardens*, New Kent Road, *Bethnal Green Gardens, Cannizaro Park*, Wimbledon, *Kelsey Park*, Beckenham, and so on. In mid-summer London from the air appears to be one big park.

It is more difficult to think of areas without parks than of parks themselves.

First the sad ones. It's hard to find anything encouraging about *Finsbury Park, Shepherd's Bush Green, Brockwell Park* (OK for tobogganning), the *Rookery*, Streatham Common – a pretty name though – or *Gunnersbury Park*. One walks sadly in them head lowered to avoid the turds; this is no way to be in parks.

But then consider the glories of *Regent's Park*, which originally contained 'wooded glades and lairs of wild beasts, deer, both red and fallow, wild bulls and boars'. Study the roses, the water, the bandstand, and the general air of privilege and power.

Hyde Park was once Henry VIII's deerpark, then a popular race-course, a duelling ground, the site for the Great Exhibition, and a training ground for demagogues. It has a bird sanctuary and some fine statues. *Kensington Gardens* which adjoins it is best bib and tucker – *Green Park* and *Hyde Park* are more suitable for courting in. *Holland Park* is to do with a hill and the remains of a fine house and an open air theatre and a fine avenue of trees. *St James's Park* has herons and mallards and guards being changed and diplomats taking the air. James I had camels (an unusual gift from the King of Spain) grazing there. As with the rather boring *Green Park*, there's too much walking through it and not enough lounging around in it.

People are possessive about the smaller parks. *Waterlow Park* is regarded with obsessive jealousy by Highgate's inhabitants; one can understand their feelings; it's delightful. *South Park*, Fulham, is used and loved by all Fulhamites, who are engaged in fighting the threats of the Hammersmith bureaucrats as I type these words. *Greenwich Park* has everything to recommend it, the Maritime Museum, Croom's Hill, plenty of wild flowers and a spectacular view over the river to the City, but Greenwich residents often prefer the lesser known *Cutty Sark Gardens*, where concerts and children's shows add to the gaiety of the nation. *Golders Hill Park* is also very much for the residents, with fine tennis courts, excellent refreshments, a secluded garden and deer, though nothing like as prolific as the deer in the magnificent *Richmond Park*.

Battersea Park belongs too much to some of the people – the violent ones – and consequently too little to the others. Which is a shame because it has a fine history. It was laid out by Sir James Pennethorne, Nash's pupil, and boasts such features as a 16-acre lake, a flower garden, a children's zoo, and much else, especially for children. It is the site for the annual Easter Parade, for the Royal Tournament march past, and provides concerts at the Pavilion in North Carriage Drive.

But I have no hesitation in nominating *Regent's Park* as the finest in London, and *Finsbury Park* as the least fine. Indeed on a fine summer's day I can imagine no nicer place in the world than *Regent's Park*, and on a murky February evening during the Friday rush hour I can imagine few places more dispiriting than *Shepherd's Bush Green*.

Best park: *Regent's Park*.
Worst park: *Finsbury Park* (*Shepherd's Bush Green* being too small to qualify).

For details of entertainments in the Royal Parks in the summer telephone: 01-212 3434; for entertainments in the other parks try: 01-633 1707. For a full review read Hunter Davies's book, *A Walk Round London's Parks*.

Peacocks

There are peacocks at the *Belvedere Restaurant* (which also incorporates *The Fisherman's Warf* restaurant), Holland Park, W8 (01-602 1238). They are arrogantly tame and live on steak, strawberries and dry-roasted nuts. A stuffed peacock guards the banisters at *Leighton House*. More plebeian peacocks (three of them) strut about the garden of the *Prince of Wales* pub (37 Fortune Green Road, NW6; 01-435 0653), and lounge around the animal enclosure in *Clissold Park*, N4. There are white peacocks in the enclosure at *Golder's Hill Park*. The peacocks at *Chessington* and London zoos are less willing to display their tails than those at *Whipsnade*. If you want to buy a peacock, *Palmers* (33-37 Parkway, NW1; 01-485 5163) is your best bet, but *Harrods* will probably be able to help you if *Palmers* can't. I expect there are peacocks at the *Peacock Club*, 225 Streatham High Road, SW16 (01-769 3300), but I haven't yet visited it.

I can't recommend best or worst peacocks. They are volatile creatures, and by the time you read this they may be quite altered.

Antique dealers regard peacocks as unlucky, and don't care to stock them. Owls on the other hand bring great good fortune.

Pens and Pen-Nibs

> They come as a boon and a blessing to men
> The Pickwick, the Owl and the Waverley Pen.

Thus runs the centrepiece in what is one of the most remarkable window-displays in London – at *Philip Poole & Co Ltd* (182 Drury Lane, WC2; 01-405 7097). Prominently on view is a display of William Mitchell pen-nibs against a stained glass catafalque – the whole a bit like a miniature Wurlitzer organ. The window, lit flickeringly at night by gas, is an unforgettable monument to The Pen. Mr Poole, known I expect as His Nibs, has a stock running into millions and many of the nibs have marvellous names such as the Figaro, the Times, the Empress, the Flying Dutchman, and others. Some are shaped like a human hand or the Eiffel Tower. The best buy must be the Time Is Money pen which 'may be left in the ink-pot' and does not 'flood, choke, splutter or need shaking'. Despite the obvious claims of the admirable *Wheatsheaf Art Shop* (76-78 Neal Street, WC2; 01-836 7186/01-379 7215), you would be callous indeed not to patronise . : .

Best pen shop: *Philip Poole & Co Ltd.*

Pet Shops (see Tropical Fish)

Pillar Boxes

> The pillar box is big and red,
> Its mouth is open wide,
> It wears a tammy on its head,
> It must be *dark* inside!

> Rose Fyldeman.

The redness of its red pillar boxes and telephone booths was the best thing which the GPO had to offer a weary world, and it was crass beyond belief when the newly formed British Telecom (what can you expect from a body with a name like that?) decided to paint its booths yellow. A few experimental ones survive in the *Edgware Road*, but fortunately they never got around to pillar boxes.

My favourite pillar box is built into the ancient walls of *Hampton Court Palace*. I like to feel that Cardinal Wolsey used it to pop a card in the post to Henry but I don't suppose he did.

All pillar box designs have been successful although none has quite come up to the octagonal Victorian pillar box, a fine example of which may be seen on the corner of Bedford Road and The Orchard in *Bedford Park*, Chiswick. Even the Royal monograms are a pleasure to look at.

Eccentricities abound. In *St Paul's Churchyard* is a double box reminiscent of those conjurors' cupboards in which spangled ladies disappear and reappear, and there is a handsome Victorian one set into the old brickwork of *3, Hampstead Lane*, N6. But almost every pillar box is a happy marriage between the arts and the sciences. If only they cleared them more often.

Best pillar box: *Hampton Court Palace.*

PS It may be worth remarking that old telephone booths retail at a cool £200. Why? Because they make ideal shower booths.

Pipes etc

Give a man a pipe he can smoke
Give a man a book he can read,
And his home is filled with a calm delight
Though the room be poor indeed.

Alfred Dunhill

The meerschaum is so called from its likeness to petrified sea-foam (*l'ecume de mer*), and in the old days as a captain in the Guards you would have had a young subaltern smoke one in for you. Now you visit *Astley's* (109 Jermyn Street, SW1; 01-930 1687) for antique meerschaums which don't need to be run in. *Smokes* (24 Upper Street, N1; 01-226 0266) specialise in tobaccos, cigars and imported cigarettes, but for lovers of the Turkish *Sullivan Powell* (34 Burlington Arcade, W1; 01-629 0433) is the place. Snuff boxes may be elegantly purchased from *Eric Graus* (125 New Bond Street, W1; 01-629 6680) or *S. J. Phillips* (139 Bond Street, W1; 01-629 6261), where the directors' lunches served in the basement are a great comfort to the afflicted soul. *T. H. Gilbert* (11 Gray's-in-the-Mews, Davies Street, W1; 01-408 0028) has nice pipes, but knows how to charge for them. *Nathan's Pipe Shop* (60 Hill Rise, Richmond, Surrey; 01-940 2404) is a little like a pipe shop in a Beatrix Potter book – very pretty. At *Alfred Dunhill* (30 Duke Street, St James's, SW1; 01-499 9566) you are in the presence of the experts, but can see your money go up in smoke too. *Desmond Sautter's Pipe Shop* (91 Piccadilly, W1; 01-499 4319 and three branches) will actually repair pipes. To a pipe-smoker that is really something. *Astley's* also repair them but charge more.

Best pipe shops: *Desmond Sautter's* and *Astley's*.

Poetry

My friend, Alan Jackson, believes that poetry should be made illegal, and that all poets who persist in writing the stuff should be sent to prison where at least they would be fed and housed and encouraged to suffer, thus deepening and enlarging the scope of their poetry.

In the meantime there are occasional poetry competitions – the biggest being those run by the Cheltenham Festival and the Arvon Foundation – and plans for a poetry olympics to coincide with the Los Angeles games.

There are a few remaining venues in which poets may read their works; *Bunjie's Coffee House* (27 Litchfield Street, WC2; 01-240 1796) is one, and the *Cockpit Theatre* (Gateforth Street, NW8; 01-262 6935) another. The Pentameters organise poetry readings at the *Three Horseshoes* (Heath Street, NW3; 01-435 3648) and programmes of forthcoming fests are on display in the bar. At the *Crown and Greyhound* (73 Dulwich Village, SE21; 01-693 2466) there is poetry on the last Wednesday in each month, and the Barrow Poets, strongly recommended, perform on Wednesdays at the *Sir Christopher Wren* (28 Paternoster Row, EC4; 01-248 1707), a new pub with 17th-century fittings. Other poetic happenings are advertised in the events magazines.

Poets may be hired from the *London Poetry Secretariat* (25 Tavistock Place, WC1; 01-388 2211). Fees range from £40 upwards, depending upon the poets' rating in the charts. The best meld is one established poet and one young and hungry one.

The National Sound Archive at the British Institute of Recorded Sound (29 Exhibition Road, SW7; 01-589 6603) holds one of the largest collections of recorded literature in the world, including Brecht giving evidence to the Un-American Activities Committee, Tennyson reciting 'The Charge of the Light Brigade', and the only recording of Sylvia Plath – just three of the treasures. Also available there and in record shops spoken word recordings by Argo, Caedmon, Listen (especially Stevie Smith) and Stream, who produced a recording of Basil Bunting reading his superb 'Briggflats'.

The Poetry Society and *Centre* (21 Earls Court Square, SW5; 01-373 7861) has useful facilities for poets and a 'critical service' which will analyse your poem for a fee. Try sending them a little known work by Andrew Marvell, appending your name to it, and . . .

The Arts Council Library (9 Long Acre, WC2; 01-379 6597) is well worth an afternoon and the *Association of Little Presses* (262 Randolph Avenue, W9; 01-824 8565) can give you all the information that you need about magazines which publish poetry, and have produced an excellent guide: *Getting your Poetry Published* (20p excluding postage). But avoid publishers who require a fee to publish your verses.

Poet's Corner in Westminster Abbey is where poets who have been mocked and starved during their lifetimes are honoured in perpetuity. In the South Transept it includes Wordsworth in a dressing gown and Dr Johnson splendidly sculpted by Nollekens. Said Johnson of this bust: 'I think my friend, Joe Nollekens, can chop out a head with any of them'.

An engaging anthology of London poetry is: *London between the Lines* compiled by John Bishop and Virginia Broadbent. (Simon Publications 1973).

Police

I have had my brushes with the Met. I spent a particularly nasty hour in the cells at *Camberwell Green* and I was unexpectedly kicked by an over-zealous 'special' in *Richmond*, but there have also been occasions when I have found the London Police, if not wonderful, at least civil and good-natured. Of course they are getting younger every year and I recently had to remind a traffic cop in *Chelsea*, who looked as though he should not be out without his mother, that he had forgotten to caution me. He blushed.

The statistics for 1982 are interesting. A very poor 'clear-up' rate was recorded for auto theft (7%) and burglary (8%) in London, but serious crime was less successful; 70% of murders and 65% of kidnappings in London were solved. 688,000 notifiable offences were recorded in the year although the real figure may be four or five times as high.*

If one believes the superannuated investigating officers from the Countryman inquiry, the Flying and Fraud Squads are

*Statistics from Report of the Commissioner of Police of the Metropolis 1982, Command 8928 (HMSO £9.10).

riddled with corruption, and on balance I think it is probably true. The *Hackney* Police – or some of them – have shown racist tendencies and the policy of some *Brixton* coppers of strip-searching black Londoners in the streets is hardly neighbourly. The *Stoke Newington* Station has to live down the unhappy Colin Roach affair. Marie Lloyd's old song: 'If you want to know the time ask a Policeman' slyly referred to the London policeman's habit of confiscating the watch and chain of well-heeled drunks.

However I have heard nothing but good about the *West Hampstead* and *Rosslyn Hill* forces in general and PC Andy in particular.

Best police station: *West Hampstead.*

Post Offices

The *Dulwich Post Office* sells knitting patterns and knicker elastic along with the latest commemoratives. *Kew's* post office in the station precinct is like a little brick gazebo, bright blue with a red letter box. Though charming it is currently under threat of demolition along with the whole of the north side of the precinct.

Lisson Grove Post Office is well sited. It is opposite the Actors' Labour Exchange and Phillips' Marylebone auction rooms. On Friday mornings there is a lot of action in *Lisson Grove*. The post office itself is minute and crowded with notices about colorado beetle and such adorning the walls. It conjures up an age when London still consisted of village communities, when people went to the post office for a gossip. The Ugandan Asians who run so many of the suburban post offices are competent, kind-hearted and industrious, but they are not yet very good at gossip.

The *Trafalgar Square* branch office (22-28 William IV Street, WC2 – alongside St Martin-in-the-Fields) is open all night and on Sundays for telephone, telegraph business, and the sale of stamps. The *Chief Post Office* is in King Edward Street and has a 150-feet counter. It also contains the National Postal Museum (see under Stamps) and is opposite the Postal Headquarters Building. Adjacent too is the statue to Rowland Hill, responsible for the whole thing, and the Postman's Park. Beneath the post office is the *Post Office Railway*, which runs between Whitechapel and Paddington by a circuitous route. It conveys 40,000 mailbags a day at 35 mph, which is a lot of letters per foot per second.

Best post office: *Lisson Grove.*

Prostitutes

Men are all right so long as they are regularly despunked. If they're not getting their oats, they're bloody pests.

Cynthia Payne

Nearly 2,000 women a year are convicted of prostitution (a 'common prostitute' can be picked up for loitering or soliciting after three cautions), but none of their customers are picked up for anything. Average fines are £50 for a first offence; £200 thereafter. The law is absurd in any case. It permits prostitution but not if there are two or more girls in the room, in which case it's a brothel, nor if the prostitute's husband or boy friend takes the money (pimping) nor if the girl or boy solicits openly on the street. A spanking parlour is only illegal if more than one person is operating it, and so on.

Prostitutes have been back on the London streets in force, particularly since the Yorkshire Ripper terrified so many girls into coming south. The classiest pros operate from smart hotels; sit in the lobby or at the bar and if they think you can afford them they will approach you. Recent British Rail concessions have made it profitable for parties of prostitutes to come up to town from South Wales at excursion rates. There must be a television play in that! The saddest girls operate from 'walk-ups' (small upstairs flats usually in *Soho*). If you press the bell saying 'Linda – Model with Large Chest' you will find yourself negotiating with the 'maid' before you meet Linda by which time it may well be too late. 'Clippies' who take your money and give nothing in return, operate from *Soho* streets, in particular from *Peter Street, Meard Street, Bateman Street, Greek Street, Archer Street* and *Great Windmill Street*. A better class of prostitute (i.e. more expensive) may be observed in *Bourdon Street* and in the area contained within *Curzon Street, Half Moon Street, Piccadilly* and *Park Lane*. But as a general rule *Soho* is where you get clipped, *Mayfair* is where you get laid, and the *King's Cross* area is where you get V.D. Many of the kids operating in King's Cross are main-lining. It's tragic.

A hint: If you *must* pay the girl or boy in advance, tear the note/notes in half. Give him/her half and promise the other half after you've been despunked. This ensures good faith on both sides.

See also under Brothels.

Pubs

(For a full survey of this subject see either the *London Pub Guide* compiled by Judy Allen (Robert Nicholson Publications) or the less reliable *Egon Ronay Raleigh Pub Guide*, (Penguin).

First the licensing laws. These allow drinking in pubs between 11 a.m. and 3 p.m. and between 5.30 p.m. and 11 p.m., but in the City of London the evening drinking hours are usually between 5 p.m. and 8 p.m. On Sundays one may drink in pubs between noon and 2 p.m. and between 7 p.m. and 10.30 p.m. There are exceptions and, where food is served, drink may accompany a meal.

In 1831 there was a pub in London to every 168 people; in 1931 there was a pub to every 535 people, and now it is a pub to every 600 people.

I shall divide pubs into the following categories:

(a) Real ale pubs   (d) Gay pubs
(b) Riverside pubs   (e) Straight pubs
(c) Pubs with entertainment (f) Pub food

(a) Real Ale pubs

The Campaign for Real Ale (CAMRA) has been astonishingly successful. Not only has it promoted the re-introduction of real ales even in pubs tied to the big breweries, but it has started running its own pubs. One such is *The Nag's Head* (79-81 Heath Street, NW3; 01-435 4108) and here you can pamper yourself with such exotic brews as Brakespeare's Bitter, Green King Abbott Ale, Wadsworth 6X, Gale's HSB, Sam Smith's Old Brewery Bitter, Ruddles' Country and Simon's Tower Bridge Bitter. *The Windsor Castle* (The Walk, Church Lane, N2; 01-883 5763) stocks fifteen real ales on a rota of seven pumps; there's also a large walled garden for the children. *The Ship and Shovel* (2 Craven Passage, WC2; 01-930 7670) serves three real ales and the best bacon and kidney rolls this side of Tel Aviv. *The Hole in the Wall*, 5 Mepham Street, SE1 (01-928 6196) has eight real ales in stock, including Godson's. Try ordering Red Barrel in this fanatical place and you'll end up *in* a barrel. The Wall and the Hole it is in is part of Waterloo Station.

The Crown (24 Aberdeen Place, NW8; 01-289 1102) has six real ales, a ghost, and live entertainment, while at *The Worcester Arms* (89 George Street, W1; 01-935 6040) there is a guest 'beer of the month'. *The Man in the Moon* (392 King's Road, SW3; 01-352 5075) is a theatrical pub with beautifully engraved glass for the actors to look at themselves in, and five real ales. Another fantasy in glass, with real ale to boot (nine varieties) is the enchantingly Victorian *Princess Louise* (208-209 High Holborn, WC1; 01-405 8816). *The Lamb* (94 Lamb's Conduit Street, WC1; 01-405 0713) is a Bloomsbury Young's pub with gorgeously engraved glass snob screens and sepia fin de siècle celebrities on the wall. *The Sun Inn* (63 Lamb's Conduit Street, WC1; 01-405 8278), just down the road from *The Lamb*, has vast cellars awash with real ale – seventy varieties, some say, but no one has lived to tell the tale – and twenty varieties on tap; *The Bricklayers Arms* (63 Charlotte Road, EC2; 01-739 5245) has twenty-one real ales and beer-drinking contests as well as Morris Dancing, which often comes to much the same thing. One cautionary word. A kind of shrill Real Ale fascism infects some of these pubs, and a trendy snobbism drives out the regulars.

Best real ale pub: *The Bricklayers Arms.*

(b) Riverside pubs
It would be contempt of Parliament to call the *House of Commons* a riverside pub, but the cheapest beer in London is served on the terrace, and the licensing laws don't apply. So get yourself elected. *The London Apprentice* in Isleworth (62 Church Street; 01-560 6136) is the pub at which the young apprentices to the London Guilds would celebrate their holidays. Under its pretty Italianate ceiling you can drink Watneys beer, and in the restaurant upstairs you can eat duck, but the best thing to do is drink on the terrace and watch the barges; its opening times are irregular.

For riverside pub-crawling Strand on the Green and Hammersmith Mall offer plenty of ports of call. My favourite at Strand is the *Bull's Head* (01-994 0647) where Cromwell was nearly caught by the pursuing Cavaliers, and the pleasantest at Hammersmith is *The Dove* (Upper Mall; 01-748 5405). It is also known as *The Doves*; it is not easy to count doves after a pub crawl. *The Dove* is not *quite* on the river, which the neighbouring *Old Ship* (25 Upper Mall, 01-748 2593) is, but it is nearly 300 years old, has a fructiferous vine and is where James Thompson allegedly, wrote Rule Britannia.

Also recommended: *The Grapes*, 76 Narrow Street, E14; (01-987 4396) with an extensive view of the river as well as oysters in season; *The Dickens Inn*, St Katherine's Way, E1 (01-488 1226), a converted docks warehouse, rather modern and touristy but serving a useful choice of food and Ruddles, and exuding optimism; *The Anchor*, Bankside, SE1 (01-407 1577) for Mrs

Thrale's steak and kidney pudding and a first edition of Johnson's dictionary; also three restaurants, the obligatory minstrels' gallery, real ale (Courage), an outside urinal of the old-fashioned type and a terrace overlooking the Thames.

The Prospect of Whitby (57 Wapping Wall, E1; 01-481 1095) is noisy and raucous; tourists are unwisely encouraged to sing. It was best in the days of Queenie Watts, but it's too loud for me.

Best riverside pub: *The Bull's Head.*

(c) Pubs with entertainment (see also Theatres, Fringe)
   A selection:

The Bridge House, Barking Road, Canning Town, E16; 01-476 2889. A big stage, a committed audience, and its own record label. Two groups every night with admittance at £1 can't be bad.

The Green Man, Stratford High St, Carpenter's Road, E15. Wednesdays and Fridays in the Lounge Bar. Tricky Dicky hosts an increasingly popular cabaret disco. Predominantly gay.

The Half Moon, 93 Lower Richmond Road, SW15; 01-788 2387. A rough and ready sort of place which specialises in bands and artists from the 60s and 70s. The customers are walk-ons from Woodstock, but the night Roy Harper played was unforgettable.

Hope & Anchor, 207 Upper Street, N1; 01-359 4510. Barrels to sit on and a concrete floor, this is rougher and readier than *The Half Moon*. But if punk can be said to be serious, here is where you'll find it. Inexpensive.

The Kensington, Russell Gardens, Holland Road, W14; 01-603 3245. Principally for the studded leather crowd, and the music rocks. Inexpensive.

The King's Head, 4 Fulham High Street, SW6; 01-736 1413. Pub rock with dancing Thursdays to Sundays. Admission charge varies.

Old Queen's Head, 133 Stockwell Road, SW9; 01-734 4904. Rock till eleven, then two hours of jazz almost every evening. A West Indian landlord and a great future. Inexpensive.

The Railway Hotel, West End Lane, NW6; 01-624 7611. Within the hotel are the Moonlight Club (rock and blues, dark and moody) and the Starlight Room (jazz, funk and punk – cheap and basic). Hendrix played here. Admission charges vary.

The Ruskin Arms, 386 High Street North, Manor Park, E12;

01-472 0377. Loud rock, but not on Tuesdays or Wednesdays. The manager is a boxer and keeps the customers sweet, no matter how heavy the music. What would Ruskin have thought?

The Spurs, Great Cambridge Road, Lordship Lane, N17; 01-808 4773. Used to be the heaviest of the heavies but has gentled into rhythm and blues. Wednesday to Sunday. Free admission.

The Star and Garter, Lower Richmond Road, SW15; 01-731 4255. An ugly pile of a place, overlooking the river. Rock and rhythm and blues Wednesday to Saturday; popular with hooray henries. Inexpensive though.

The Wellington, 102 Uxbridge Road, W12; 01-743 4671. Strippers on Mondays and Tuesdays, heavy metal the rest of the week; though not as heavy as it used to be. Admission free.

Should all this pall try *The Gilbert and Sullivan* (23 Wellington Street, WC2; 01-836 6930) and listen to G & S on the juke box. Or take in *The Pindar of Wakefield* (see under Music Halls).

Best pub with entertainment: *The Bridge House.*

(d) Gay pubs
At last the Gay Movement is acquiring a sense of humour. There is, for example, an organisation called GOGOL for Gay Oxford Graduates Of London (ring John on 01-373 4234) and another called The Pink Wrinkle for, well, mature gays (ring Leslie on 01-272 1927). One can befriend former members of the armed forces (ring John on 01-730 6889 or Mark on 01-858 3495) or speak Gay Esperanto (Peter on 01-892 6536). Details of these and numerous other unusual possibilities in *Gay Reporter* (Denis Lemon's new magazine), *Time Out*, or from *Gay Switchboard* (01-837 7324). To tide you over a short list of predominantly gay recommendable pubs.

Bolton's, 216 Old Brompton Road, SW5 (01-373 8244). An old-fashioned three-bar Victorian pub, predominantly male, all ages from winkle to wrinkle.

Campion, 1 Wellington Terrace, W11 (01-229 5056). Large bar with snuggery for snuggers. Predominantly male, predominantly local, predominantly second time around.

Coleherne, 261 Old Brompton Road, SW5 (01-373 5881). Has the reputation of being rough and not for nice boys, but the reality is reassuring – there is even a grandfather clock. Male.

The Cricketers, 317 Battersea Park Road, SW11 (01-622 9060). Gay and straight. A unique landlady in Viv Spanton. Drag acts Thursdays to Mondays. Tuesdays are for girls and feature a girls' band.

The Euston Tavern, 73 Euston Road, NW1 (opposite King's Cross – 01-387 4566). A gay disco operates on Fridays through Sundays with drag acts etc. Resident DJ is Tricky Dicky; don't miss Mrs Shufflewick on her rare appearances. Downstairs is straight.

The King William IV, 77 High Street, Hampstead, NW3 (01-435 5747). A barbecue in the garden on Fridays and Saturdays. Very Hampstead. Trendy T-shirts. On the electronic game a sign: 'By hitting tail the enemy becomes shorter'. Predominantly male.

London Apprentice, 333 Old Street, EC1. Where the action currently is Macho, cruisy, and very busy.

New Black Cap, 171 Camden High Street, NW1 (01-485 1742). Drag acts throughout the ages photographically recalled; the real thing every night and Sunday lunch. Mixed.

Royal Vauxhall Tavern, 372 Kennington Lane, SE11 (01-582 0833). Drag acts nightly and Sunday lunch times. Noisy and friendly. Predominantly male with apprehensive tourists.

The Salisbury on the corner of St Martin's Lane and St Martin's Court is high camp. Plenty of engraved glass, gilt, and mirrors; plenty of engraved gilt actors admiring themselves in the mirrors. Extremely theatrical.

Ship and Whale, 2 Gulliver Street, SE16 (01-237 3305). Closed Mondays; discos Wednesday to Sunday and Sunday lunch. A pool table, a flood-lit garden (spoilsports), and electronic games. Male.

The Sussex Arms, 107a Culford Road, N1 (01-254 3965). 'A beautiful pub for beautiful people'. Resident groups Wednesdays and Saturdays.

Union Tavern, 146 Camberwell New Road, SE5 (01-735 3605). Discos Tuesday and Thursday; cabaret acts – can get quite lively – other evenings. Predominantly male with theatrical overtones, and a few jock-sniffers.

If it seems from the above that lesbians are ignored in London pubs, it should be understood that most gay girls prefer clubs to pubs. For latest information ring the Lesbian Line (01-837 8602) or the London Friend Women's Line (01-354 1846). Their information will be more reliable than mine!

Best gay pub: *New Black Cap.*

(e) Straight pubs
This list is for those who believe that London pubs are being over-run by CAMRA fascists, punk rockers, gay libbers, and just long for some peace and quiet.

Blackfriar, 174 Queen Victoria Street, EC4 (01-236 5650). A louche hymn to art nouveau; the 'side-chapel' is unforgettable in the way that peritonitis is unforgettable. If you don't go, you'll never know. Charrington Bass, Wethered, Directors Bitter.

The Brewery Tap, 69 Wandsworth High Street, SW18 (01-870 2894). Attached to Young's Brewery, so see under Breweries.

The French House (officially the *York Minster*), 49 Dean Street, W1 (01-437 2799). The centre for the Free French during the war, and the centre for the Soho Set after the war. Dylan Thomas, Francis Bacon, Colin MacInnes, and Brendan Behan, all appreciated its qualities, but it doesn't welcome tourists. Champagne is served in half bottles to celebrate a minor success.

Lamb and Flag, 33 Rose Street, WC2 (01-836 4108). Run by an author, ex-farmer and wine merchant, this pub was once known as *The Bucket of Blood*. Agents for the Duchess of Portsmouth, who fancied herself libelled, here made an attempt on Dryden's life. There used to be bare-knuckle boxing in the upstairs room, now often used for poetry (q.v.). Dryden Night is December 19th, and Burns Night is also celebrated. Sadly it lost its stucco façade a few years ago. Strong real ale, excellent food, Courage.

Pontefract Castle, Wigmore Street, W1 (01-486 3551). The most interesting feature of this interesting pub is that it serves in the Balcony Bar twenty varieties of malt whisky; obviously several visits are called for.

Queen's Elm, 241 Fulham Road, SW3 (01-352 9157). A Bohemian pub which has always been popular with writers. In the upstairs room the successful Public Lending Right campaign was masterminded by such stalwarts as Brigid Brophy and Maureen Duffy. Courage. (What else?)

Red Lion, 2 Duke of York Street, SW1 (01-930 2030). Not to be confused with the other Red Lion in Crown Passage just a couple of hops away. Your reception here may be surly (mine was) but there's no denying the ravishing glitter of the engraved mirrors, each bearing a different British flower. It's not unlike drinking on an old-fashioned merry-go-round. Ind Coope. Crowded.

Rose of York, Petersham Road, Richmond (01-940 0626). One of the prettiest pubs in one of the prettiest settings (Ham Common). A carvery on Sundays, and Samuel Smith beer. Classy.

Still and Star, 1 Little Somerset Street, E1 (01-488 3761). In the middle of Jack the Ripper land which may account for the welcoming atmosphere inside, the *S and S* is run by a lady Freeman of the City of London. Charringtons and IPA.

The Gunmaker's Arms, Eyre Street Hill, EC1 is a charming curiosity on a miniature scale. Natural to feel 'tight' here.

The Opera Tavern opposite Drury Lane in Catherine St, is also small, highly ornate and atmospheric. A delight.

I am not enamoured of any of the following: *Windsor Castle*, Campden Hill Road, W8 (despite the tortoise); *The Coal Hole* (the Strand, WC2); *The Hour Glass* (Brompton Road, SW1); *Cockney Pride* (Jermyn Street, SW1); *The Norbury* (Norbury, SW16); the *Bricklayers Arms* (Beckenham, SW7); *The Tournament* (Old Brompton Road, SW7).

Best straight pub: *The Opera Tavern.*

(f) Pub food
If you can get to the *Coach and Horses* (29 Greek Street, W1; 01-437 5920), which is the *Private Eye* pub, early enough, you will be served by a little old West Indian lady-chef, who is indestructible. She does bangers and mash the way they ought to be done, and similar delicacies. The proprietor is a dead ringer for Walter Matthau, which is only of interest, I suppose, to the two parties concerned.

Other recommendations:

Simpson's Tavern, Ball Court Passage, 38½ Cornhill, EC3 (01-626 9985) for a stewed cheese speciality; *Ladbroke Arms*, 54 Ladbroke Road, W11 for an excellent carvery; *Queen's Head*, 13 Brook Green, W6 (01-603 2696) for their freshly homemade buffet; *Ye Olde Cheshire Cheese*, 145 Fleet Street, EC4 (01-353 6170) for game puddings (from October); the *Grenadier*, 18 Wilton Row, SW1 (01-235 3074) for good, if expensive English food; the *Bunch of Grapes*, 207 Brompton Road, SW3 (01-589 4944), a pretty pub with lip-smacking food; the *Fox and Anchor*, Charterhouse Street, EC1 (01-253 4838) for homemade soups, mixed grills and breakfasts; the *Grafton Arms*, 72 Grafton Way, W1 (01-387 7923) for Scottish food; the *Warwick Castle*, 6 Warwick Place, W9 (01-286 6868) for shepherd's pie; the *Cutty Sark*, Lassell Street, SE10 (01-858 3146) for whitebait; the *Samuel Pepys*, Brooks Wharf, Upper Thames Street (01-248 3048 for the restaurant) for game pie and spotted dick; the *Wattenden Arms*, Old Lodge Lane, Kenley for fresh crab salad; the *Dover Castle*, 43 Weymouth Mews, W1 (01-636 9248) where children are welcome.

An inadequate list, I'm afraid. Book in advance in those pubs which accept bookings. If not, arrive before 1 p.m. and, if there is a 'today's special', have it! It is less likely to have been recently defrosted.

Best pub food: *Queen's Head*, Brook Green.
Worst pub food: *instant mash, technicolour peas and tired lettuce are the give-aways.*

Pub Signs

The Blind Beggar, a pub notorious in the past for murder and mayhem, has a fine sign overhanging the Mile End Road, Stepney. It shows the eponymous beggar accompanied by a rather stout young lady who has him by the arm. Is she his wife, his daughter, his fancy woman? Is she helping him, robbing him, or interviewing him for market research? We have no way of knowing. *The Hog in the Pound*, 28 South Molton Street, W1, is a prime (sic) example of what posh art dealers call *genre art*. It shows two pigs, trotters hanging over the fence, considering the world and all its follies from their superior position. The sign itself is rectangular with hemispheric extensions at either end. It's not a thing of beauty, but it's original and well-conceived, with graphics in a sort of Wild West script.

However, I think my favourite pub sign must be the staid, unshowy, but entirely satisfactory *Builders Arms*, in St Paul's Road, N1. The builder in question is a brickie, but perhaps when the sign was commissioned it was thought that there were already quite enough *Bricklayers Arms* in London. Anyway there he is with brick and trowel, his body much lived in, the same shape as Nye Bevan's, the forearms massive, the head behind its moustache and underneath its flat cap owing nothing to anyone. He is neither proud of his calling nor ashamed of it. He just goes on adding brick to brick, the way most of us have to, whatever kinds of bricks we deal in. All praise to the anonymous artist.

Best pub sign: the *Builders Arms*.
Worst pub signs: *Those which merely show the logo of the brewery to which the pub is 'tied'*.

PS A good game for children on a car journey. Give them a point for each leg (human, animal or heraldic) visible on pub signs.

Race Tracks (around London)

Ally Pally was the only genuine London race track and now it's gone and we mourn its passing. Known disrespectfully as the Frying Pan (from its shape) it was primitive. Once I remember the starter barricading himself in his shed after being stoned by the crowd; the favourite had been left many lengths at the start, which was in front of what passed for a grandstand. There on summer evenings we'd plunge on ageing Doctor Blimber, the ugliest horse in racing, and sometimes he'd win.

Of the courses adjacent to London, *Kempton Park* is like an old whore who's run to seed, and *Epsom* is even worse. The trek from the stand to the paddock is exhausting, the crowds on Derby Day cannot be coped with, and the whole place reeks of dilapidation. But it's exciting to back a fast short-runner there over the quickest five furlongs in racing.

Sandown has lost much of its charisma since the new stand was built, but visibility is good, crowds are well contained, and the curry in the hors d'oeuvre bar has become essential before the first race on a winter's day.

The Royal Meeting at *Ascot* offers the best racing, the priciest women and the most valuable horses, but I am not impressed by a Royal Enclosure which admits me. Though fields are small, the jumping meeting in the spring is to be preferred. A Monday evening meeting at *Windsor* can be a pleasure, though finding the winner of a 23-horse selling handicap there poses problems to test an Einstein (the draw is not as significant as it used to be); but it's informal and amiable.

The best tipster used to be Robin Goodfellow of the *Daily Mail* (Arthur Salter) who went through the card on three successive days – a unique 18-horse accumulator. Currently Richard Baerlain of the *Guardian* and *Observer*, is enjoying an Indian summer. Never afraid to put his money where his mouth is, he tipped the unraced Morston to win the Derby at 25/1, and during 1982 consistently tipped Soba, who kept winning races, even the Royal Hunt Cup at 16/1.

Best racecourse: *Sandown Park.*
Worst racecourse: *Epsom.*

Railway Lines

> How noble was her carriage,
> How first-class was her brain,
> She was not of my station,
> But love came in her train.

The *Broad Street Line* (otherwise known as the *North London Line*) is the best in London. Hampstead to Richmond in twenty minutes during the rush hour is not to be sneezed at. It runs three times an hour from Richmond to Broad Street and back through back gardens hung with washing. Children still wave at Broad Street trains as they pass, and the graffiti tend to be richer in sexual imagery than on the more populated lines. For as long as I can remember the line has been under threat of permanent closure, but we shall fight on.

The Drain (*Waterloo and City Line* running between Waterloo and the Bank) is a law unto itself. Moving walkways and a single ticket price are just a part of its old-fashioned charm. The *Bakerloo Line* beyond Queen's Park is hair-raising. Like as not you'll end up (sic) at Watford Junction.

Best line: *Broad Street.*
Worst line: *Southern Region to Blackheath and beyond.*

Records/Tapes

A selection:

(a) General
HMV (363 Oxford Street, W1; 01-629 1240) is the daddy of them all, and claims to be the largest record store in Europe. Their stock (on three floors) is certainly comprehensive, but the

assistants lack the enthusiasm of those in smaller emporia. You can get steel needles for 78s here.

Beggars Banquet (8 Hogarth Road, SW1; 01-370 6175) specialises in independent labels and has its own. Second-hand and trade-in facilities. Branches throughout west London.

(b) Classical
Orchesography (10 Cecil Court, WC2; 01-836 2314). Cut-price, deletions and special offers, mainly in the classical range.
Harold Moore's Records (2 Marlborough Street, W1; 01-437 1576). A similar policy to *Orchesography*, but a wider selection of rarities.
Covent Garden Records (20 James Street, WC2; 01-379 7674). Principally deals in popular classics. The two marmalade cats, Figaro and Aida, are not for sale.

(c) Opera
Collector's Corner (62 New Oxford Street, W1; 01-580 6155). New and second-hand opera recordings – especially rarities.

(d) Jazz – See entry under Jazz.

(e) Musicals
That's Entertainment (43 The Market, WC2; 01-240 2227) not only stocks a vast selection of sound tracks of films and stage musicals, but produces its own records, which are often sold by subscription to American universities. A delightful place.

(f) Rock
Daddy Kod (94 Dean Street, W1; 01-437 3535) for reggae music.
Summit Records (45 Camden High Street, NW1; 01-380 1068) Reggae, independents, new wave, deletions and posters.
Vintage Record Centre (91 Roman Way, N7; 01-607 8586). Old recordings, including rock 'n' roll and blues; also second-hand and trade-in. Fanatical.
Virgin Megastore (14-16 Oxford Street, W1; 01-636 1771). A company whose history has been not unlike an MGM musical of the thirties. Their success with discount records led them into record production, publishing and associated areas. A bit complacent these days.
Rough Trade (202 Kensington Park Road, W11; 01-229 8541). Independent labels representing the very latest in musical fashions.
Record and Tape Exchange (38 Notting Hill Gate, W11; 01-727 3539 and three branches). The claim is that *everything* brought in

for exchange will be accepted at prices from 1p to £2.50. All the shops are open *every* day of the year 10 a.m. to 8 p.m. Wholesale discounts for dealers. Rarities upstairs at the Notting Hill branch. Obviously the place to go at 7.50 p.m. on Christmas Eve when you've got no money to buy presents, just a few old discs.

Best record shop: *depends on what you want.*

Rivers/Streams

London is a city of lost rivers, and one which has been refound. The lost rivers are reflected in street names. There used to be a river which descended from Kilburn (the *Kil Bourne*) via Westbourne Grove (*West Bourne*) to Bayswater (*Baynard's Water*) and Knightsbridge (the bridge over which the knights used to fight in armed combat) to Sloane Square – if you look up from the tube station you can see the conduit which carried it underground at this point – after which it was dammed to make the Serpentine before entering the *Thames*.

Then there was the *Ty Bourne*, which flowed from the heights of Hampstead, via Hyde Park (Tyburn Hill), Stratford Place (the Street Ford), to Green Park, where it created the Bason, a valuable reservoir. The *Fleet* descended from the Vale of Health via King's Cross (it wisely went underground for part of its passage here) to where it met the *Hol Bourne* (Holborn), and the two rivers continued jointly via Ludgate Circus and, of course, Fleet Street, into the *Thames*. Remarkably the Holborn Viaduct still has the look of a bridge over a river, although the *Hol Bourne* was never much of a river. What was once the insalubrious *Fleet Ditch* is now a perfectly sanitary sewer, although no longer visible to city workers crossing the viaduct. Also in the City was the *Walbrook*, and in south London such poetically named streams as the *Falcon Brook*, the *Neckinger*, and the *Tygris*. The *Wandle*, rising in Carshalton Ponds, is still a familiar feature of the Wandsworth area.

The *New River* was manmade by Sir Hugh Myddelton's engineers, who brought the water a distance of thirty-eight miles from Chadwell Springs in Hertfordshire. The water flowed for the first time on September 29th, 1613, and the New River Company still exists (30 Myddelton Square, EC1; 01-837 2105). Although straightened in the 19th century, it was still permitted to meander, as a river should, through the meadows of Enfield. Equally picturesque for much of its length is the poet laureate's favourite river, the gentle *Brent*, which undulates through Hanwell, swallows up golfballs in Brent Lodge Park, passes under the Wharncliffe Railway Viaduct – Queen Victoria used to instruct the driver to slow down here while she enjoyed the view – and the horrific Uxbridge Road. On a recent reconnaissance I am happy to report that I found clumps of willow-herb, was stung by nettles, and stared at by a man with a wheelbarrow. Exploring the *Brent* is rewarding, and useful hints may be picked up at the Grange Museum of Local History on a traffic island in the inappropriately named Blackbird Hill.

As for the *Thames*, what a success story this continues to be! It is clean, it is fresh and yet still, along the eel-filled Twickenham stretch, untamed. As Rupert Brooke put it:

> One may not doubt that, somehow, good
> Shall come of water and of mud . . .

But the *Quaggy* (Lewisham area) is not so happy. Choked with abandoned supermarket trolleys, unwanted prams and babies, and other unmentionables, it is not a subject to dwell on.

Best river: *Thames.*
Best stream: *Brent.*
Worst stream: *Quaggy.*

Roller Skating

The Covent Garden Roller Disco in the Jubilee Hall Recreation Centre, Central Market Square, WC2 – well, it isn't a disco really – is ideal for a family outing, particularly on Sunday mornings. I rollered there with a rabbi – a holy roller, I guess.

Other skating places include *Finsbury Leisure Centre* (Norman Street, EC1; 01-253 4490), *Pickett's Lock Leisure Centre* (Pickett's Lock Lane, Edmonton, N9; 01-803 4756) and the *Tottenham Sports Centre* (703 High Road, N17; 01-801 6401). It's not a bad idea to telephone any of the above to check that you can hire your own particular size in skates.

For the man who thinks he has done it all there is a gay roller disco every Tuesday in Lavender Gardens, SW11.

Best roller skating: *Jubilee Hall.*

Roofs/Chimneys

One could not ignore the claims of the *Battersea Power Station* chimneys (Gilbert Scott 1934) even if one wanted to. Beside them most other London chimneys shrink into insignificance, as Hemingway's did when he looked at Scott Fitzgerald's in the rive gauche lavatory. But I must put in a word for the crooked chimneys of *44-52 Waterloo Gardens*, E2 and of *2 Flask Cottages*, NW3. Curiously patterned pots, as on the *Hampton Court* chimneys, were much imitated, notably on *The Lodge*, Waterloo Park, N6, where a row of six such chimneys look like sticks of rock.

Harrods roof is an amazing sight; you feel you ought not to be looking at it, as you might feel you ought not to be looking down a duchess's cleavage. *St Pancras's* roof is, of course, pure Gothic Disneyland. Then there is the roof of Nash's *Cumberland Terrace* at the east end of Regent's Park. The statues seem designed to stand in silhouette against the dawn. Glance too at the roof of the *Royal Geographical Society* (corner of Kensington Gore and Exhibition Road), at the *Bishop of Southwark's house* in Tooting Bec Gardens, at the *Ritz Hotel*, at the houses in *Welbeck Street*. The Great Hall of *Lambeth Palace* has a marvellous seventy-feet-high hammerbeam roof.

The flamboyant vaulting atop Henry VII's chapel in *Westminster Abbey* is sublime, but it is scarcely a *roof*.

Best roof: Great Hall, *Lambeth Palace.*
Best chimneys: *Battersea Power Station.*
Worst chimneys: the flats in *Peabody Avenue*, SW1.

Rugby Football

Although there are those who would lie down and die for the Harlequins or the Barbarians, there is really no question but that *Twickenham's* the place. Actually the headquarters of rugby is in Whitton (next to All Hallows, a Wren city church re-erected in a leafy suburb). The turf drains effectively so that seldom if ever do matches have to be abandoned. The only problem is visibility. In mid-December when the Varsity Match is played, during what Ivor Brown calls 'the dull droop of a short mid-winter afternoon', and the sun sinks low behind the huge western stand and the mist rises then the figures on the field acquire the reality of crowds during the showing of a D. W. Griffith film on a badly-adjusted portable television set, when Concorde is flying low overhead. The England/Wales match in January is always likely to be fogged out, but England/Scotland in March is worth waiting for, as are the Middlesex Sevens in May. The vast new video screen aids visibility at the expense of atmosphere.

The most loved rugby player of my generation was Gareth Edwards. And of my father's generation: Prince Obolensky. And today? Erica Roe. *Sic transit gloria mundi.*

Best rugby: *Twickenham.*

Sauna/Massage Parlours

You are safer in these joints than visiting a prostitute (q.v.) although the most you can expect is 'hand-relief', which may be from two topless girls and will cost about £20 for approximately 15 minutes – they won't wait for ever! Quite a squalid experience but far better than the Arab sauna I visited in Jerusalem. A short while before my visit a client had fallen into the furnace and been scalded to death.

The following parlours may have more to offer than the average:

Cleo's, 23 Greek Street, W1 (01-734 7348). A 'luxury Roman sauna'. Infra-red and ultra-violet treatment, a solarium, and trained 'maidens' to reach those parts which other maidens can't reach.

Ann Coult's, 55 Blandford Street, W1 (01-486 6482). Enemas of soapy water, colonic irrigation (for that stuffed up feeling – I used to think colonic irrigation was to do with a dam on the Zambezi – ah, youth! youth!), and birching in the sauna are available here, but not on the National Health. Closed at weekends.

The French Connection, 36 Store Street, WC1 (01-637 8179). Even the two-girl, topless, VIP treatment is not the ultimate here. Inquire for further details.

Finland House Club, 56 Haymarket, SW1 (01-839 5400). Altogether rather classy with many sophisticated additions to the regular range. In the next edition I'll tell you about my experiences in your actual Finnish sauna. In your actual Finland.

The saunas at the *Green Park* and *Clarendon Court Hotels* are perfectly respectable (as indeed are most hotel saunas in London).

Best sauna/massage: *Finland House Club.*
Worst sauna/massage: establishments in the neighbourhood *of Euston Station.*

Schools

This is serious business. All I can do is pass on recommendations for six state and six private schools, about which I have heard or at which I have observed only good. I should welcome more comments, especially about schools in tougher areas of the capital.

State
Fitzjohn's Primary, 86 Fitzjohn's Avenue, NW3. 01-435 9797.
Fleet Primary, Agincourt Road, NW3. 01-485 2028.
Fox School, Kensington Place, W8. 01-727 7637.
John Ruskin Primary, John Ruskin Street, SE5. 01-703 5800.
Pimlico School (comprehensive), Lupus Street, SW1. 01-828 0881.
White Lion Street Free School, 57 White Lion Street, N1. 01-837 6379.

Private
Arnold House, 3 Loudoun Road, NW8. 01-286 1100.
The Hall School, Crossfield Road, NW3. 01-722 1700.
The Mall School, Hampton Road, Twickenham, Middlesex. 01-977 2523.
St Paul's Boys School, Lonsdale Road, SW13. 01-748 9162.
St Paul's Girls School, Brook Green, W6. 01-603 2288.
Westminster School, Dean's Yard, SW1. (various numbers).

The London school with the highest recorded lead pollution level is *Telferscot Primary* (Telferscot Road, SW12) in Balham; *St. Bernadette Primary* (4 Atkins Road, SW12; 01-673 2061) has the lowest.

Sermons

Father Charles-Roux of *St Etheldreda's* Roman Catholic Church gives the best damn sermons in London. An ex-diplomat, he is wise in the ways of the world and his jokes reflect this. Nor is he the only reason for visiting *St Etheldreda's*, for some of the best music may be heard at this 12th century church of the Bishops of Ely, whether it be Mozart or seldom heard Victorian masses.

Philip Boss preaches 'intelligent and enthusiastic and simple' sermons at *Christ Church*, Fulham. At *Farm Street Church* (114 Mount Street, W1) they take their sermons seriously and, at the *Liberal Jewish Synagogue* (q.v.) the sermons by Rabbis Rayner and Goldberg should be listened to attentively, for they are pertinent and hard-hitting.

Best sermons: *Father Charles-Roux.*

Sex shops

According to the Williams Report the statistics for sex crimes in Britain have remained remarkably stable since we became 'permissive' – not that London, compared with most European capitals, is 'permissive' at all. The Williams Committee suggested that such outlets as sex shops do serve a valuable social function, but the squalor of these places is endlessly disheartening. The coin-in-the-slot movie shows are gloomy beyond belief and the cubicles smell like monkey houses. Avoid them.

Hereunder are some of London's less unpleasant sex-shops:

Doc Johnson's (Coventry Street, W1 and branches). An American chain with transatlantic sex aids featured. Nancy Reagan and Margaret Thatcher dolls not yet on sale.

Harmony Time (Wardour Street, W1 and branches). Modern and brightly lit which make the dildoes etc look all the less enticing.

Lovecraft (Coventry Street, W1 and branches). Wide-ranging stock and clean.

Janus Books (Greens Court, W1 and branches) specialise in spanking, domination and bondage. Cheeky.

Josephine (New King's Road, by Putney Bridge). Old-fashioned lingerie, pin-up magazines of the 40s and 50s. Seven minutes of American porn for 50p – not worth it.

Ann Summers (Marble Arch, W1 and branches). More civilised than the competition. Stocks well displayed. Take credit cards. Keep it up, Ann.

Newport Sex Shop (Little Newport Street, WC2). Tiny. Scarcely room to swing a . . .

Private Shops (numerous branches throughout the suburbs and elsewhere). The fastest growing sex-shop operation with the main emphasis on video-hire and magazines. Overpriced, even at sale time, which is most of the time.

To recommend any shop in this list would imply that they have anything truly erotic to sell, which they seldom have. Beware of anything shrink-wrapped. Demand to see some footage of any film or video before buying. Most tourists face a sad disappointment when they return to the solitude of their hotel room. Still, as Woody Allen memorably said, masturbation is having sex with someone you love.

Best sex shop: *Ann Summers.*

PS As I write, legislation that sex shops should be licensed is being effected. Many will not survive.

Ships

The Cutty Sark, a tea-clipper of the 1860s, preserved in dry dock at King William Walk, Greenwich, was built to the highest specifications and is one of the most beautiful ships ever created. Her collection of figureheads is worth a study. Nearby too is Sir Francis Chichester's *Gipsy Moth IV*, looking frail. Other fine ships include the cruiser, *HMS Belfast*, commissioned in 1939. She it was which opened the bombardment of the Normandy Coast on D Day, and she may be seen at Symon's Wharf, Wine Lane, Tooley Street, SE1.

The Tate and Lyle Sugar Ship, moored at Woolwich, is a beauty. Captain Scott's *Discovery*, presently in St Katherine's Docks Ships Museum, is fascinating, and other fine maritime survivals may be seen there and at the National Maritime Museum in Greenwich.

Best ship: *The Cutty Sark.*

Shirts

If one demands to have one's shirts made-to-measure, a great luxury, then *Harvie & Hudson* (77 Jermyn Street SW1; 01-930 3949), classic shirt makers, or *Hilditch & Key*, almost next door at 73 Jermyn Street (01-930 5336), or *Turnbull & Asser* at 71/72 Jermyn Street; (01-930 0502), gently trendy, may be relied upon to pamper and flatter and cosset. As a general rule any establishment in Jermyn Street whose name includes an ampersand will be All Right.

For a bespoke shirt visit *John Langford* (23 Woodfield Road, W9; 01-289 0066) or the elegant *Deborah & Clare* (14b Beauchamp Place, SW3; 01-584 0641) or the *Sale Shop* (2 St Barnabas Street, SW1; 01-730 5913 and 5 Park Walk, SW10) whose traditional shirts are sold at better than traditional prices. *Ted Lapidus* (164 New Bond Street, W1; 01-629 2323) has such beautiful clothes that he can afford to be surly. Also recommended are *Crolla* and *Paul Smith* (see also under Tailors).

Best shirts: *Turnbull & Asser.*
Worst shirts: *nylon ones which cling.*

Shoe Shops

In shoes more than in anything else – except possibly life insurance and coffins – you get what you pay for. If you buy your shoes at the Oxford Street chain stores or their high street branches, you won't of course, get originals, nor shoes in half sizes. *Lilley and Skinner's* (various branches) do specialise in smaller or larger than average feet, so give them a try. But even smaller (sizes 13-3 for women) and larger (women's sizes 8-11) feet can be accommodated at *Sally Small* (71 York Street, W1; 01-723 5321) who will also send shoes on approval and at *Crispins* which has two branches in Chiltern Street, W1, and also caters for narrow feet (AA & AAA). Women who are able to pay for original shoes might try *Clive Shilton*, where leather is stocked in 800 colours, or *Manolo Blahnik* (49-51 Old Church Street, SW3; 01-352 8622) who makes the most beautiful shoes in London. Très glam (as they used to say in bad American musicals) are the shoes there and at *Santini e Dominici* – well, the name hardly suggests slipper socks, does it? – at 14 and 16 South Molton Street, W1 (01-629 9617). But for classic women's shoes try either *H. & M. Rayne Ltd* (57 Brompton Road, SW3; 01-589 5560 and branches) or *Charles Jourdan* (39 Brompton Road, SW3; 01-581 3333). Since the two shops are adjacent it's possible to test your purchases by walking from one to the other.

Men with small feet (from size 5) are catered for at *William Timpson* (424 Brixton Road, SW9; 01-274 4735 and branches) and handmade, handsewn shoes may be ordered from *H. Maxwell & Co Ltd* (11 Savile Row, W1; 01-734 9714). According to John

Taylor, who ought to know, the best shoemaker in London is *G. J. Cleverley*, who made shoes for Valentino in 'Blood and Sand'. Does he still make shoes? Ring him up (01-530 4797) and ask. Awkward feet are fitted and difficult repairs undertaken at *Gohills Footwear* (246 Camden High Street, NW1; 01-485 9195), but for fine Italian shoes in traditional or flamboyant colours, *Fillirosetti* (177 New Bond Street, W1; 01-491 7066) is the place. Then of course there's *Kickers* (331 Kings Road, SW3; 01-352 7541), whose boots are cheerful and durable.

If I were rich, which I shall be if you buy enough copies of this book, I should get my shoes at *Lobb's* (9 St James's Street, SW1; 01-930 3664), which, besides being one of the handsomest shops in London and having cut shoes for Queen Victoria, makes a wooden last for each customer's foot and cuts and sews each piece of leather by hand. They do everything except milk the cow. Allow six months.

For children's shoes you should go to *Johnson's* (37-39 King's Parade, Twickenham, Middlesex; 01-892 9012, and branches in west London). Nothing is too much trouble for them and time seems limitless even for sneakers. High fashion children's shoes come from *Instep* (118 New Oxford Street, WC1; 01-637 7594). Continuous cartoons are played and the shoes are on specially low stands. *The Children's Foot Health Register* (84-88 Great Eastern Street, EC2; 01-739 2071) will help with all queries.

Best shoes: (women) *Manolo Blahnik*.
Best shoes: (men) *Lobb's*.
Best shoes: (children's) *Johnson's*.

Shop Fronts

The most famous shop front in London is *James Smith and Sons*, 53 New Oxford Street, WC1 (01-836 4731). With wrought-iron above and sensationally good Gothic lettering everywhere, it seems churlish not to buy an umbrella or a shooting stick. Architecturally the most interesting is a Huguenot (c 1757) shop front with a fine double bow-window at *56 Artillery Lane*, Stepney (next to E. Patston and Son, scale makers) but *Berry Bros & Rudd* in St James's, that street of excellent shop fronts, is perfect 18th century. Nothing is more charming than *Woburn Walk* in Bloomsbury, where in 1822 Thomas Cubitt created a small shopping precinct, which has fortunately been preserved. For restrained good taste I recommend *Purdey & Son*, the gun makers, in South Audley Street, W1, while *Gucci* in Bond Street and *Andrew Grima* in Jermyn Street are brilliant modern designs. I don't know which is more vulgar, *Denisa* (with a coronet over the D), the Lady Newborough, who spreads over several shop fronts in White Horse Street, W1, or *Jones* in Beauchamp Place, whose name is proclaimed in a kind of cable-knit script on a red marbled ground. At 46 South Molton Street, a street of restrained opulence, is *Widow Applebaum's*, a deli of such exuberant crudity that one can only warm to it.

Other recommendations: *Penhaligons*, parfumiers of Covent Garden; *John Martin*, wine merchants of Eastcheap; *J. Wippell and Company*, haberdashers of Tufton Street, W1; and the minuscule but delightful headquarters of *Twinings*, tea merchants, in the Strand.

Quite the worst is *McDonalds* with their hideous logo. The trouble is there are so many branches; quite takes the appetite away. And *Kentucky Fried Chicken* is not much better. *Conduit Office Supplies* present a hardboard fascia to Conduit Street, which is lowering for Mayfair. Oh dear.

Best shop front: *Berry Bros & Rudd*, St James's.
Worst shop front: *McDonalds Hamburgers*.

Shove Halfpenny

The shove halfpenny championships of the world are held at the *Heroes of Alma Pub* (11 Alma Square, NW8; 01-286 3195). It should be added that this is emphatically not a spectator sport, and as yet the tobacco firms have not moved in as sponsors.

The Old Nun's Head (15 Nunhead Green, SE15; 01-639 1745) runs several teams of shovers, and at the *Rose and Crown* (47 Colombo Street, SE1; 01-928 4285), a lively family pub, halfpennies are shoved with great élan.

Signposts

Pleasantly old-fashioned signposts, some with pointing fingers, can be found in and around *Dulwich Village* and in the *Brent* area of north west London. The most poignant signpost is the one at *Streatham Vale*, SW16. It combines two signs on a single post. One

170

says 'Lonesome Depot', the other 'South London Crematorium'. In *Hoe Street*, E17, there is a large and fierce sign reading: 'HALT Beware of Pedestrians'. It's as bad as being told to beware of low flying aircraft or, in France, of beetroots. The coyest sign is in the *Bayswater Road* – No 123 – where it announces: 'Decency Forbids – Lavatory Opposite'.

The best signpost in London – well, in the world really – is the one which announces the Prime Meridian of the World (Latitude 51°28′ 38″ North, Longitude 0°00′00″); this, of course, is at the *Royal Observatory* in Greenwich.

The most ineffective signpost in London is the one in *Trafalgar Square* which announces that the west side of the square is open only to buses and taxis. Hardly anyone sees it, and many of those who do, fail to understand it.

Best signpost: *The Prime Meridian*, Greenwich.

Skating

For a country which continues to produce such fine skaters, there are surprisingly few rinks. In London I can recommend the *Richmond* rink (Clevedon Road, East Twickenham; 01-892 3646), *Queens* (Queensway, W2; 01-229 0172), the *Sobell Leisure Centre* (Hornsey Road, N7; 01-607 1632) and *Streatham* (386 Streatham High Road, SW16; 01-769 7861), though this can get rowdy.

Old-fashioned it may be, but *Richmond* still has the best reputation.

Best rink: *Richmond.*

Snacks

See under Budget Restaurants, Fish and Chips, Take Away Food etc.

Solicitors

Amongst the best:

Ashurst, Morris, Crisp & Co. 7 Throgmorton Ave, EC2; 01-283 1070.
Dawson & Co. 2 New Square, WC2; 01-404 5941.

Charles Doughty (civilised divorces). 20 Essex Street, WC2; 01-836 8400.

Harbottle & Lewis (theatrical). 34 South Molton Street, W1; 01-629 9871.

Hicks, Arnold, Rose, Johnson. 6 Exchange Court, WC2; 01-836 4234.

Kennedy, Ponsonby & Prideaux. 46 Cannon Street, EC4; 01-248 4741.

Lovell, White & King. 21 Holborn Viaduct, EC1; 01-236 6011.

Rubinstein Callingham (literary). 6 Raymond Buildings, Gray's Inn, WC1; 01-242 8404.

Spanish Restaurants

Not much competition here. The choice lies between the old established *Martinez Restaurant* (25 Swallow Street, W1; 01-734 5066) and the more up-to-date *Dulcinea* (29 Ebury Street, SW1; 01-730 4094). I prefer the latter. The decor is creamy and seductive and, if you need music, then the Aranjo Guitar Concerto is preferable to Manuel and his Music of the Mountains. My table d'hôte – excellent value at £7.50 – entitled me to choose from consommé regional (cherry and almond soup), tortilla, or mussels in cream, followed by monkfish, veal or chicken, and oranges in caramel or blackcurrant cassis. The spices were tactfully chosen, almost bland, and although the tortilla was a disappointment, the fried courgettes were the best I have ever eaten. There was an interesting choice of wines with a selection from eight half-bottles. It is rare these days for half-bottle men to receive much encouragement from wine-waiters, but as I was dining alone, I was grateful. If you don't care for garlic, give the *Dulcinea* a miss. Otherwise you should be well pleased.

The *Martinez* has its hand-painted tiles and its choice of excellent Riojas to recommend it.

Best Spanish restaurant: *Dulcinea.*

Squares

There is a popular misconception that *Bedford Square* is the last *complete* Georgian Square in London. Well, it isn't. It is the last complete *early* Georgian Square in London, but the unheralded and unsung *Wilmington Square* in Finsbury is uniform and complete and dates from the early 19th century. Other little known delights from that period include *Cleaver Square* in Kennington, *Canonbury Square* (J. Leroux), *Trinity Church Square*, SE1, and *Cloudesley Square* (church by Barry); while off the Commercial Road in Stepney, *Albert Gardens* is a regular three-sided square of early 19th-century houses, unpretentious and charming. Indeed there are plenty of good old squares to choose from, as the actress said looking down from the gallery of the House of Commons.

Initially the squares were built by aristocrats and their agents, latterly by speculators who sometimes were, shamefully, aristocrats. The earliest (*Bloomsbury Square* and *St James's Square*) were planned before the Great Fire (1666) but most of the square-building took place in the century after the ashes stopped smouldering. The names of the speculators, Bond and Clarges, Frith and Neale, Panton and others, are familiar to us from street names. Nicholas Barbon, who laid out £200,000 in building costs but economised by standardising the designs, was for a time the most successful, but he was a hard bargainer and when he died I'm sorry to say that his will stipulated that none of his enormous debts should be paid. Typical Barbon houses may be studied in Bedford Row.

Sadly much of what the 19th-century speculators put up, the 20th-century speculators pulled down. Whatever happened to *Portman, Tolmer, Grosvenor, Sloane, Tavistock, Berkeley* or *Audley Squares*? In *Union Square* the square-bashers left half of the square intact to display most eloquently the mess they had made of the other half. Occasionally the squares were unpleasant from the start, and *Milner Square* is very strange. In the words of the great Sir John Summerson: 'It is possible to visit Milner Square many times and still not be absolutely certain that you have seen it anywhere but in an unhappy dream.'

For myself I like *Lincoln's Inn Fields* and *Old Palace Yard*, Westminster hugely, but they are not what one means by a London square. While *Golden Yard*, Hampstead (tiny, Elizabeth Gouge-ish), *Percy Circus* (crazily planned at an angle of 35° from the edge of Lonsdale Square), and *Smith Square* (Headquarters of the Conservative party and a dignified setting for the prettiest concert hall in London), deserve to be mentioned, my choice will be *Manchester Square* (1776-1788) because, although dominated by Hertford House, the home of the Wallace Collection, and otherwise little regarded by the architectural historians, it is green and pleasant, and less disturbed by traffic fumes than many of the grander squares. Runners-up include *Dorset Square, Bedford Square* (inevitably), *St James's Square* (very fine, excellent to park in, with an enchanting vista of the Haymarket Theatre), *Mecklenburgh Square* (J. Kay, 1812), *Kensington Square, Lonsdale Square* and *Paulton's Square*.

Disasters include, besides those named above, *Leicester Square* and *Finsbury Circus*.

Best London square: *Manchester Square.*
Worst London square: *Leicester Square.*

Stamps

The cutest stamp shop must be the one on Waterloo Station with this endearingly candid notice: 'My entire stock is in the window'. Stamp dealers may be found in improbable places, such as *Cranbourn Street*, WC2, *Tooting Bec* (Mr Stockman, a most suitable name, at No 55 Trinity Road), and the *Upper Richmond Road* (Phil's Stamp Shop is at No 370). At the latter I have always received a very fair hearing; I say 'hearing' advisedly, for it is very unusual for a stamp shop actually to *want* to buy stamps from a customer.

Most London stamp shops are in and around the *Strand*, clustering around the formidable *Stanley Gibbons*, like poor relatives around a famous man. At *Stanley Gibbons* one expert on Rhodesia told me that my £5 Rhodesia stamp of 1903 was a real treasure and that the last one they had like it had been sold privately for £900, but at the end of the week his colleague dismissed the 'treasure' to me as an 'obvious fake'. Try to sell stamps at the *Strand Stamp Centre* opposite *Stanley Gibbons*, and they look at you much as if you'd asked whether Edward VIII should abdicate over Mrs Simpson. The conglomerate of collectors opposite the Embankment tube station and under the arches at Charing Cross are more accommodating.

It can all be most frustrating. I invited *Robson Lowe's* comments on a hand-stamp from the first Paris Commune. They had never seen anything like it, they said, and photocopied it, sending the original to their agent in Paris. He had never seen anything like it either, and *Robson Lowe* (50 Pall Mall, SW1; 01-839 4034) concluded that its very uniqueness rendered it, so far as they could tell, valueless. The politest of all brush-offs come from *Eric*

Etkin Ltd (55 New Bond Street, W1; 01-499 1781 – more or less next door to *Harmer's*). There ever so charmingly they begin by saying: 'You're going to hate us after we've told you our view of your stamps . . .' But the last time they said that I sold the same stamps by public auction for £470.

Phillips (17 Blenheim Street, W1; 01-629 6602) auction stamps most Thursdays. *Harmer's* and *Stanley Gibbons* more infrequently. *The City of London Bishopsgate Auctions* (170 Bishopsgate, EC2; 01-283 7968) hold fortnightly lunch-time sales, which are principally for City businessmen. They are extremely jolly, but like to be paid in cash.

The National Philatelic Society is at 1 Whitehall Place, SW1 (01-839 1987) and the *Royal Philatelic Society*, unparallelled for solemn elegance, is at 41 Devonshire Place, W1 (01-935 7332). A certificate of authentication from the RPS is as eagerly sought after as a safe conduct out of hell, but their consultations are very slow. The finest stamp collection in the country is in the Stamp Room at *Buckingham Palace*. No problem about getting in to see that. Just shin up a drainpipe . . .

The *Penny Black* public house (Tentor House, Moorfields, Moorgate, EC2; 01-628 3675) is a philatelists' pub and has a large exhibition of photostats from the GPO Museum, while the *Mayflower* pub in Rotherhithe St, SE16, is the only pub in the world licensed to sell postage stamps.

Best stamp dealer: *The GPO.*
Best for accessories: *Harris Publications* (42 Maiden Lane, WC2; 01-240 2286).

Stationers

At *Pen to Paper* (11 Long Acre, WC2; 01-379 6560) I bought 500 sheets of good quality weave – A4 in a tasteful shade of mauve – and set about trying to find a printers or stationers who would print my name and address at the top of it in a type of my choosing. The price quoted by commercial printers was close on £50. Obviously too extravagant. *W. H. Smith* said they *would* have done it, and quoted a sensible price, only it was the firm's policy never to print on somebody else's paper. In the end I was reduced to having a rubber stamp made (£8). A bit non-U, déclassé, arriviste and naff.

Despite strong recommendations for *Scribner's* (29 James

Street, WC2; 01-240 7640) with contemporary importations from France and the USA, *Smythson* (54 New Bond Street, W1; 01-629 8558), *Chisholm's* (four branches), where you can buy the Filofax system, without which governments fall and worlds collide, and the *Walton Street Stationery Co* (97 Walton Street, SW3; 01-589 0777), which is so seductive that it almost makes you *want* to pay bills, the verdict lies between *Paperchase* (213 Tottenham Court Road, W1; 01-580 8496 and a Fulham Road branch), to be avoided at Christmas, and *Lamley and Co* (5 Exhibition Road, SW7; 01-589 1276), a somewhat haphazard stationer and bookseller, whose leisurely concern for the customer is welcome.

The best specialist paper retailers is *Falkiners Fine Papers* (117 Long Acre, WC2; 01-379 6245) with a range of over 1,000 papers and such accessories as gold leaf and calligraphy supplies. At *Cass* (various branches) you can buy nice quality paper and envelopes *by weight*; an eminently sensible policy.

Best stationer: *Lamley and Co*.

PS Would it not be agreeable if you could buy stamps wherever you buy envelopes and postcards?

Statues/Sculptures

> Queen Victoria's
> statue is
> the work of her
> daughter Beatrice.
> The shape's all wrong,
> And the crown don't fit,
> but – bless her old heart!
> She was proud of it – Humbert Wolfe (1885-1940)

There are nine statues of *Queen Victoria* in London and five of *Shakespeare* – a most undistinguished selection for our greatest poet and playwright. Until recently there were two statues of *Pocahontas*. One of them, opposite Cassell's in Red Lion Square, was naked and would have turned the head of a less susceptible man than Captain Smith. But the rotters took it away.

On the subject of nakedness, Canova's *Napoleon* in Apsley House is nine feet tall in white marble and naked except for his marshall's baton and victorious fillet. Outside on Hyde Park Corner and on an even grander scale is Sir Richard Westmacott's 30-feet-high nude of *Achilles* (1822), cast from French 24-

pounders captured at Salamanca, Vittoria, Toulouse and Waterloo. The statue was subscribed for by the gentlewomen of England in honour of the Iron Duke. They were more than a little alarmed when they saw what their money had got them. Even Achilles's fig-leaf (he is not really Achilles, but the sculptor had to call him something) was scarcely enough to pacify their beating hearts. It may be that some of the gentlemen of England found him provocative too, for his fig-leaf was chipped off in 1871 and 1961, the present one having survived for over twenty years.

Also on Hyde Park Corner is *King David*, representing the artillery; he is said to have a most fetching bottom, and since the traffic passes close by this, numerous accidents are caused to and by drivers of a certain persuasion. *Sir Arthur Sullivan* has a naked lady weeping at his ankles – successful composers get these – together with a misspelled quotation from 'The Yeomen of the Guard', but the most erotic nude statue in London is *La Déliverance* by Emile Guillaume. It may be seen at the junction of Finchley Road and the North Circular. A naked girl, symbolising the emotions felt by the allies at the conclusion of the battle of the Marne (1914), stands on tip-toe on a globe with a sword upraised. Someone with a sense of humour chose Lloyd George to do the unveiling.

Many of London's finest statues are grouped together in Victoria Embankment Gardens, Leicester Square and Waterloo Place. In the first named, besides *Sir Arthur Sullivan*, you may find a charming memorial by Major Cecil Brown to the *Camel Corps* (1920). It's a camel, and there's another camel at the foot of the *Albert Memorial*. Also a fine bronze of *Robert Burns* sitting on a tree trunk and composing poetry (Sir John Steell), and statues to an advocate of temperance, the founder of the Sunday Schools, and others. A wall fountain to *Henry Fawcett* (no pun intended, one supposes), the blind statesman, refreshes.

Leicester Square, once a duelling ground and now a pedestrian precinct, offers statues of *Shakespeare, Reynolds, Hogarth* and *John Hunter*, the founder of modern surgery; also a sentimental figure of *Charlie Chaplin* by John Doubleday (1981), and a most inadequate memorial to *Sir Isaac Newton*.

In Waterloo Place, besides the National Memorial to Edward VII and various military men, *Captain Scott* may be observed sculpted by his wife in antarctic kit (he wears it; I doubt whether his wife when she sculpted him did), and *Florence Nightingale* next to her friend and victim, *Sidney Herbert*. A less formal *Florence Nightingale* is on the North Terrace of St Thomas's Hospital. She wears a cap and frilled cuffs and carries a lamp, but she is only a replica, for the original was stolen by thieves. Also at Thomas's a delightful bronze of *Edward VI*, 'a most excellent prince of exemplary piety, and wisdom above his years. The glory of his reign and most magnificent founder of this hospital'. Another king well served by his sculptor is *Charles I*. Hidden during the Civil War, the statue of him which now stands at the top of Whitehall is simple, dignified and venerable.

In Kensington Gardens may be found two of London's most loved statues, *Physical Energy* by G. F. Watts (1906) and *Peter Pan* by George Frampton. The *Peter Pan* tableau, which derives from Barrie's *The Little White Bird*, which he set in Kensington Gardens, includes mice and rabbits and fairies and such, and has been polished smooth by generations of posh children playing on it. The actress Nina Boucicault modelled for Peter. Just along the road at Bowater House, the main entrance to the Park, is a group which is circumvented by a vast tonnage of traffic every day. This is Epstein's work; some know it as *Pan*, others as *The Family of Man*. A mother and father, two children and an excited dog, are permanently frozen as they run towards the trees. Close on their heels and playing his pipes is the untrustworthy figure of Pan (not Peter).

London contains several *boys on dolphins*, easily the most attractive being the one by David Wynne on the corner of Victoria Embankment and Oakley Street. The boy is airborne but keeps hold of the dolphin's fin with the tips of his fingers. David Wynne was also responsible for a *girl on a dolphin* (in front of the Tower Hotel, St Katharine's Way), and the grandiose figure of *Guy the Gorilla* at London Zoo, the same Guy who died in 1978 at the age of 32 and is still mourned.

The oldest statues in London are the marble sculptures found in the *Temple of Mithras*, Walbrook, and presently to be seen in the London Museum. *King Alfred* in handsome Trinity Church Square, SE1 (formerly in Westminster Hall) is thought to date back to the 14th century. He looks wise but worried, perhaps because nobody is sure whether he *is* King Alfred.

The best statue of *Churchill* (Ivor Roberts-Jones 1973) is in Parliament Square. Impressive and business-like, this Churchill is striding off the plinth as though he cannot wait to get back into the debating chamber and at the throats of the mining MPs. Together with *Freud* (near the Swiss Cottage Library), *Gandhi* (in Tavistock Square), and *Sir Thomas More* (handsomely represented on the Embankment outside Chelsea Old Church) he has not been diminished by his statue.

Although I'm fond of Barbara Hepworth's *Winged Victory* excitingly placed on the wall of John Lewis's at Oxford Circus, and of the charming lady shoppers outside Jeeves in Pont Street (black cement by Derek Holmes/Kate McGill) who are obviously hell-bent on a cup of tea and a Kunzle cake in Harrods, the award must rest between Henry Moore's *Draped Seated Woman* on the Stifford Estate, Jamaica Road, SE1 and Epstein's bronze *Madonna and Child* (inspired, I believe, by Michelangelo) on what was once the Convent of the Hold Child, Cavendish Square. This piece he called his 'passport to eternity', but both the Moore and the Epstein are deeply serious and unforgettable. For an expert analysis see *London Statues* by Arthur Byron (Constable).

Best statues: *Draped Seated Woman* by Henry Moore; *Madonna and Child* by Jacob Epstein.

Most inadequate statues: *Sir Isaac Newton; Dr Johnson* (behind St Clement Dane's).

Steak

Curiously difficult to get a decent steak in London. The chains of steak restaurants – *The Aberdeen Steak Houses, The Garner Steak Houses, The Berni Inns* and such – do a job. The first named do it best. Then there are the hamburger (q.v.) joints. Of these *Clouds* (6 Kingston Hill, Kingston, Surrey; 01-546 0559), the *Hard Rock Cafe** and *Benson's** do a fair steak. *C. J. Kane's* (3 Campden Hill Rd, W8; 01-938 1830) is a pleasant American-style establishment, which means of course that you can get a twelve-ounce steak there. *Surprise* (12 Gt Marlborough St, W1; 01-434 2666) is a good deal grander and has a lavish array of salads to complement the steaks. *Chateaubriand* (48 Belsize Lane, NW3; 01-435 4882) specialises in fillet steak, and does it very well. But the best bet is *Le Steak Nicole* (72 Wilton Road, SW1; 01-834 7301) which – the name is a heavy hint – is not American at all but French. Good steaks, good salads, reasonable prices – if you need good red meat when the moon is full, you could do worse. Another French place, the pretty *Cafe Jardin* (10 Lancashire Court, 122/123 New Bond Street, W1; 01-493 2896) serves a steak in herbs with salad and chips for £6.95 including VAT.

Best steak: *Le Steak Nicole*.

*For addresses see under Hamburgers.

Steps/Staircases

The grandeur of the steps leading up to the *Albert Memorial* (designed by Sir Gilbert Scott for £120,000 which Albert would have considered excessive) represents the optimism of an age which could afford to be expansive. *The Duke of York Steps* which descend from Waterloo Place to the Mall and St James's Park are much loved. They form a matching set with the *Duke of York's Column* (Benjamin Wyatt, 1833) – steps should lead to something *high* – which marks the site of Carlton House, built by John Nash between 1827 and 1832 for Crockford, the fishmonger turned bookmaker who wished to put Buckingham Palace in the shade, and did. From these steps one has a fine view over the park to Big Ben, the House of Commons and numerous high-rise blocks, and having climbed the steps, one can enjoy the statues before relaxing for a refreshing cup of tea at the Ceylon Tea Centre in Lower Regent Street. I'm also delighted by *Holly Bush Steps*, which descend into Heath Street from Holly Bush Hill in Hampstead. They are charming, but the steps leading up to *St Bride's Institute*, just off Fleet Street, are gloomily impressive. Best for sitting on are the steps at the *National Gallery* and the *Tate* (but the *Metropolitan Museum* steps in New York are the *very* best for sitting on).

Dirty, windy and bleak are the steps at *Bromley South Shopping Precinct*. Even worse are the steps at most multi-storey carparks. Disastrous are the steps at *Waterloo Station*. Exhausting are the steps up to the *Monument*.

There are fine staircases everywhere in London. The *Tulip Staircase* at Queen's House, Greenwich; Wyatt and Barry's *Grand Staircase* at Lancaster House, St James's which uses the full height of the building; the magnificent Cromwellian staircase in the finest oak at *Cromwell House*, Highgate; the staircase of exceptional splendour at 44 *Berkeley Square*; the fine iron staircase (c 1700) at *37 Stepney Green*; the elliptical staircase (1810) in 7 *Albemarle Street*; the painted staircase (1720) of 8 *Clifford Street*, W1, and the fine mid 18th-century staircase in the *Skinners' Hall* (8 Dowgate Hill, EC4); represent everything that staircases are about. An unusual open-air staircase is the one in the Italian manner starting up the side of the threatened Broad Street Station. I could continue. But space requires me to choose . . .

Best staircase: *Cromwell House*, Highgate.
Best steps: *Waterloo Place*.

Stores

There is a rumour, possibly apocryphal, that there is a lady living just two blocks from *Harrods* to whom a single small carton of yoghurt is delivered every morning – free of delivery charge, of course. Certainly *Harrods* (motto: 'Omnia, Omnibus, Ubique' – 'All things to all people everywhere') is the best place for changing unwanted Christmas presents and they will even take back sales goods, which very few other stores will do. One can even haggle at *Harrods* and then demand a further reduction by paying cash. If you have an account at *Harrods*, you are permitted to reserve sale goods on the day before the sales open to the public. I have found it a useful rule of thumb to patronise sales only at high class stores since the substantial discounts offered on classic goods constitute real bargains, where rubbish remains rubbish no matter how cheap it may have been.

Of course *Harrods* is not the only London store. *Liberty's* in Regent Street is splendid for walking through and – inevitably – getting lost in. The only vulgar goods I have ever seen in *Liberty's* were those leather rhinos. *John Lewis* and the various stores linked to the partnership pride themselves on never being knowingly undersold; they are strongest in textiles and furnishing fabrics; however they do not accept credit cards. *Harvey Nichols* are old-fashioned but courteous, while *Fortnum and Masons*, whose salesmen wear tailcoats, is not so much a shop more a trip to the moon on gossamer wings. *Heal's* in Tottenham Court Road is spacious and county and at Christmastime on the ground floor young musicians from the Royal Academy of Music play to you while you spend money you haven't got on presents you don't particularly like for people you never see. *Heal's* is strongest in bedding, lighting and art.

At *Marks & Spencers* the clothes are slightly old fashioned, as they have to be when such huge quantities are involved, but they are excellent value. There is never any unpleasantness about taking unsatisfactory purchases back; if you are unprincipled you can get cash back for goods which you have purchased by cheque; a useful standby in times of crisis. Once when I had wrecked a corkscrew trying to decork a bottle of wine bought at M & S, they gave me a replacement bottle of wine *and* a pound to buy a new corkscrew with. *Woolworths* is not to be derided. The counters loaded with sticky sweets are *not* an inspiring sight on Monday mornings, but for goods such as watering cans, giant boxes of matches, light bulbs etc you can travel a lot further and pay a lot more.

Probably the best of the old-fashioned family stores is *Barbers* in the North End Road, Fulham; a splendid place particularly for Christmas presents. I have also heard good reports of *Ely's* of Wimbledon (for courtesy), *Bentall's* of Kingston, and the *Pantheon* in Oxford Street. This is the exception, because for most of its length Oxford Street is a shopping disaster area. *Selfridges*, which used to be such an Aladdin's cave of delights has become a giant's dungeon of despair. Only Miss Selfridge and the kosher food department redeem the place, but these departments are splendid.

Of all the stores which London has recently lost I mourn *Whiteley's* most; without it the Queensway and Westbourne Grove area lacks dignity and seriousness of purpose.

Best store: *Harrods.*

Street Lights

Many of the early gas-holders are magnificent. Look, for example, at the bold lamps, guarded by winged dragons, on *Holborn Viaduct*. Almost anything may hold or guard a lamp. Serpents do it (*1 Wimpole Street*, W1; *193 Euston Road*, NW1; *23 Queens Square*, Isleworth), winged mermen do it (*15 Harrington Road*, SW7), Atlas does it on holiday from carrying the world (*18 Finsbury Square*, EC2), a Viking ship does it (the Norwegian Church, *Albion Street*, SE16), and even an owl does it sleepily and slyly (the Bank of England).

Most impressive are the ironwork lamp-holders (c 1750-1760) by Isaac Ware outside 44 *Berkeley Square*; most dignified are those along the north face of *Drury Lane Theatre* (the only original section remaining); most delightful are the cluster of converted gas lamps opposite the *Garrick Theatre*. Covent Garden is the area for hunters of old gas-lamp-holders; there are several in *St Martin's Court*.

London bridges are particularly well lit. From the frivolous clusters on *Putney Bridge* to the outrageous nautical nonsenses on *Lambeth Bridge*, from the solemn dignity of *Westminster Bridge* and *Tower Bridge* to the cheerful silliness of the lighting on *Hammersmith Bridge*, all enhance their function.

After the advent of electricity designers of street lamps were able to direct the light source downwards, but greater freedom did not necessarily mean that their designs were more imaginative. I seem to have seen the celebrated four-sided lantern in the *Strand* with 'Savoy Theatre' engraved on the glass in countless films of the forties and fifties. If Edgar Lustgarten didn't stand in front of it to deliver his homilies he ought to have done. In *Carting Lane* alongside the Savoy is another famous street lamp. Lit by gas, it is never extinguished.

The most elaborate of all and probably the most loved are those lamp standards along the *Thames Embankment*. Sir Joseph Bazalgette gave us twisting dolphins above lion masks along the *Victoria Embankment;* the *Chelsea Embankment* is even more elaborate with children clambering up the lions and fish bearing torches to light the lamps. In *Trafalgar Square*, close to Admiralty Arch, the lamp standards are encrusted with fat putty amidst a wild cluster of animal and marine life. But I think that despite the claims of these and of the fine lamps which illuminate the Nash terraces, the best street lights in London are those in *Lincoln's Inn Fields*. Have a look at them.

Best street lights: *Lincoln's Inn Fields.*
Worst street lights: *Cromwell Road Extension.* Though the lighting in Jermyn Street is an opportunity sadly wasted.

Street Markets

There have been three books on London street markets in recent years. Jeremy Cooper's *Guide to London Street Markets*, Alec Forshaw and Theo Bergstrom's *Markets of London* and Kevin Perlmutter's *London Street Markets*. The last named (published by Wildwood House), being the most comprehensive, is required reading for anyone seriously into the fascinating business of street marketeering. It lists some 150 markets (and even that is not the full complement).

Everybody must know by now that *Petticoat Lane* (Middlesex Street, E1) is more for tourists than for bargain hunters; not many antiques there, except the jokes told by the stall-holders. And keep your hands in your pockets. They used to say that you could walk through *Petticoat Lane*, and see your own handkerchief for sale on a stall by the time you got to the end. But V. S. Pritchett tells how at the old dog market in *Bethnal Green* you could buy your own beloved airedale painted black and offered as a retriever! While on the subject, the continuing market in lost and stolen animals, often kept in degrading conditions, at *Club Row*, E2, on Sunday mornings, is an outrage. So is *Southall Market*, the only weekly horse market in Britain. Most of the horses sold here (and many of them have been stolen) are bound for butchers' shops in France and Belgium.

For fruit, vegetable and junk, *Whitechapel* is good, but *Hoe Street Market*, Walthamstow, E17, is better; there's a mile of it. *Brick Lane*, E1, early on a Sunday morning is over-rated, although it's lively enough and almost the only place to go for plastic flowers. *Brixton* is excellent (cut price reggae music), and the *Lower Marsh Market* in the Cut, Waterloo Road, is delightfully eccentric. Professor Burchett, tattoo artist (his son now) has his premises at No 217; any design can be copied.

For antiques, *Bermondsey Market* (the New Caledonian, on Fridays) is among the cheapest, but you need to get there exceptionally early (about 4.30 a.m. in summer) and you'll not make it without private transport. Take a torch too or you'll regret it. *Portobello* (Saturdays) has a quarter of a million customers through its market; specialists can usually find their stall somewhere – and don't ignore the covered arcades, where most of the better quality items are to be found. I sold a Japanese print there for £25 that I couldn't get 50p for in my shop. *Cutler Street* (just off Petticoat Lane, Fridays to Sundays) is for silver, coins, medals and stamps; *Farringdon Road* (weekdays and Saturdays, lunch-time) is for books, but only about six stalls survive and it is a shadow of past glories. *Columbia Road Market* (Bethnal Green, Sunday mornings) is superb for gardeners, but they don't sell tools; these you should get at *Leather Lane* in the City (Monday to Friday 11 a.m. – 3 p.m.) or at *Franklin's Camberwell Market* (159/161 Camberwell Road, SE5 – closed Mondays) where Reuben Reubens, collector of banjos and dealer in toys may be found.

Camden Passage, Islington, is for good quality antiques with prices to match. Better value on Wednesdays (from 7.30 a.m.) than on Saturdays (from 9 a.m.). *Camden Lock* is too trendy for my taste, but it's useful if you want to discover the latest collecting craze (currently old linen). I sometimes have a stall at *Streatham Market* (not a street market because it's in a church hall between the ice rink and the bus station) on Thursday mornings (7 a.m. to 1 p.m.). It's principally for dealers, but the public can do well too – especially at my stall.

Best street market: (for food) *Berwick Street*, W1; (for antiques) *Bermondsey*.

Worst street market: *Club Row*.

Street Names

The street names of the City of London give a vivid picture – sometimes all too vivid – of what life must have been like in medieval London. Under Henry I's laws a 'street' had to be wide enough for two loaded carts to pass each other and for sixteen armed knights to ride abreast; a 'lane' had to be wide enough for a cask of wine to be rolled along it transversely with a man on either side – staggering probably.

Some of the more colourful names have not survived. There used to be a *Gropecuntelane* in St Pancras, and *Sherborne Lane*, EC4, used to be Shitebourne or Shiteburgh Lane, the place where the privy was to be found. *Pudding Lane*, where the Great Fire started, is not named after a homely pud, but after the bowels and entrails which the butchers of Eastcheap would cast into the Thames. (A *Cheap*, by the way, was a market.) *Addle Street*, EC2 derives from the Old English adela, meaning stinking urine or manure, while *Stinking Lane* was renamed King Edward Street in 1843. Could this have been the unamused Victoria's doing? Even the familiar *Houndsditch* was the trench into which dead dogs were thrown. But the trade is not entirely one way. *Spital Street*, E1, is a diminution of Hospital Street.

A study of London street names is endlessly fascinating. *Old Jewry*, EC2 was the area in which the Jews used to live before their expulsion in 1290. *Jewry Street*, EC3, used to be known as *Poor Jewry* – the change, it seems, was a conscious one! *Crutched Friars*, EC3, meant originally the friars of the Holy Cross, for 'crutch' or 'crouch' in Middle English meant 'cross', and *Bevis Marks*, EC3, which sounds so aristocratic, derives from a simple mistake, an 'R' being misread for a 'V', the name meaning the boundaries (marks) of the bury (abbey). *Threadneedle Street*, EC2, derives not from an inn sign nor from the arms of the needlemakers' company, but from the children's game of *threatneedle*, an early form of oranges and lemons. As for *Turnagain Lane*, that merely means a cul-de-sac. Much of the charm of the City of London would be lost if we were not constantly reminded of an earlier city in such street names as *Distaff Lane, Beer Lane, Bread Street, Milk*

Street, Ironmonger Lane, Honey Lane, Sugar Baker's Court, Old Fish Street and *Wood Street*. These need no explanation.

Moving beyond the square mile of the City of London, there are some delightful groups of names. In the Borough, for instance, we are deep in Dickens country, so we find *Pickwick Street, Marshalsea Road, Sawyer Street, Quilp Street, Dorrit Street, Weller Street, Doyce Street, Copperfield Street*, etc. These are some of the streets which Dickens used to tramp nightly in search of inspiration.

Down in the Surrey Docks things become romantic and piratical with *Dock Head, Muscovy Street, Cathay Street, Pickle Herring Street* and *Shad Thames*, while in Dulwich a whole area is named after that local benefactor, Edward Alleyn, and his thespian colleagues. The streets around Charing Cross used once to spell out in acrostic: 'George Villiers, Duke of Buckingham', but, alas, *Duke Street* is gone and *Of Alley* has changed its name.

Here at random are a few of my other favourites: *Perkin's Rents, Rabbit Row, Dog Kennel Hill, Electric Lane, Nevada Street*, SE10, *Bleeding Heart Yard, Edith Grove, Haunch of Venison Yard, Wapping High Street, Straightsmouth, de Crespigny Park, Frying Pan Alley, Crooked Usage*, and *Tranquil Vale*, Blackheath (anything but).

And some of the worst: *Coldbath Square*, EC1, *Glamis Way*, Northolt, *Industry Terrace*, SW9, *Tweezer's Alley, Little Plucketts Way*, Buckhurst Hill, *Freke Road, Ogle Street, Organ Lane, Thermopylae Gate*, E14, *Balls Pond Road* and *Quex Road*.

There are many excellent books on the subject: *Street Names of the City of London* by Eilert Ekwall (OUP 1965) is just one.

Best street name: *Amen Corner*.
Worst street name: *Roxy Avenue*, Romford.

PS Camden Council and the GLC have changed the name of Selous Street, NW1 (named after Henry Selous, a Victorian painter, but with unfortunate Rhodesian associations) to Nelson Mandela Street.

Streets

In spring the best street in London is *Vicarage Gate*, Kensington. The blossom is overwhelming in its pinkness. In autumn it's *Maida Avenue*, Little Venice. *Doughty Street* in Bloomsbury is not just an architectural delight – south of Guilford Street it is intact almost exactly as it was in 1790, except for the traffic wardens – but full of happy memories. The publisher of my early novels had his offices there and threw parties in his back garden. That's the thing about streets, they swarm with ghosts. *Pont Street*, SW1 for instance, which is amusing – those tall, red, fin de siècle monsters which Osbert Lancaster calls 'Pont Street Dutch', that fine austere St Columba's Church of Scotland (Sir Edward Maufe 1950-1955) – is haunted by the ghosts of Lily Langtry, who lived at No. 21, and Oscar Wilde, arrested at the Cadogan Hotel. *Meard Street*, W1 with its dignified Georgian houses is haunted by ghosts who want to show you a good time; and the liveliest of them all, Nell Gwynne.

Streets in which one has been happy... *Croom's Hill*, Greenwich, *Frognal*, NW3, *Lamb's Conduit Street*, WC1 and the adjacent *Rugby Street*, WC2, *Keats Grove*, the erratically meandering *Marylebone Lane*, *Marylebone High Street*, *Percy Street*, *Gainsborough Gardens* and *Riverside* at Twickenham; it's partly because of the street that one was happy. It is natural to feel a touch of excitement in what remains of *Regent Street*, and a touch of alarm in *Pall Mall*. There's hardly a dull street in *Westminster* amidst all those Anns and Peters and Pyes. *Lord North Street* is exceptional. And *Beauchamp Place*, SW3 is so frivolous it's irresistible. The best street in Chelsea is the secluded *Margaretta Terrace*, SW3. This is a street which shines out like a good deed in a naughty world. *Melbury Road* in Holland Park, where many pre-Raphaelites lived, is full of good things. *Tavistock Terrace*, N19, is another charming street; exceptionally pretty.

But then what can one say in favour of *Oxford Street*? Or *Tottenham Court Road*? Only Heal's and the fact that Gissing lived there. They've changed the name of *Rillington Place*, where Christie did his women in, but the East Enders are rather proud of Jack the Ripper and the alleys in which he did his messy work. And what about *Beech Street*? Where's *Beech Street*? Why, it's only the principal thoroughfare to the Barbican Centre, and look at it! Graffiti ('LEB Dry Riser Inlet'), debris and a tunnel of such hideosity that Dante should have set his motto over this hell-hole.

Best streets:
Clarges Street, W1 (for architecture).
Church Row, NW3 (for elegance).
Godfrey Street, *Melbury Road* and *Margaretta Terrace*, SW3 (for charm).
Lamb's Conduit Street, WC1 (for interest).
Beauchamp Place, SW3 (for frivolity).
Worst street:
Beech Street, EC2.

Striptease

> After a time you can get very tired of chicken.
> (Though they'll never believe that, back on the farm).
>
> from *Striptease* by Gavin Ewart (b 1916)

Very few are left. Even fewer, I expect, by the time this is published. The discreditable fashion for 'peep-shows' – you put 50p in a slot and watch a nude swanning around through a letterbox, for heaven's sake – nude encounter parlours, and suchlike, and the anonymity of the sex cinemas have cut a swathe through the striptease business, and only the oldest established have survived. These include:

Raymond's Revuebar (6 Walker's Court, W1; 01-734 1593). Very plush, very vulgar, very successful. Cheap rates for OAP and members of the armed forces. I once saw a stripper at the *Revuebar* called Rita Himalaya.

Sunset Strip (30 Dean Street, W1; 01-437 4842) has a projecting stage and a reputation for 'going further' than the competition. *Doll's House* (4 Carlisle Street, W1; 01-734 8396). The first strip club to be licensed by the GLC. Small and moderately priced; fairly squalid. *Carnival Strip Club*, 12 Old Compton Street, W1 (01-437 8337). Continuous business for twenty-three years. What can there still be to amaze and astonish its many regulars?

There are also lunch-time striptease shows at various pubs, such as the *Artesian* (80 Chepstow Road, W2; 01-229 5912) and the *Queen Anne* (139 Vauxhall Walk, SE11; 01-735 2079) at which the excellent strippers include several original and good-humoured acts.

Best striptease: the *Queen Anne*.

Supermarkets

What I ask for is that the supermarket stocks everything I want at prices I can pay without an endless queue; the staff should be helpful, the trolleys should be steerable, and the car park should be within easy reach.

What I do not ask for is 'Ave Maria' played on an electric organ and piped to all parts of the store through crackling loudspeakers.

The most helpful assistants are to be found at *Marks & Spencers*, whose convenience foods are almost as good and almost as cheap as the real thing. There too you can buy a small selection of English cheeses packed together as a single item and their cheap and cheerful wines are just that. Also recommended: Chinese chicken, sausages, pies, croissants and scones.

Waitrose has the most comprehensive stock, with everything that a nuclear family could possibly need for its housekeeping requirements. The presentation of the food is wholesome and the best branches are at East Sheen, Finchley Road, and Brent Cross.

At *Sainsbury's* in Vauxhall the aisles are too narrow, at *Sainsbury's* in Muswell Hill I am told that 'you can't get out' (*can* that be true?), and at *Sainsbury's* in Richmond the atmosphere is distinctly unenthusiastic – but they stock the best brown sugar and soft margarine in town. At its best *Sainsbury's*, who are about to open one of the biggest supermarkets in Europe in the Cromwell Road extension to add to huge new emporia in Nine Elms and at Crystal Palace Football Ground, give good value for money and helpful service.

The best thing about *International Stores* is that you can buy your food with a Barclaycard if you are lucky enough to have a Barclaycard, but shopping there can be confusing and discouraging. *Safeway*, being American run, is strong on ethnic goods and health foods, while *Tesco's* is, on average, the cheapest of the major London supermarket chains. The Wandsworth branch has not been well reported on, but *Tesco's* seldom disappoint. I have no good reports of *Bags*, in Kentish Town Road, of *Shepherd's* in Chiswick High Road, or of *Europa* (except the branch in St John's Wood High St, which is fine). My chief grouse, however, is that having spent £15 for a week's groceries you are everywhere expected to pay for a carrier bag, and only rarely can you get your purchases delivered.

Cheon Leen (4-10 Tower Street, WC2; 01-836 3478) presents all the wonders of the orient available in wire baskets.

Best supermarket: *Waitrose*, Brent Cross.

Surprises

Once travelling on the top of a West End bus I heard an English lady identifying to her American friend various tourist attractions. Pointing to the National Gallery she announced that it was Buckingham Palace. Pointing to Eros she announced that he was

Nelson, and the Knightsbridge Barracks she identified as the Horse Guards Parade. Enigmatic and unexplained, this incident was just one of many surprises daily to be experienced in London. Here are some more:

There is a *Tudor House* in Petersham much admired by those casual passers-by who see its twisted chimneys from the 65 and 73 buses. Yet it appears in no antique maps of the locality. Why not? Because it was removed just a few years ago brick by brick from Kent.

The biggest room in the world is 340 feet long and may be found in *Lloyds*. The biggest black cat in the world may be seen at *Catford Shopping Centre Precinct*, while a giant watch hangs like a symbol from an early Bergman film above a watchmaker's in *Southampton Row*. In *Lancaster House* (Stable Yard, St James's St) there is a Great Gallery, over 120 feet long, and the best painted ceilings in London, including one by Veronese. (Open Sats, Suns and Bank Holidays 2-6). The Gothic Castle in *Green Lanes*, Stoke Newington, contains no princes or princesses, merely a pumping station.

From the grandiose to the miniature: there is a model of *St Paul's Cathedral* on the struts of Vauxhall Bridge along with other miniature symbols of the arts, and *No 49 Strand-on-the-Green* has a front door large enough only to admit midgets.

It is always worth looking up when walking along London Streets. From the M3 flyover near *Teddington* you can see on the roof of Job's Dairy a series of brown and white cows grazing placidly in silhouette. And high up on the *Royal Exchange* you will see a model grasshopper, the symbol of the Gresham Family.

Numbers 23 and 24 Leinster Gardens, *Bayswater*, are not houses at all, merely a dummy façade concealing the extension of the Metropolitan Railway from Edgware to Westminster (1868).

And what is the mystery of the huge office building in *Bloomsbury* bounded by Bucknall Street, Earnshaw Street, Dyott Street and St Giles High Street? Nowhere is its purpose identified, and yet many hundreds must work there. Any suggestions?

If you are bored with London *and* bored with life, a phone call to *Pranksters* (01-348 7596) will secure you a singing telegram, a custard pie message, a look-alike celebrity, or a personalised prank, stunt or hoax.

Finally when all else fails (even *Feminist Tarot Readings* – phone Marlene at 01-226 8451) do not forget to visit the squirrel-racing at *Kenwood*. This unique event is held annually; the preliminary heats are on 31st February, the all-England championships on 1st April. See you there.

See also Unusual Shops.

Swimming

Swiss Cottage Pool (Winchester Road, NW3; 01-278 4444) is clean and big and well attended, but there is a danger of chlorine inhalation. The new *YMCA* in Tottenham Court Road has a fine pool, and you are likely to make new friends there. It also has rock climbing facilities in its magnificent gym. *The Crystal Palace Sports Centre*, (Ledrington Road, SE19; 01-778 0131) has a sophisticated modern pool to championship standards, but membership and entrance are expensive. *The White City Pool* (Bloemfontein Road, W12; 01-743 3401) has its own wave machine and tropical plants. Here and at the *Elephant and Castle Leisure Centre* (Elephant and Castle, SE1; 01-582 5505) there are gently sloping bottoms so that children and non-swimmers feel as secure as when they're on the beach. The *Kensington Baths* (Walmer Road, W11) are also ideal for children and *Richmond Pool* (Chertsey Road, Richmond) was, until the Council cut the staffing levels dangerously. The *Porchester Baths* at the top of Queensway are splendidly period. If you can afford to, try the pool at the *RAC Club* (89 Pall Mall, SW1; 01-930 2345) or the even more exclusive one in the *Berkeley Hotel* (Wilton Place, SW1; 01-235 6000) – not advised unless you can boast an overall tan. At the *Holiday Inn* (17 Sloane Street, SW1; 01-235 4377) you can eat a leisurely roast Sunday lunch (£8.50 inclusive) while your children disport themselves in the pool in front of you. All Holiday Inn hotels have pools.

Sadly I cannot speak so highly of *Kentish Town, Wandsworth* (mucky), *Whitechapel*, the *Brockwell Park Lido, Chelsea, Camberwell*, or *Forest Hill* pools, although I suspect that my friend who says of the last-named: 'Frogs and cockroaches abound' is exaggerating.

If you like skinny-dipping, try *Kenwood* or *Highgate Pond* (men only) or the Ladies' Pool on *Hampstead Heath* (women only). *Lordship Lane*, N17 is agreeable for open-air swimmers; also *Parliament Hill Fields*. The *Serpentine Swimming Club* is for hardy lunatics who like to swim every day of the year. Sometimes they break the ice with their heads, which accounts for a lot.

Best swimming: (indoor) *White City*, (outdoor) *Parliament Hill Fields*.

Synagogues

The oldest and most beautiful synagogue in London is the *Spanish and Portuguese Synagogue* in Dukes Place, Bevis Marks. Rebuilt after the Great Fire, it survived the Blitz, and is still in use, though only on high days and holidays. During run-of-the-mill days it remains locked up and access is only gained by prior arrangement. The design is similar to many Wren churches, and the wood was carved by the same craftsmen. The next oldest synagogue in London, the *German Synagogue* (James Spiller 1788-1790) was comprehensively bombed by Hitler; a tragic loss. But of course a synagogue is more than bricks and stones; essentially it is a community of ten men or more, and an ark, and the Law and the Prophets, and one person to bake a strudel, and lots of people to claim that they have a better recipe.

The *Liberal Jewish Synagogue* (28 St John's Wood Road, NW8; 01-286 5181) is not to be confused with the *St John's Wood Synagogue* in Grove Road NW8, which is small, intimate and orthodox. The *LJS* has a large and fashionable congregation who come to shul three times a year, and when they need to be confirmed, married or buried. It has an excellent choir and two rabbis, John Rayner, sonorous and dignified, and David Goldberg, witty and worldly-wise, whose sermons are always pertinent. It was the first Liberal synagogue in London and in 1922 it appointed a young rabbi from America, Harold Reinhardt, who moved after a year to the *West London Synagogue* (33 Seymour Place, W1; 01-723 4404) when the *LJS* refused to pay his fare home. Reinhardt inspired loyalty from his new congregation, until a further schism in 1958-9, when he founded the *Westminster Synagogue* (Kent House, Rutland Gardens, SW7; 01-584 3953). The *West London Synagogue* is sometimes referred to as a banqueting suite with a synagogue attached – but in Hugo Gryn it has a fine preacher and an excellent pastoral minister, who stops this Sephardic and Moorish institution from becoming too stuffy. The *Westminster Synagogue*, in a building in which the young Queen Victoria received the momentous news that she was to become Queen of England, is the most expensive synagogue in the country. Members are expected to pay £500 a year or more, with no guarantee of life after death, but, since the Rabbi, Albert Friedlander, is a theologian of parts, they should at least receive the best advice that money can buy. No riff raff get in and there are beautiful old (Jacobean?) seats in the ante-room.

The *New West End Synagogue* (10 St Petersburgh Place, W2;

01-229 2631) is an Ashkenazi establishment which has lost something of its former glory. Former rabbis included Ephie Levine and Louis Jacobs. Ephie enjoyed the best that life had to offer. When offered the traditional tip after conducting a wedding or funeral, he would say: 'Don't thank me now; thank me *by post*.' Louis Jacobs was and is a fine, contentious scholar and preacher, whose appointment the United Synagogue refused to endorse.

Shorter reports: *Greatorex Street*, E1, contains a survivor of the old East End synagogues; here something of the old *heimische* atmosphere lingers. The East End Jews moved to Cricklewood (the synagogue is in Walm Lane) then on to Finchley. The *Finchley Synagogue* (Kinloss Gardens, N3; 01-346 8551) is – how shall I put this tactfully – architecturally uninspired. There is a golf club attached. The friendliest synagogue is the *Liberal and Reform* (Alyth Gardens, NW11).

The most civilised congregation is to be found at the *Hampstead Synagogue* (1 Dennington Park Road, NW6; 01-435 1518); the congregation at the *Edgware United Synagogue* however, under their powerfully rhetorical Irish Rabbi Bernstein, supported Begin in his worst excesses. One has to admire the courage of the congregation at the *Kingston Liberal Synagogue* (Rushett Road, Long Ditton, Surrey; 01-977 4640) which literally built its synagogue around it. The *South London Synagogue* (Prentis Road, SW16; 01-769 4787) is distinguished both by its choir and by its rabbi – in this case a lady rabbi (one has abbesses but not rabesses) who was also an SDP PPC (if you follow me) at the last general election and whose energy and cheerfulness are infectious.

Best synagogue: (architecturally) *Bevis Marks*.

Tailors

The four best tailors in Savile Row are *Huntsman H. & Sons Ltd* (tailors and breeches makers), *Anderson & Sheppard, Hawes & Curtis*, and *Kilgour, French & Stanbury. Huntsman* (11 Savile Row, W1; 01-734 7441), who prefer their suits to be square-shouldered, require three fittings and charge currently something in the region of £850. If you wish to be attended by the nabob himself – Colin Hammick – you have to join a waiting list. *Anderson & Sheppard* (30 Savile Row, W1; 01-734 1420 and 01-734 1960) eschew stuffing; their clothes are therefore of an exceptional softness and durability. *Hawes & Curtis* (2 Burlington Gardens, W1; 01-493 3803), who are also shirtmakers and hosiers, have an imposing list of clients, so that if you like the way Princes Philip, Charles and Andrew dress, these are the tailors to patronise. As for *Kilgour etc*, (33a Dover Street, W1; 01-629 4283 and 01-629 5074), they are the international tailors for those with Porsches in the trunks of their Rollses; they made Fred Astaire's tails in 'Top Hat', which can't be bad.

But none of these tailors, howsoever grand, can measure up to the great Henry Poole. He it was who when the Prince of Wales at the turn of the century dared to complain about one of his suits, took some chalk from his pocket, drew white marks all over the Prince's jacket, barked out: 'Bring it in for alterations!' and marched off.

I can also recommend for ready-made as well as for made-to-measure, *Jaeger's* (204-206 Regent Street, W1; 01-734 8211), *Crolla* (35 Dover Street, W1; 01-629 5931) with a fine selection of shirts, *Paul Smith* (44 Floral Street, WC2; 01-379 7133), *Webster Brothers* (56 Cornhill, EC3; 01-626 5838 – also shirts) and *Chamberlain and Jones* (877 High Road, E11; 01-989 1271) who made me a dinner jacket a quarter of a century ago, and it still looks pretty good – at least I think so.

The best range of ready-made suits come from *Simon Ackermann*. Chester Barrie suits are also available at *Austin Reed* branches.

For repairs and alterations, *Stitch in Time* on Waterloo Station (01-928 5593) undertakes men's and women's tailoring repairs to be collected the same day, while the gentleman at 36 Worple Street, Whitton, Middlesex charged me a mere £4.75 for repairs to a silk Paris suit by Ted Lapidus, which I bought for a tenner at an antiques fair, and completed an excellent job in three days. Altar Ahmed of the *5-Star Cleaners* (339 Upper Street, N1) will also undertake any repairs, and will clean anything graciously and expeditiously.

Best tailor: *Huntsman H. & Sons Ltd.*

Take Away

It is now possible to fool just about all the people all the time. Quite apart from Butchers (q.v.) who prepare their meat to gourmet standards, there are now an increasing number of delicatessens, where home-cooked and frozen food is available for the overworked hostess or inept bachelor. Here are four of the best:

Acquired Tastes, 9 Battersea Rise, SW11 (01-223 9942), is open until 9.30 p.m. seven days a week. Renowned locally for their pâtés and terrines – most of them are *made* locally – they also do an excellent line in Mushrooms à la Grecque, and have an exceptional counter of some 50 cheeses, all of them fresh. Also a wide choice of teas, wine, herbs etc.

Big Mamma, 70 Lupus Street, SW1 (01-834 1471). A huge pot of lasagne and a fine selection of salads (95p for a generous portion of Niçoise) distinguish this life-enhancing establishment from similar delis. Hot dishes (or at least they will be hot when you heat them) include Chicken Chasseur (£1.25 a portion compared to three or four times as much in a restaurant).

Joanna's (between Lots Road and Cheyne Walk, SW6). A miniature shop stuffed full of croissants, baguettes, spicy sausage rolls, home-made chocolate chip cookies, fresh fruit, sorbets and such. A freezer is crammed with home-made supper-dishes in foil. But the assistants ought not to smoke in a shop such as this.

For fresh take-away pasta go to *Pasta Pasta* (52 Pimlico Road, SW1; 01-730 1435). The pasta is made daily in the basement (£1.20-£1.60 per lb) and a selection of classic sauces (£2.50 per lb) is also available. To be encouraged.

Best Take-Away: *Acquired Tastes*.

See also Fish and Chips, Delicatessens, Butchers etc.

Taxis and Taxi Ranks

The London taxi is designed as a taxi and not as a car. Regulations require that there should be seating for five adults, with enough headroom for a man to keep his top hat on, and that the privacy of the passengers be protected at all times. This means that the driver's rear view mirror must not be angled so that he can see what is going on in the back of the cab. A taxi is also required to have a narrow turning circle. As Nubar Gulbenkian who owned one put it: 'It can turn on a sixpence – whatever that may be. A London cabby must have 'the knowledge', which means that he must have passed a vigorous test on London's geography. The passenger has pullywag loops to hang on to, control of heat and light, ashtrays and a tinted rear window. I am old-fashioned enough slightly to resent the advertisements on the tip-up seats, but they can hardly be said to scream at you. It is also remarkable how rarely a taxi breaks down.

The best ranks to find taxis at are outside the Law Courts in the *Strand; Sloane Square; Hanover Square*; and *Cadogan Gardens*, where the Squire Bancroft shelter has miraculously survived. The worst ranks are in *Leicester Square, Charing Cross, King's Cross* and *Euston Stations*.

And always bear in mind that if several of you are making a London journey it will probably save you money to take a taxi now that public transport is so expensive.

Best taxi rank: *Cadogan Gardens.*
Worst taxi rank: *Charing Cross Station.*

Tea

When Dr Johnson paid his visits to Mrs Thrale at Streatham it is recorded that he sometimes drank as many as twenty-five cups of tea in rapid succession. His tipple was a mild *bohea*, and the cups he drank it out of would be the tiny ones without handles after the Chinese manner. (Incidentally tea is cheaper to buy now than when it was first imported.) Other celebrated tea-fanciers include Lord Petersham, who had *pekoe, souchong, congou* and *gunpowder* in his caddies, and Edmund Waller, who was told by a Jesuit who had been to China that the boiling water should remain on the leaves 'while you say the Miserere Psalm very leisurely', thus ensuring that 'the spiritual part of the tea' was not wasted. In those days, of course, you blended your own in the bowls provided in the caddies.

All of which is preamble, for I had intended to tell you about the firm of *R. Twinings & Co* who have been selling tea in London since the year 1710 or thereabouts. And the old firm is still where it has always been, in a tiny shop in the Strand opposite the Law Courts and underneath those familiar sculpted Chinamen. It's still the same family there, and it would be disloyal surely to recommend that you went anywhere else for your tea. However the *Ceylon Tea Centre* (22 Regent Street, SW1; 01-930 8632) and the *India Tea Centre* (343 Oxford Street, W1; 01-499 1975) permit you – *encourage* you – to taste your tea in congenial surroundings before committing yourself to buying the leaf.

Best tea: *R. Twinings & Co.*
Best cuppa: *Ceylon Tea Centre.*

PS I bet you didn't know that Widow Twankee was named after a brand of China tea.

Tea Houses/Cream Cakes

Julius Caesar and Mark Antony; the Duke of Wellington and Napoleon; Sherlock Holmes and Moriarty; *Maison Bertaux* (28 Greek Street, W1; 01-437 6007) and *Patisserie Valerie* (44 Old Compton Street, W1; 01-437 3466); accuse me of hyperbole if you wish but cake lovers would agree that this is one of the great struggles of world history. *Bertaux* is perhaps a touch suaver; *Valerie* marginally more lively; try them both and make up your own mind.

   Many armies are engaged in the battle of the cream cakes. There are those who swear by *Maison Sagne* (105 Marylebone High Street, W1; 01-935 6240); a true Viennese flavour distinguishes it, and, if the sachertorte or the almond pastries don't blow your mind, the mural certainly will. In competition with Sagne is *Gloriette* (7 St John's Wood High Street, NW8; 01-732 1039 and various branches), a highly professional patisserie; *Louis* (32 Heath Street, NW3; 01-435 9908 and 12 New College Parade, NW3; 01-722 8100), where you can almost always find a table free; and *Maison Bouquillon* (41-45 Moscow Road, W2; 01-727 4897 and 28 Westbourne Grove, W2; 01-229 2107). At either branch of *Maison Bouquillon* you can sink your teeth into a *tarte aux fraises du bois*, for the merest taste of which I would have the children of my best friend shipped off to a white slaver in Buenos Aires. They also do an excellent line in made-to-order birthday cakes. But there is still better . . .

   Pechons Restaurant and *Tea-rooms* (127 Queensway, W2; 01-229 0746) has a selection of over 100 cakes; scope here I should have thought for a sponsored charity event. Most of them are memorable. Tea at the *Ritz* is for those suffering a crisis of confidence, but remember to wear a tie; until recently it was the only meal the Ritz provided which was satisfactory. If you can bear ravishing fashion models with legs like fork-lift trucks swanning around you (most of their energy is taken up with fluttering those massive eye-lashes) then *Fortnum's* is the place. It would have amused Jerry Cornelius. On Fridays and Sundays (3.30-6.30) at the Palm Court in the *Waldorf* (Aldwych, WC2;

01-836 2400) there are *thés dansants* (£6.95) to an elegant quartet, but for the true sophisticate the *ABC* in Euston Road cries out to be visited. If it isn't full of Bulgarian spies being 'turned' by *Smiley's People*, then it ought to be.

While recognising that *Richoux* (41a South Audley Street, W1; 01-629 5228 – my typewriter gave me South Awfly Street which is rather good) has claims to be considered among the greats, and that at *Konditorei Manfred* (Lichfield Terrace, Sheen Road, Richmond) the kindest lady in the GLC area dishes out wonderful rum truffle biscuits, the best cake in London, or anywhere in the world, is an *Original Maid-of-Honour*, as served at the café of that name (288 Kew Road, Kew, Surrey; 01-940 2752) in a fine Georgian terrace opposite the gardens. A mélange of almonds, pastry, honey and eggs, it is the sort of confection for which saints would cast down their golden crowns around the glassy sea. An astonishing survival for both the cake (which may be taken home and heated for five minutes in a moderate oven before eating) and the café are of ancient renown. It also serves chocolates and other superior delicacies of a pastrified nature.

Best tea-house: *Maison Bouquillon.*
Best cake: *The Original Maid-of-Honour.*
Worst cakes: *Any with a glacé cherry on top.*

Tennis

The most delightful place to play tennis in London must be the court which adjoins *St Botolph, Bishopsgate* (be warned: there are three St Botolphs within a few hundred square yards). Keys may be obtained from the verger.

The three courts at the north end of *Regent's Park* may be confidently recommended; so may the courts in *Golders Hill Park, Battersea Park, Belsize Park*, and *Waterlow Park*. The courts in *Parliament Hill Fields* are not so hot. On these park courts you do not need white clothes, sweat bands or bad manners like the professionals. If you wish to pay half a ransom I can recommend the *Holland Park Lawn Tennis Club* (1 Addison Road, W14; 01-603 3928) or the *Hurlingham Club* (01-736 8411) in Fulham. It was at *Hurlingham* that a friend of mine was asked to make up a four and found herself playing mixed doubles with three ex-Wimbledon champions. But to be sure of playing with the best join the exclusive and expensive *Queen's Club* (Palliser Road, W14; 01-385

3421). At the *Wimbledon Club* (Church Road, Wimbledon, SW19; 01-946 6959) not to be confused with the All England Lawn Tennis Club, the setting is splendid and there is no shortage of courts.

There are real (or royal) tennis courts at *Lord's, Queen's Club*, and *Hampton Court Palace*. This is a game of great and complex antiquity; since very few people can understand it – I can't understand it, even though I've played it – the courts are frequently available.

Best tennis court: (for tennis) the *Centre Court*, the *All England Lawn Tennis Club*.

Best tennis court: (for atmosphere) *St Botolph*, Bishopsgate.

Theatres (Fringe)

The London fringe, which has extended to the London suburbs and beyond, has become vital to the commercial theatre, producing many of the writers, actors and directors, upon which it depends. Nobody gets rich doing fringe work, but the possibility of a West End transfer glimmers fitfully like St Elmo's Fire. While lunch-time theatre has become less popular, evening shows on the fringe have improved and we are now living through a golden age of alternative theatre. At least we would be were many of the shows genuinely *alternative*; politically they remain naive and uninformed.

Each fringe theatre has its own personality. *The King's Head* (115 Upper Street, N1; 01-226 1916) is claustrophobic and loud with the clatter of cutlery as rather hectic meals are served before the performances begin. The productions are usually more satisfying than the food and can be memorable; the most recent West End transfer was the delightful *Mr Cinders*. In the adjoining pub the barmen and barmaids refuse to deal in decimal currency.

The Riverside Studios (Crisp Road, W6; 01-748 3354), once BBC rehearsal rooms, have been under constant threat of closure, but their adventurous policy of playing host to avant-garde dancers, musicians and theatre companies has given exposure to some of the most brilliant international talents. Since the sad loss of the *Round House* it is more than ever important that we should fight to preserve *Riverside*.

The *Bush Theatre* (Shepherd's Bush Green, W12; 01-743 3388), above a pub, has always been a theatre without frills, a theatre in which excellent writing and acting talent can be seen at very close quarters, British talent predominating. *Hampstead Theatre Club* (Swiss Cottage Centre, NW3; 01-722 9301) has tended to concentrate on starry casts in literate plays with more than an outside chance of a transfer. Civilised, but none too radical. *The Tricycle Theatre* (269 Kilburn High Road, NW6; 01-624 5330), originally formed by actors from the Pindar of Wakefield pub (see under Music Halls), is one of the pleasantest of the fringe theatres, but the choice of plays and casts is, to put it politely, whimsical. *The Almeida Theatre* (Almeida Street, N1; 01-359 4404) takes a commendable interest in avant garde music notably with a John Cage festival; its experimental policy makes it always worth a visit. *The Gate* at the Latchmere (503 Battersea Park Road, SW11; 01-228 2620) has a handsome restaurant attached to its small theatre. The menus complement the plays. Thus, when I saw the apocalpytic piece *The Bed Sitting Room*, I ate baked potato skins. God help us if they mount *Titus Andronicus*. The pub in which it is established is a handsome Victorian pile. Exhibitions and plays at the *ICA* (The Mall, W1; 01-930 3647) often excite hostility from the press and other guardians of our morality (dirty nappies in a feminist exhibition caused a furore) and the theatre itself ('like a VD Clinic', comments a friend) cannot always be relied upon for a comforting night out for a family party from Penge. However, the snack bar is one of the very best around and the bookshop stocks some interesting radical paperbacks.

The highly professional *Greenwich* and *Lyric*, Hammersmith theatres are only fringe theatres geographically, although the *Lyric* (King Street, W6; 01-741 2311) has a studio theatre, which is an excellent example of what an established theatre can provide in the way of small cast productions. Also at the *Lyric* is a first-rate snack bar. The Theatre Upstairs at the *Royal Court* (Sloane Square, SW1; 01-730 2554) mounts socially concerned productions which can be stunning or which can be bullshit. It frequently enjoys full houses.

There are four theatres in London principally devoted to Theatre in Education, but where splendid visiting companies such as Shared Experience and The People Show may sometimes be found. These are the *Cockpit Theatre* (in the north), the *Curtains Theatre* within Toynbee Hall (in the east), *Oval House* (in the south) and the *Questors*, Ealing (in the west). Of these the *Questors* (Mattock Lane, W5; 01-567 5184) is the handsomest, the *Cockpit* (Gateforth Street, NW8; 01-402 5081) the best equipped and the most professional, the *Curtains* (Arts Workshop (01-247 3633) has the greatest community concern, and *Oval House* (54 Kennington Oval, SE11; 01-582 7680), with its agreeable tattiness, the most energy.

The *Young Vic* (66 The Cut, SE1; 01-928 6363) has a marvellously versatile acting area, splendid refreshments, and excellent atmosphere, but no very clear policy. The *Albany Empire* (Douglas Way, SE8; 01-691 3333) in Deptford is a power-house of talent in an under-privileged area. In the modern and intelligently designed main hall you can eat and drink while watching anything from Tommy Cooper to Rastafarian rapping. It is a noticeably *young* theatre, but allow plenty of time to find it.

It is a long journey, geographically and aesthetically, between the best two London fringe theatres. At the *Half Moon Theatre* (213 Mile End Road, E1; 01-790 4000) a production of *Trafford Tanzi* by Claire Luckham, which deservedly transferred to the *Mermaid*, was all that fringe theatre ought to be. The enthusiasm at the box office was infectious in contrast to the surliness that greets you at most West End theatres. *The Half Moon*, currently building two new theatres on the site of the old one, enjoys great local support. It remains to be seen whether the new artistic director can continue the success of Robert Walker (twenty-stone, shaven-headed and determined).

The *Orange Tree Theatre* (45 Kew Road, Richmond, Surrey; 01-940 3633), run by Sam Walters (genial, cultured, and fraught-looking), also draws most of its support locally, and the character of the place reflects life in Richmond as the *Half Moon* reflects life in the East End. In a tiny ninety-seat room above a pub, local actors perform plays by local authors to local audiences, but cosiness is avoided by excursions into the classics (*King Lear* and *Peer Gynt* in miniature); the place respects the intelligence of its clients. Here lunch-time performances have been discontinued, but the summer festival of children's plays has become something to look forward to.

Tickets for many fringe productions can be centrally booked at the *Fringe Box Office*, Duke of York's Theatre, St Martin's Lane, WC2 (01-379 6002). For a fuller survey of fringe theatre see the excellent publication: *The British Alternative Theatre Directory* by Catherine Itzin (John Offord).

Best fringe theatres: the *Half Moon*; the *Orange Tree*.

Theatres (Open Air)

Occasional theatre performances take place against the backcloth of *Holland House*, a Jacobean mansion, much restored, in Holland Park (no advance booking), but although this romantic ruin would be ideal for a number of plays (*Nightmare Abbey*, *The Cenci*, *Thieves Carnival*), no impresario has yet taken it upon himself to set up a regular company there. Performances of Shakespeare in the galleried yard of the *George Inn*, Southwark (77 Borough High Street, SE1; 01-407 2056) attract tourists but Sam Wanamaker has plans to build a facsimile of Shakespeare's Globe Theatre, which will be more authentic. In recent years the *Tower of London* has been used as scenery for an open air performance of *The Yeomen of the Guard* during the London Festival, but this is all prevarication, because there is really only one full-time (well, summer-time) professional, open air theatre in London, and that is David Conville's outfit in *Regent's Park*. Competition from Concorde, thunderstorms and bike boys is fierce, but the actors manage to make themselves heard most of the time, especially now that they're acting in a 1200-seat, steeply-raked, amphitheatre. Snacks are excellent. On my last visit I enjoyed wurst sausages and loganberries and cream. Ticket prices are modest (£2-£6) but the standard of productions varies alarmingly. As a general rule choose Shakespeare plays set in forests and avoid productions by Richard Digby Day in favour of Conville productions. The theatre faces west so, even if the play isn't worth watching, the setting sun behind the fine trees is. Blankets may be hired, but remember to bring cushions, thermos flasks of coffee or something stronger. Despite the bugs there cannot be many pleasanter ways of passing a fine summer's evening.

Best open air theatre: *Regent's Park.*
Worst open air theatre: *The Beating of the Retreat.*

Theatres (West End)

There are London theatres which actors dread. The *Phoenix* is one and the *Piccadilly* another – especially since no one can find it. Actors are not over the moon about playing in the *Westminster Theatre* either. It can mean that they are being employed by Moral Rearmament, and a morally rearmed audience is not a barrel-load of laughs. I find it impossible to enjoy anything at *Sadler's Wells Theatre*. The *Whitehall* has had a strange career. As the home of the *Whitehall* farces in the post war years it was hugely popular; as the home for Paul Raymond's nude farces in the seventies it was not hugely popular, although I preferred those to the tepid milk-and-water satire of *Anyone for Dennis?* The *Prince of Wales* is hideous (the theatre, that is); the *Prince Edward Theatre* has the rudest box office staff (or had) which is saying something, bearing in mind how much competition there is for this award, and at the *Queen's Theatre* the attendants always chatter and bang doors before the interval. The *Shaftesbury* has a crowded foyer but a charming front of house manager. The *Vaudeville* has been nicely renovated inside and out with *Mousetrap* money, but the front of the *Adelphi* has been wrecked, although you can still see in the lettering of 'Royal Adelphi' a touch of genuine deco wit. Somebody *must* visit the *Strand Theatre*, but nobody has ever been seen going in or, more ominously, coming out. The *Cambridge Theatre* seems to have gone.

The *Haymarket* is a gloriously theatrical building, and backstage it has the loveliest star dressing room in London. The *St Martin's* is special because it's where I had my only West End play performed. ('You and you alone, sir,' wrote one of my fans, 'have been responsible for the disintegration of the British Empire)'. And the *Savoy Theatre*, the first to install electric lights, kept my wife happily employed for nearly a year. The *Duke of York's* reeks with charm; it is usually host to a classy and successful play. The *Palladium* is expensive enough mid-week and charges an extra £2 on Fridays and Saturdays. The *Aldwych*, where Ben Travers farces ran so successfully during the twenties and thirties, is acoustically difficult; I worked on *London Assurance* there; a happy time in a happy place. The *Old Vic*, now expensively renovated, used also to be bad for seeing and hearing, but the air at the *Old Vic* was always rich with the expectation of pleasure.

The *Royal Court* lives in the shadow of its history. Those who remember the regime of George Devine and the sense of occasion which informed each new play there, have little time for Max Stafford Clarke, but he is not a negligible figure.

Cut price tickets (half the regular price plus 50p service charge) for some West End plays are available at the *SWET Theatre Booth* in Leicester Square (2.30 p.m.-6.30 p.m. non-matinee days; 12 noon-6 p.m. matinee days – no telephone). Cut price tickets for the *Royal Shakespeare Company* at the *Barbican* are sometimes available on the performance day after 10 a.m. at £4; for the

National after 10 a.m. at £4.50; previews and midweek matinees £3.50.

Best West End Theatres: the *Duke of York's* (for atmosphere); the *Haymarket* (for architecture).

Worst West End Theatres: the *Prince of Wales* and the *Apollo*, Victoria.

See also Arts Centres, and Theatres, Fringe.

For full details of London theatres – useful when booking tickets – I recommend: *The Playgoer's Companion* by Barry Turner and Mary Fulton (Virgin Books).

Tiles

The most beguiling tiles are to be found in the foyer of the *Whitechapel Public Library*, Whitechapel High Street; they were removed thither from a building demolished in 1963 to make way for the new traffic roundabout. The tiles form a mosaic of Whitechapel Haymarket in 1878. Amongst the vignettes two young men, one a townee, one a rustic, are about to indulge in a meaningful relationship while a merchant in a purple hat is passing a posy of flowers via his riding crop to a girl in orange stockings on a hayrick. One can understand his partiality. Since this delightful mise-en-scène (the horses are wearing ear muffs) is next door to Bloom's kosher restaurant and the Whitechapel Art Gallery and opposite the City of London Polytechnic, a detour is obviously called for.

Other good tiles may be seen on the *Victoria Line* of the Underground (q.v.), in the *Martinez Restaurant* (25 Swallow Street, W1; 01-734 5066), decorating the *Michelin Building* in the Fulham Road, and in the *Princess Louise* pub (208 High Holborn, WC1; 01-405 8816), which also has fine engraved glass ceilings, but has replaced its original cubicles.

Best tiles: *Whitechapel Public Library*.

Toll Gates

Only one toll gate remains, but it's a beauty. The toll gate in *College Road*, Dulwich, was built in 1789 by Mr Charles Morgan of

Penge, who needed easy access to some fields he had rented from Dulwich College, and he could see no reason why others who wished to use it should not pay for the privilege. The college took it over on Morgan's death, continued to charge travellers and still do. The table of tolls on a board beside the road charges for every 'horse, mule or donkey drawing any vehicle' as well as for 'lambs, sheep or hogs, per score', but it also taxes motorists 5p, though not at night. Between 1901 and 1958 the tolls were collected by the same loyal lady.

In *Barnes High Street* I spotted 'Ye Old Toll Gate Antiques' and I can believe that the pretty house was indeed a toll house, but it isn't now.

Best toll gate: *College Road*, Dulwich.

Toys

The children I know best are just as happy cutting a hole in the side of a cardboard box or climbing a tree and creating a tree house than playing (for more than a few minutes) with the latest electronic video game. But an old cardboard box and a pair of scissors don't make much of a birthday present.

Robert Louis Stevenson wrote: 'If you love art, folly, or the bright eyes of children, speed to Pollocks', and *Pollocks Toy Museum* (1 Scala Street, W1; 01-636 3452) is still there. Not only can you study the old theatres and plays, but you can also buy equivalents of the antique – usually Victorian – toys. A magical place. *Pollocks* has opened a second branch (Unit 44, The Market, Covent Garden, WC2; 01-379 7866) recently, and it too is a delight. Beatrix Potter postcards are cheaper here than at W. H. Smith.

Also to be found in the new Covent Garden complex (Unit 32 – 01-379 7681) is *Eric Snook*, who concluded a remarkable coup when he secured the rights to marketing ET spin-offs. His best traditional lines are his rag dolls and his mechanical chicks and rabbits. He took back a defective pencil box with very good grace. (Incidentally there is a *Doll's Hospital* at 16 Dawes Road, SW6; 01-385 2081.) *Eric Snook* stocks some Galt toys, which are extremely ingenious and popular with children, but for the best selection you should hop along to *Galt's* (30 Great Marlborough Street, W1; 01-734 0829).

The toughest toys of all are Tonka trucks and tractors; they are indestructible. For teddy bears try *Carrie's* (32 Pembridge Road, W11; 01-727 4805). For collectable toys – not to be played with – try *Stuart Cropper*, Stand L/14 Grays Mews Antique Market, 1 Davies Mews, W1 (01-629 7034). I can powerfully recommend *Tridias* (44 Monmouth Street, WC2; 01-240 2369 with a branch in Richmond), *Tigermoth* (166 Portobello Road, W11; 01-727 7564) for stocking fillers as well as trendy clothes, *Tiger Tiger* (219 King's Road, SW10; 01-352 8080) for dolls houses, puppets, and jokes, *John Turnbull* (Hercules Road, SE1) for model soldiers, *Bagatelle Toys* (79 High Street, Wimbledon, SW19; 01-946 7981) for general toys.

What about *Hamley's* (188 Regent Street, W1; 01-734 3161), the largest toy shop in the world, and *Selfridge's* toy department (Oxford Street, W1; 01-629 1234) at Christmas? Between them they stock just about every toy ever made, but go there sober and it's like walking into the world of Hieronymous Bosch.

There are over 100 toy libraries in London, a full list of which may be obtained from the *Toy Libraries Association* (Wyllyotts Manor, Darkes Lane, Potters Bar, Herts; 0707 44571), which also produces a *Good Toys Guide*.

Best toys: *Pollocks Toy Museum.*

PS Don't forget *The Museum of Childhood, Bethnal Green*.

Train Spotting

The best places for train spotting are *King's Cross* and *Paddington* stations. You see a good variety of engines at *Clapham Junction*, but it can be cold enough to freeze your dead man's handle. The worst places for train spotting are *Fenchurch Street* and, of course, anywhere on the *Northern Underground line*.

Best train spotting: *Paddington.*
Worst train spotting: *Fenchurch Street.*

Trees

> Poems are made by fools like me
> But only God can make a tree.

Joyce Kilmer (1888-1918)

The interesting question is why God also made the beetle which carries Dutch Elm Disease, thus killing more than 9,000 matured elms in the royal parks alone. Students at Chelsea College of Art have transformed three of these into an abstract sculpture (between the Magazine and Rima in Hyde Park), but I would have preferred the trees.

London is full of arboreal wonders, from the oaks in *Greenwich Park*, which would have been 300 years old when Shakespeare admired them, to the superb oak on the Green at *Northolt Village*. There's a plane tree on the banks of the Wandle in Festival Walk, *Carshalton* which, at 125 feet, is the tallest plane in Britain. A yew in the Old Vicarage Garden at *Enfield* is reputedly over 400 years old, and in the *Chelsea Physic Garden* (see Gardens) grows the biggest olive tree in the country, an *olea europaea*, which also ripens fruit in December – seven pounds were harvested in 1976. Also in this garden a cork oak, a pomegranate, a fine Chinese Willowpattern tree, a maidenhair tree, an Indian bean tree, a cucumber tree, and many other varieties, including a black mulberry (*morus nigra*). Many mulberries grow in south London, and from their leaves came the caterpillars which made the silk which made the dress which Lady Di wore on her wedding day. South London is also notable for its box elders.

There's a wild cherry in *Highgate Woods*, which is said to have inspired Housman ('Loveliest of trees, the cherry now . . .'); there's a fully matured palm in *Isleworth Cemetery*, beneath which lie victims of the Great Plague – the burial ground itself has been vandalised; there's a black walnut in *Marble Hill Park*, which is of vast circumference and considerable dignity, and there is a huge horse-chestnut in the middle of *Richmond Terrace Gardens*, perfect for playing under after your picnic. Growing out of the stone of that fine Wren church, St Magnus the Martyr, *Billingsgate*, is one of those twisted old trees which have long since, like an old dog, forfeited any claim to pedigree; but it is much loved. So is the tree which grows through the middle of the PEN Club headquarters in Glebe Place, *Chelsea*; and the beech tree at *Kenwood*.

But it is not merely single trees which so delight the eye. There's that avenue of limes giving a vista to Holy Trinity, *Brompton*, and a superb avenue of planes in *Chingford Mount Cemetery*. Around the *Albert Memorial* and in Queen Mary's Gardens, *Regent's Park*, are such generous agglomerations of trees that it scarcely matters what they are; what matters is that they survive to give us all, or those of us who are not past caring, a moment's reflection, 'a green thought in a green shade'.

Best tree: The oak at *Northolt*.

PS If you wish to endow a tree to commemorate a person or a special event contact *The Tree Council* (35 Belgrave Square, SW1X 8QN; 01-235 8854) who will welcome your interest.

PPS Of the ten million trees planted in 1973 ('Plant a Tree in '73') between a half and two-thirds survived.

Tropical Fish (and other pets)

No sooner do fish pass my threshold than they give a little sigh and turn their toes to the stars. We no longer have them in the house. But for those who do a visit to *Palmer's*, *Animal Fair*, or *King Fisheries* is called for.

Palmer's (33-37 Parkway, NW1; 01-485 5163) is an exotic pet shop, where you may find, between the talking parrot and the red-kneed bird-eating spider, your required fish. If you don't *Animal Fair* (17 Abingdon Road, W8; 01-937 0011) may be relied upon to be helpful with puppies, kittens and white mice as well as tropical fish. But the specialists are *King Fisheries* (Tropical and Marine Fish) of Beckenham. This is a fascinating place with healthy fish and knowledgeable staff; furthermore they will buy back at half price any fish which you buy from them and with whom you don't hit it off. In County Hall may be seen two large aquaria filled with fish from the Thames. Sadly Harrods pet department has closed.

Best tropical fish: *King Fisheries*.

Tunnels

There are eleven tunnels under the Thames in London, five for tube trains, three for cars, and three – one disused – for pedestrians.

The most romantic tunnel is the *Thames Tunnel* (Rotherhithe to Wapping). For nineteen years after a company had been formed by Marc Brunel (Isambard Kingdom Brunel's father) disasters attended the project. There were floodings in which six men drowned, and bankruptcies, and many workers, suffering from 'tunnel disease' went blind. Brunel spent his savings and those of his wife on this dangerous and speculative venture, until at last the tunnel was opened in 1843. Within a year, two and a quarter million people (more than the population of London) had passed through it, but without vehicular traffic it could never pay its way, and in 1864 the tunnel, which had cost a million pounds to build was sold for £200,000 to the East London Railway Company. Still in use, the *Thames Tunnel* carries the Wapping to New Cross trains.

Tower Subway (Tower Hill to Tooley Street – completed August 1870), originally carried a sub-aqueous omnibus service, but it proved unreliable. Closed to the public in 1897, it now serves as a duct for pipes and cables.

The *Blackwall Tunnel* (Blackwall to Greenwich 1890-1897) was the first to be lit by electricity. This required a special power station to be built but the light was sufficient for a gentleman to read *The Times* in any part of the tunnel. It took 17,000 lbs of iron, 1 million tiles and 7 million bricks in the building. A second tunnel became necessary and this was opened in 1966.

The two *Dartford Tunnels* (opened 1963 and 1980 and costing £6 million and £36 million respectively) currently carry between twenty-five and forty thousand vehicles a day. The walls are faced with vitreous mosaic designed to reflect the light without causing glare. The *Greenwich Subway* (Island Gardens, Poplar to Church Street, Greenwich – opened 1902) is for pedestrians only and exceptionally squalid. For more details I recommend *Tunnels Under London* by Nigel Pennick (Electric Traction Publications, Cambridge).

Best tunnel: *Thames Tunnel.*
Worst tunnel: *Greenwich Subway.*

Underground Lines and Stations

The *Victoria Line* (opened between 1968 and 1972) is the best underground line in London. Where other lines have scheduled speeds of between 16 and 23 mph, the *Victoria* rolling stock can roll along much faster by virtue of 'longer station spacing', as they say. Only on the new Heathrow extension of the *Piccadilly Line* and on suburban sections of the *Metropolitan Line* is it possible to travel faster, although paradoxically on the countrified stretches of the *Metropolitan* you would not wish to. Apart from its speed and regularity, the *Victoria Line* adopted the imaginative scheme of having tile murals at each station so that regular passengers could get their bearings with a shock of friendly recognition. The trains on the *Victoria* and *Jubilee lines* are automatically controlled which means that, if you have greater faith in computers than in human beings, you should feel safer on these lines than on the older ones.

But while the *Victoria* and the *Jubilee* are all sweetness and light, weepings, wailings, and gnashings of teeth may be heard the length of the notorious (and dirty) *Northern Line*, while the *Bakerloo* is a law unto itself. The *Circle* trains always come when you want the *District*, and vice versa. In 1973 the *Piccadilly Line* replaced its electro-pneumatic braking system with the Westcode electrically-controlled mechanism, which is why you no longer hear that poignant sigh just before the train pulls out of the station. The average length of a traveller's journey on the underground system is 4.7 miles, a journey which takes him or her less than fifteen minutes; not, all things considered, bad.

The stations are idiosyncratic. *Earls Court* has a greengrocers (not cheap), a fine Victorian overhead roof, an overhead duct which carries a river, and handsome veteran destination boards. You can drink at *Kew, Baker Street, Sloane Square* and *Liverpool Street* stations; you can buy antiques at *Edgware Road* and stamps at *Waterloo*. At *Bank* station, which connects with *Waterloo* via 'The Drain' (the Waterloo and City Railway and the oldest surviving part of the underground system), there is a travolator, similar to the one at Heathrow. The *Barbican* station (formerly Aldersgate Street and Barbican) is most elegant, while *Uxbridge* is aggressively bold in an uncompromising thirties style. *Baker Street* has a cartoon cinema and Sherlock Holmes on the walls; *Bond Street* is like a modern shopping precinct – damn it, it *is* a modern shopping precinct – suave and expensive-looking – damn it, it *is* expensive, while *Goodge Street* and *Hampstead* (once *South Kentish Town*) are little architectural revolutions in the tiled neo-Georgian manner. *St John's Wood* station (c 1940) is curved and low and pleasantly bricked; entering it is like walking into the mouth of a friendly fish. *Great Portland Street, Hanger Lane* (1947 but tatty), and *Arnos Grove* (1933) are circular. *South Kensington* is all red tiling and witty iron scrollwork, a bit arty but fun, just what *South Kensington* ought to be. At *Holborn* you have to walk miles for your interline connection. *Highgate* and *Barons Court* are nasty; *Chalk Farm* and *Gunnersbury* and *Mornington Crescent* worse. *Camden Town* is the draughtiest station in London. But worst of all must be *Oxford Circus* in a wet afternoon rush hour; almost unendurable.

A hint to strap-hangers. Supposing you have to make the daily trek from *Victoria* to *Wimbledon* on the *District Line* at 5.30 p.m. It is worth while travelling east for a few stops, say to *Blackfriars*, and then west, thus ensuring a seat for the journey home.

The London transport map of the London Underground is, of course, a triumph of graphic art, clear and satisfying. It must also have been looked at longer and with greater concentration than the *Night Watch*, the *Mona Lisa* and the *Laughing Cavalier* together.

Best line: *Victoria*.
Best station: *Kew Gardens* (with a pleasant concourse and a civilised bar).
Worst line: *Northern*.
Worst station: *Chalk Farm* (also *Oxford Circus* in the rush hour).

Universities, Colleges, Polytechnics, etc.

Good ones: The *Royal College of Defence Studies* in general, and the pink gins in the officers' mess in particular. Also the *Institute for Strategic Studies*. Do these two have war games together and, if so, who wins? The *City of London Polytechnic, the North East London Polytechnic, Imperial College, Goldsmiths' College, City Lit, King's College*.

At the *South Bank Poly* brilliant and cheap language laboratories may be found. The *South Lambeth Evening Institute* is celebrated for its pottery courses at the *Elmwood Pottery*, and I have heard nothing but good of the Drama and English faculty at *London University*.

Not such good ones: The *Architectural Association* (it produces, says a friend who may have an axe to grind, 'smooth talking con-men with little or no architectural interest'); *University College*, Gower Street; *South West London College*, Tooting.

As for the *London School of Economics* (LSE) what can I possibly say that has not already been said about an institution that has already produced both my mother and Mick Jagger, bless them.

Unusual Shops

The following are all recommended. I have excluded from this list unusual shops featured elsewhere in the book.

Astroturf, and avant-garde technological furniture and effects, from *Astrohome*, 47/49 Neal Street, WC2; 01-240 0420.

Beautiful Bodies from *City Gym* (Murray's), New Union Street, EC2; 01-628 0786.

Beehives, complete with bees (£45+), from *John Davies*, 66 Embercourt Rd, Thames Ditton, Surrey; 01-398 3277.

Capes from *Born and Bred*, 85 Bourne St, SW1.

Electric Art from *Argon*, 3 Theberton St, N1; 01-359 3845.

Ephemera from *Dodo*, 185 Westbourne Grove, W11; 01-229 3132.

Flying Ducks, and kitsch generally from *Schram & Scheddle*, 262 Upper St, N1; 01-226 4166.

Frames from *Evans the Frame*, 71 Regents Park Road, NW11; 01-722 2009.

Frozen Reindeer from *The Swedish Shop*, 7 Paddington St, W1; 01-486 7077.

Herbs from *Meadow Herbs Shop*, 47 Moreton St, SW1; 01-821 0094 and from *Culpeper*, 9 Flask Walk, NW3; 01-794 7263.

Holograms from *The Light Fantastic Gallery*, Unit 48, Covent Garden, WC2; 01-836 6423.

Home Making Wine and Brewing Equipment from *W. R. Loftus*, 1/3 Charlotte St, W1; 01-636 6235.

Interpreters from *Ethnic Switchboard* 01-993 6119.

Keyboard Hire from *Keyboard Hire*, 8 Thornhill Rd, N1; 01-607 8797.

Lavatory Seats from *Sitting Pretty*, 131 Dawes Rd, SW6; 01-381 0049.

Left-Handed Shop from *Anything Left-Handed*, 68 Beak St, W1; 01-437 3910.

Lighting from *Christopher Wray*, 591/593/600/602/606/613 New King's Rd, SW6; 01-736 8008 and from *Roger of London*, 344 Richmond Rd, Twickenham; 01-891 2122 and very cheap from *Mr Resister*, 267 New King's Rd, SW6; 01-736 7372.

Magic from *Davenport's*, 51 Gt Russell St, WC1; 01-405 8524.

Movie Memorabilia from *The Cinema Bookshop*, 13 Gt Russell St, WC1; 01-637 0206.

Personalised Presents (your name or monogram on almost anything) from *Eximous*, 12a Maddox St, W1; 01-629 3152.

Sci-Fi Magazines etc from *Al Reuter*, Reedmore Books, 1 Midland Crescent, NW3; 01-435 4634 and from *Forbidden Planet*, 58 St Giles High Street, WC2; 01-379 6042.

Murals (commissioned, mainly for children) from *Hippo Hall*, 65 Pimlico Rd, SW1; 01-730 7710.

Painted Furniture (for adults) from *Shop for Painted Furniture*, 95 Waterford Road, SW6; 01-736 1908, (for children) from *Dragons*, 25 Walton Street, SW1; 01-589 3795.

Patchwork from *Patchwork Dog and Calico Cat*, 21 Chalk Farm Road, NW1; 01-485 1239.

Polo Sticks etc from *Holbrows*, incorporated within George Parker & Sons (saddlers to the Queen Mother) 12 Upper St Martin's Lane, WC1; 01-836 1164.

Posters from *Poster Shop*, 168 Fulham Road, SW10; 01-373 7294.

Saxophones (and other brass instruments) from *Paxman's*, 116 Long Acre, WC2; 01-240 3647.

Scaffold Furniture from *One Off*, 31 Shorts Gardens, WC2.

Shells (very beautiful) from *Eaton's Shell Shop*, 16 Manette Street, W1; 01-437 9391, (opposite Foyles).

Spectacles (fantastic frames) from *Cutler & Gross*, 18 St Christopher's Place, W1; 01-486 4079.

Stained Glass (ready made, DIY or made to measure) from *Lead and Light*, 15 Camden Lock, Chalk Farm, NW1; 01-485 4568.

Stoves from *Stove Shop*, Camden Lock, Chalk Farm, NW1; 01-969 9531.

Swizzle Sticks (and cocktail paraphernalia) from *The Cocktail Shop*, 5 Avery Row, W1; 01-493 9744.

Tapestry from *Ehrman*, 21-22 Vicarage Gate, W8; 01-937 4568.

Telephones from *The Telephone Shop*, 339 Fulham Road, SW10; 01-352 4574.

Umbrellas, walking sticks etc. from *James Smith*, 53 New Oxford Street, WC1; 01-836 4731 (one of the most extraordinary and best loved shops in London).

Uniforms (for chefs, waiters, butchers etc) from *P. Denny & Co.*, 39 Old Compton Street, W1; 01-437 1654.

Videos from *The Video Palace*, 100 Oxford Street, W1; 01-637 0366.

Vegetarian Food

What is distressing about vegetarian and health food establishments is that the clients and even the staff frequently look so unhealthily like vegetables. But the food is usually good, sensibly priced, and well served, at least in the restaurants.

The four *Cranks* restaurants, the original one at Marshall

Street, also at Covent Garden, Heal's 4th Floor and Peter Robinson 1st Floor, are typical of the genre. Soups, quiches, salads and crumbles, are what you can expect, and a bill of about £4.50 a head is what you will have to pay. The drawback is that *Cranks* is (are?) very crowded.

Less crowded and rather cheaper are my two favourites. *Wilkins Natural Foods* (55 Marsham Street, SW1; 01-222 4038) opposite the depressing Dept of the Environment, is unassuming but serves deliciously fresh and appetising food. *The Wholemeal Vegetarian Restaurant* (1 Shrubbery Road, SW16; 01-769 2423), unlike the other places mentioned above, is open in the evenings. It serves excellent soups and vegetable casseroles (menu changes daily) and is famous locally for its hot banana pudding.

Also powerfully recommended:

Cherry Orchard (241 Globe Road, E1; 01-980 6678; closed evenings). Buddhist-run for vegetarians and vegans with 16 herb teas to choose from.

Food for Thought (31 Neal Street, WC2; 01-836 0239; open till 8 p.m.). Very popular, partly on account of its delectable puds.

The Garden (616 Fulham Road, SW6; 01-736 6056). Charles Brodie, the successful entrepreneur of La Poule au Pot and Maggie Jones, has started this restaurant 'for vegetarians and their meat-eating friends'. A good idea. Open evenings. Reports please.

Healthy, Wealthy & Wise (9 Soho Street, W1; 01-437 1835; open till 8 p.m.). Headquarters of the Hare Krishna Society. The food is more adventurous (deep fried vegetable balls in thick tomato sauce for example) than at most vegetarian cafes.

Neal's Yard Bakery and Tea Room (6 Neal's Yard, Shorts Gdns, WC2; 01-836 5199; closed evenings). It only seats 24 and long queues testify to the success of quality vegetarian food. The cakes are baked without sugar, and in the various shops you can buy whatever's good for you, including a vast selection of aperients.

Slenders (41 Cathedral Place, Paternoster Square, EC4; 01-236 5974; closes 6.15 p.m.). Popular, largeish, modern, self-service restaurant near St Paul's.

There are numerous excellent health food shops in London, and a useful guide through the maze (or maize) is: *Guide to Good Food Shops* by S. Campbell (Macmillan).

Best vegetarian Restaurant: *Wholemeal Vegetarian Restaurant*, Streatham.

See also under Indian Restaurants.

Vets

When Magpie, my 15-year-old Geordie mongrel bitch, was a mere pup-in-arms and was taken for her first ride on the London Underground, all hell broke loose. Leaping from my arms she caught her paw in the Oxford Street escalator. She howled. A middle-aged lady trotted up, brandishing a handkerchief. 'Don't worry,' she cried, 'I'm a midwife.'

Having bandaged the paw, she directed me to an animal clinic where the paw was set, but upside-down, and I was instructed to keep the bandage on for at least a week. Long before then the putrefaction was such that a local vet in New Cross had to repair the damage as best he could.

This was the same bitch, whose pregnancy at the age of seven was wrongly diagnosed by a vet as 'a phantom'. So we starved the poor creature (she had always been greedy) when we should have been feeding her up.

But there are competent vets, and two whom I can heartily recommend are:

Andrew Carmichael, 7 Addison Avenue, W11 (01-603 4407/4094). *Peter Cronin*, 5c Bedford Corner, South Parade, W4 (01-994 2387).
It would be invidious to choose between them.

The *Elizabeth Street Veterinary Clinic* (01-730 9102) is open 24 hours a day.

Views

Easy. Nobody will persuade me that there is a better view in and around London than the view from the first floor room of the Roebuck Pub at the top of Richmond Hill. In fact you don't need to be in the Roebuck, because the view looks splendid in all weathers and at all times of the year from any vantage point, but the Roebuck is ideal. Nor am I alone in thinking this. Turner, amongst numerous other artists, thought it a fit subject for his palette and it is known as *Turner's View*.

Other justifiably famous views include the palpitatingly romantic view from the *Rennie Bridge* over the Serpentine, especially on a summer's evening; the silhouette view of towers and spires and upended matchboxes from *Primrose Hill* or *Parliament Hill* looking south into the distant smoke; the view from *Westminster Bridge* ('Earth has not anything to show more fair', said Wordsworth, and he was an authority), but the view from *Hungerford Bridge* runs it close; the view from *Battersea Old Church* looking west along the river – Turner was there too!; the *Haymarket Theatre* at night from St James's Square; the view from William and Mary's bedroom in *Kensington Palace* along the Serpentine, which is why the Serpentine was moved to its present position; the view from *Greenwich Observatory* towards the river; the view down *George Street* from the north side of Hanover Square to the portico of St George's Church; the view up *Fleet Street* to St Paul's (partially obscured by a crass development); the view of *Cannizaro Park*, Wimbledon from the big house; the view from the top of the *NatWest Building* – but you're only allowed to see it if you're a big executive; the view of *Hertford House* across Manchester Square; the view south along *St James's*.

Best view: *Turner's View.*
Worst view: *the view from the dressing rooms of the National Theatre.*

Wall Writings

Old graffiti date you dreadfully. Remember 'Marples Must Go'? Long after he went it is still faintly visible on the *Cromwell Road* extension, as well as on the *M1* bridges. 'Springboks out' survives in *Isleworth*, and just the other day I spotted in *Wembley*: 'Radio Caroline Forever'. The plethora of 'George Davis is Innocent OK' graffiti in the *East End* must be something of an embarrassment now, but racialist graffiti, especially around football grounds, are an embarrassment to humanity.

Intellectual wall writings tend to be self-conscious. In the *Charing Cross Road*: 'The Grave of Karl Marx is just another Communist plot' sounds artful rather than spontaneous, but at the *Festival Hall*: 'Colin Davis can't tell his brass from his oboe' is witty enough to be excusable. At the *LSE* 'Lateral thinking is a con. Honest? Yes, straight up.' Since graffiti have recently been so widely anthologised (by Nigel Rees among others) it could be more interesting to study advertising slogans. Down the

Commercial Road I spotted a placard requesting: 'Boys Wanted for Plastics' and nearby in *Black Lion Yard*, E1, could be seen (and maybe still can) on some doors: 'J. D. & J. Evans, Cowkeepers' with a Hebrew inscription insisting that the milk is properly kosher. On the gasometer at the *Oval* (the most celebrated gasometer in the world) it warns: 'Use Gas Well' and on the wall of a cafe in the *Waterloo Road* one could/can read: 'The Sunday Referee. Most Enterprising Paper of the Age.' One genius inscribed his entire philosophy of life and critique of social revolution on a convenient wall along the approach to *Paddington Station*, where the commuter trains linger, and where it had once innocently announced: 'Virol – Nervous Girls Need It!'

In several places I have spotted the healthily cynical: 'If voting changed anything, then I'd make it illegal.' Facing commuters travelling east on the M4: 'Good morning, lemmings.' But my favourite has been on public display in *Dean Street* – the Soho Square end – for as long as I can remember: . . .

Best wall writing: (though it is in fact a hanging sign board):

Hospital For Women
Please Go Quietly

Weather

The meteorological variations within Greater London from Ruislip, Barnet and Southgate in the north to Epsom and Dartford in the south are significant. It is *foggiest* in the London parks, along the Thames and at Heathrow; it is *snowiest* on the borders of London and Kent, and it is noticeably *warmer* within the central London enclave. The absolute temperature range over the last 100 years at Kew is from 22.2°F (−3.4°C) on January 5th, 1894 to 93.9°F (43.4°C) on August 9th, 1911, but on that same August 9th the temperature reached an official 100°F at Greenwich.

In hot weather the *hottest* places in central London are iron railings exposed to direct sunlight, and the *coldest* places in cold weather are the conductor rails of the London Underground network. The average annual rainfall at Kew is 23.95 inches. The *driest* month is March, the *wettest* months are July and November, the *coldest* month used to be January but is now February, while the *hottest* month is July; the *sunniest* month is April, the *cloudiest* is December, and the *foggiest* is November. The *hottest* time of the year, consistently over the years, is between 3 and 4 p.m. on 29th July. Letters to *The Times* have claimed mysteriously and with authoritative backing from statistics that Thursdays are much *wetter* than other days of the week.

In short one has only to visit other capitals, such as Washington DC, Kampala, Port Stanley, or Moscow, to realise just how lucky we are.

PS Serious students should study: *The Climate of London* by T. J. Chandler (Hutchinson 1965) or other similar books.

Weather Vanes/Weather Cocks

There is a fine fat ram on top of *Young's Brewery* in Wandsworth High Street, and there is an ethereal flying horse above the *Inner Temple*. Cocks may be spotted all over the shop, notably on *All Hallows By The Tower's* steeple, and *19 Cheyne Place*, Chelsea. There is a ship, as you might expect, above *Trinity House*, Trinity Square, EC3; less predictably ships float above *Liberty's* in Great Marlborough Street and *Tooting Public Library* (a Viking vessel). But the best ship sails proudly over the restored *St Nicholas Cole Abbey* in Queen Victoria Street, having been removed from the vanished church of St Michael, Queenhithe. *Battersea Library* features an old man dozing over his books, while *Lambeth Palace* has an arrow and a crown in the finest of iron tracery. The weather cock on the roof of the *Banqueting House* (all that remains of Whitehall Palace) was placed there by James II to establish the direction of the winds when William of Orange was preparing to sail.

But the best has to be . . .

Best weather vane: *Old Father Time* with his sickle at Lord's Cricket Ground.

Windows

One of the most elaborate windows in London must be the Ruskin window at the east end of Sir Gilbert Scott's Church of *St Giles*, Camberwell. Designed when Ruskin was really only a kid – well, twenty-five – it is imaginatively coloured in ultramarine, cobalt and crimson and depicts incidents from the Old and New Testaments set in scholarly opposition. 'The purest and most thoughtful minds,' said Ruskin, 'are those which love colour the most,' and he certainly lived by this dictum. An interesting comparison may be made with William Morris's three-lancet east window in *St John the Apostle*, Whetstone, N20, and with the fine John Piper window in *St Margaret's*, Westminster. But the most impressive modern church window is Hugh Easton's vision of the Risen Christ above blitzed Stepney in the beautiful church of *St Dunstan and All Saints*, Stepney High Street.

In *Southwark Cathedral* is a stained glass window (Christopher Webb, 1954) featuring characters from the plays of Shakespeare, the adopted local lad, whose brother Edmund Shakespeare, is buried in the cathedral. Also a fine west window by the Victorian Henry Holiday. The glass in *St Paul's* was destroyed by bombs in 1941, but some old armorial glass may be found in the Great Hall of *Lambeth Palace* and in the fine hall of *Gray's Inn*. The *Great Hall of Guildhall* has new stained windows with scrolls detailing 663 mayors and lord mayors. *St Katherine Creechurch* in Leadenhall Street has 17th-century glass designed as a catherine wheel, of course, in its fine east window.

The windows in Horace Walpole's Gothic extravaganza at *Strawberry Hill* might as well be in a church; other fine Gothic windows may be seen in the *House of Commons*, at *48 Park Lane*, and, of course, at *St Pancras Station*. I have a great fondness (because I have passed them so many times) for those huge and heavily leaded studio windows along the *Cromwell Road extension*, overlooking what used to be playing fields until bureaucrats decided they had a better idea.

Christopher Wren designed some Mozartian windows in *Fountain Court* at Hampton Court Palace, and Nash's row of little windows, like aircraft propellers, above the portico of the *Haymarket Theatre*, are delightful. But then London is full of charming little windows and fanlights (q.v.).

Best windows: *St Dunstan and All Saints*, Stepney.
Worst windows: (jointly) *The Senate House*, London; *Dulwich College Great Hall* ('So ugly,' says my nephew, 'that it's permanently covered by a curtain') and the ground level windows along the north side of *William IV Street*, WC2. From these vile smells emanate.

Wine

If you buy your wine from a wine bar (q.v.) or at an auction (q.v.), you have the opportunity of tasting what you're getting before it's too late. *Christie's* hold regular auctions of wine, and for all except the rarest vintages you would not expect to pay more than in an off-licence, and could well pay a great deal less.

If the price is your concern and you can't get to an auction, you should buy your wine at *Oddbins* (various branches). In 1979 *Which* reported that *Oddbins* was the cheapest off-licence chain, and it has remained so. The best branches are 141 Notting Hill Gate, W11 (01-229 4082) and 142 Fulham Road, SW10 (01-373 5715), where the staff are particularly amiable. In the same edition of *Which* the most expensive chain was *E. J. Rose & Co Ltd* (various branches).

Gimmicks and fashions count for a great deal in such a vulnerable market; for years Bulls Blood sold on its macho name, and that nasty sparkling Mateus Rosé on the shape of its bottle. Recently wine boxes have become all the rage, and they are an excellent way of regulating your drinking, although decent wines would probably resent being boxed – and so far have not been. The gimmick at *Seven Dials Wine Co* (17 Shorts Gardens, WC2; 01-836 9851) is that their wine is delivered by tanker, stored under nitrogen in basement vats, and poured for you into litre bottles which are returnable. You choose your wine from a small selection (two French reds, two French whites) which are (currently) less than £3 a litre, the appropriate label is stuck on your bottle (16p when you bring it back) and you go on your way rejoicing.

At the *Camden Wine and Cheese Centre* (214 Camden High Street, NW1; 01-485 5895) you can select from fifty champagnes, at *Mainly English* (14 Buckingham Palace Road, SW1; 01-828 3967) from sixty English wines, and at *Harrods* from eighty-five malt whiskies.

Strongly recommended is *Buckingham's* (6 Fulham Road, SW3; 01-584 1450 and branches) and the classy *Berry Brothers & Rudd Ltd* (3 St James's St, SW1; 01-930 1888). *Bottoms Up* (various branches) is challenging *Oddbins* for the cheap and cheerful end of the market. The best of the house clarets is *Harvey's* Medoc AC, the worst *Findlater's* Côtes de Bourg. *Marks & Spencers'* Vinho Verde is a trusted favourite if you can get the cork out; it's good value. The best wine cellars in London restaurants are at the *Connaught* (Carlos Place, W1; 01-499 7070), *Oslo Court* (Prince Albert Road, NW8; 01-722 8795) and the *Tate Gallery Restaurant* (Millbank, SW1; 01-821 1313).

Best wine merchants: *Berry Brothers & Rudd Ltd* (for expensive wines). *Seven Dials Wine Co* and *Oddbins* (for cheaper wines).

PS If you need drying out, try ACCEPT, Ward 20, Western Hospital, Seagrave Road, SW6 (01-381 3155). They are used to it.

Wine Bars

At the last count – and it's not easy to count them when they won't stand still – there were more than 250 wine bars in London. Wine is no longer significantly more expensive than beer, and women are said to be safer from unwelcome attentions in wine bars than in pubs, but this is only true of the nicer wine bars and the nastier pubs. In many City wine bars women are not welcomed. In others, especially in South Kensington, they are regarded as fair game.

The king of the London wine bar scene is John Davy, who owns more than twenty of the things. The first was the *Boot and Flogger* (10-20 Redcross Way, SE1; 01-407 1184). At a Davy wine bar you get a choice of six house wines, and twenty-four more select wines, with ports, sherries and a cold buffet. The *Balls Brothers* chain (almost all in the City) offers a choice of some seventy wines, but is a bit clubby and predictable.

The *Cork and Bottle* (44-46 Cranbourne Street, WC1; 01-734 7807) is to be found underneath Chez Solange and the adjoining stamp shop just off the Charing Cross Road. It's not always easy to get served, but the wines available (details on blackboards) are varied and interesting. Don and Jean Hewitson, who also run other wine bars, organise regular festivals of wines from different regions at the *Cork and Bottle*, and always stock Antipodean wines. Expect to pay between £1 and £2 a glass. For £1.65 I enjoyed a Laboure Roi Chablis. The glass was not very full, and it would have been better value to have bought the bottle at £6.60. However the homemade snacks are tasty and, if you choose your evening, you can watch Juan Ramirez plucking with his plectrum. Unluckily, I had to settle for some turgid, taped Matt Monroish stuff.

The *Archduke* (Concert Hall Approach, SE1; 01-928 9370, closed Sundays) caters for music lovers. Hoffnung characters adorn its menus, and the rather grand food includes a wide variety of sausages. They do a nice watercress mayonnaise but use stock cubes in the pies. A variety of wines, including Chinese, is available in this cool and friendly place, which presents live jazz and blues.

Julie's Bar (137 Portland Road, W11; 01-727 7985) is currently very fashionable – which doesn't mean much in the brittle world of wine bars, but it has plenty to offer the well-heeled customer. The atmosphere is reminiscent of a Fry's Turkish Delight commercial, but there is a small back garden used for lunches in summer; they serve cream teas when the wine bar is closed, and the service is cheerful.

Tracks (Soho Square, W1; 01-439 2318) is aglitter with film people and television executives. It has an open air terrace, French, German and Italian wines, and serves excellent lunches. *Paling's* (25 Hanover Square, W1; 01-408 0935) does even better food, though the decor is gaudy.

Brahms and Liszt (19 Russell Street, WC2; 01-240 3661) is recommended by young Henrietta Browne-Wilkinson whose taste in such matters is impeccable, and hated by my ex-bank manager, whose heart I broke. It is crowded, though the old warehouse which it inhabits is not small; noisy, shabby, and fun. They do a nice line in steak-and-kidney pies, and other comestibles, but if you are serious about eating you should book in advance.

The best for food are *Daly's* (Little Essex Street, WC2) and *Mildred's* (135 Kensington Church Street, W8; 01-727 5452), where the roast pork with cream and green peppercorns was followed by an irresistible choice of puddings.

Recommended also:
Cafe des Amis du Vin, 11-14 Hanover Place, WC2 (01-379 3444) – especially the soup.
Fino's, 123 Mount Street, W1 (01-492 1640).
French's, 55 East Hill, SW18 (01-874 2808).
Draycotts, 114 Draycott Avenue, SW3 (01-584 5359).
Pontefract Castle, 71 Wigmore Street, W1 (01-486 3551).
The Loose Box (over ninety wines), 7 Cheval Place, SW7 (01-584 9280).

Not so good:
Sloanes, 52 Sloane Square, SW1 (01-730 4275).
Ebury Wine Bar, 139 Ebury Street, SW1 (01-730 5447).
El Vinos, 47 Fleet Street, EC4 (01-353 6786).
Tuttons, 11-12 Russell Street, WC2 (01-836 1167).

Best wine bar: the *Archduke*.

Zoos

Chessington Zoo is decidedly tatty. It also features a circus and fun-fair which no self-respecting zoo ought to do. The children ignore the animals or glance at them impatiently, and the animals appear (perhaps as a consequence) sulky.

The *London Zoo* in Regent's Park plays host to more than two million visitors a year. While disapproving of zoos as entertainment, I realise that they are essential for research and to ensure the survival of endangered species, and the *London Zoo* does fine work. It rejoices in some excellent architecture. The original buildings were by the great Decimus Burton, and the more recent buildings have enhanced what had been deteriorating. The Snowdon Aviary, the Charles Clore Mammal Pavilion, and the impressive Lion Terraces all pay tribute to Sir Hugh Casson, who has been in charge of the developments. But entrance for an adult is a hefty £3.50 and the snacks are dreadful. Children can stroke things and ride on them at the Children's Zoo. The Wolf Wood and the Tropical Bird House are the best bets – and the feeding of the sealions, pelicans and penguins (2.15 p.m., 2.30 p.m. and 2.45 p.m. respectively) of course. There are also Children's Zoos in *Battersea Park* and *Golder's Hill Park*.

Whipsnade, some little way up the M1, sets animals as far as possible in their natural environments, and is enjoyable.

The GLC organise a mobile zoo which tours the parks throughout the summer (details 01-633 1728). Pony rides always provided.

Best zoo: *London Zoo.*

What's Best in Each Area: A selection from each district

NORTH

N1
Fanlight
Fishmongers
Pub Sign

N6
Lion
Staircase

NW1
Disco
Fish & Chips
Park
Post Office
Pub, Gay
Theatre, Open Air
Zoo

NW3
Breakfast
Hill
Ice Cream
Kite Flying
Swimming, Outdoor

NW4
Supermarket

NW6
Chimney Sweep
Police Station

NW8
Parking Meters
Weather Vane

SOUTH

SE1
Cinema
Concert Hall
Horses, Dead

Music Hall
Obelisk
Organ
Palace
Roof
Stamps
Statue

SE6
Dog Track

SE7
Milestones

SE10
Ship
Shoes, Children's
Sign Post

SE11
Striptease

SE21
Toll Gates

SW1
Arcade
Butcher
Car Wash
Cats
Character
Chinese Restaurant
Chocolates
Clairvoyant
Gallery, Old Pictures
Hats, Men's
Hats, Women's
Horses, Live
Hostel
Library
Shoes, Men's
Spanish Restaurant
Steak
Tea, Cup of
Wine

SW3
Cosmetics
Delicatessen
Fish Restaurant
Footscraper
Garden
Shoes, Women's
Store
Taxi Rank

SW6
Croquet
Greek Restaurant

SW7
Auction, buying
Museum
Stationers

SW11
Litter Bins
Take Away Food

SW14
Tennis

SW16
Osteopath
Vegetarian
   Restaurant

SW17
Street Name

SW18
Brewery

SW19
Arch

EAST

E1
All-Night Eating

224

Kosher Food
Theatre, Fringe
Tiles
Tunnel
Windows

E16
Pub, with
   Entertainment

EC1
Birds

EC2
Church
Pub, Real Ale

EC3
Bollards
Synagogue

EC4
Bank
Cathedral
Dome
Modern Building
Tea

WEST

W1
Bread
Car Park
Chapel
Cheese
Cocktails
Coffee
Croissants
Dogs
Florists
Fountain
Gallery, Modern
   Pictures
Gambling

Hotel
Italian Restaurant
Jazz
Kiosk
Mexican Food
Night Club
Pipe Shop
Shirts
Shop Front
Square
Street
Street Market
Tailors
Toys

W2
Bridge
Darts
Tea House
Train Spotting

W4
Pub, Riverside

W6
Arts Centre
Budget Restaurant
Pub Food

W10
Cemetery

W11
Vet

W12
Swimming, Indoor

WC1
Frieze

WC2
Alley
Bookshop
Cabaret

Embassy
Fancy Dress
Ghosts
Greengrocer
Indian Restaurant
Lavatories
London Club
Opera
Pen Shop
Pub, Straight
Roller Skating
Street Lights
Theatre, West End
Wine Bar

Surrey
Auction, selling
Clock
Cricket
English Restaurant
Ferry
Fishing
French Restaurant
Garage
Garden Centre
Golf
Horse Trough
House, Big
House, Small
Pillar Box
Rugby Football
Skating
View

Bibliography

Besides the specialist volumes mentioned in the course of the text, those mentioned hereunder have proved useful and entertaining; although a full bibliography would run to the length of a Tolstoy novel.

Alternative London by various authors (6th edition 1982 Otherwise Press)

F. R. Banks: *The New Penguin Guide to London* (8th edition 1982 Penguin Books). The most comprehensive and reliable of all the guides.

Charles Dickens: *Dickens's Dictionary of London 1879* (Howard Baker Press Ltd 1972). Fascinating.

Numerous titles by *Geoffrey Fletcher*, knowledgeable, enthusiastic and crusty; and *Ivor Brown*, gentle and literary.

V. S. Pritchett: *London Perceived* (Chatto & Windus 1974). Nostalgic and elegant.

The best of the many food guides are: *The Good Food Guide* (annual editions ed. Christopher Driver); *Let's Lunch in London* by Corrine Streich (Papermac 1982); *A Guide to London's Best Restaurants* by various authors (Virgin Books 1982).

A Guide to London's Best Shops by Charlotte DuCann (Virgin Books 1982) is splendid but could have been better subbed.

Reader's Contribution Form

Return to David Benedictus, Sphere Books Ltd, 30-32 Gray's Inn Road, London WC1X 8JL

I should like to nominate:

Nominee's name ....

Address ....

Phone number ....

In existing category ....

or in new category ....

Comments ....

....

....

....

Note: any establishment in the Greater London area may be considered. Contributions from those with vested interests not welcomed! Feel free to take issue with existing entries.

My Name ....

My Address ....

....

My phone number ....

I would/would not like an acknowledgement in the book (please delete).

All nominations will be checked before being included in or excluded from future editions of this book. Thanks.

Reader's Contribution Form

Return to David Benedictus, Sphere Books Ltd, 30-32 Gray's Inn Road, London WC1X 8JL

I should like to nominate:

Nominee's name ....

Address ....

Phone number ....

In existing category ....

or in new category ....

Comments ....

....

....

....

Note: any establishment in the Greater London area may be considered. Contributions from those with vested interests not welcomed! Feel free to take issue with existing entries.

My Name ....

My Address ....

....

My phone number ....

I would/would not like an acknowledgement in the book (please delete).

All nominations will be checked before being included in or excluded from future editions of this book. Thanks.